W9-BWE-488

KILLER ON THE ROAD

Discovering AMERICA

Mark Crispin Miller, Series Editor

This series begins with a startling premise—that even now, more than two hundred years since its founding, America remains a largely undiscovered country with much of its amazing story yet to be told. In these books, some of America's foremost historians and cultural critics bring to light episodes in our nation's history that have never been explored. They offer fresh takes on events and people we thought we knew well and draw unexpected connections that deepen our understanding of our national character.

Ginger Strand

KILLER
ON THE ROAD

Violence and the American Interstate

University of Texas Press

AUSTIN

Requests for permission to reproduce material from this work should be
sent to:
    Permissions
    University of Texas Press
    P.O. Box 7819
    Austin, TX 78713-7819
    www.utexas.edu/utpress/about/bpermission.html

♾ The paper used in this book meets the minimum requirements of ANSI/
NISO Z39.48-1992 (R1997) (Permanence of Paper).

Library of Congress Cataloging-in-Publication Data

Strand, Ginger Gail.
    Killer on the road : violence and the American interstate / by Ginger Strand.
— 1st ed.
        p.   cm. — (Discovering America)
    Includes bibliographical references and index.
    ISBN 978-0-292-72637-6 (cloth : alk. paper) — ISBN 978-0-292-74210-9
(e-book)
    1. Murder—United States—History.   2. Murderers—United States—
Biography.   3. Violence—United States—History.   4. Interstate Highway
System—Social aspects—History.   5. Express highways—Social aspects—
United States—History.   6. Automobile travel—Social aspects—United
States—History.   7. United States—Social conditions—1945-   I. Title.
    HV6524.S77   2012
        364.152′30973—dc23   2011038888

≡ CONTENTS ≡

Every time we merge with traffic
we join our community
in a wordless creed:
belief in individual freedom,
in a technological liberation
from place and circumstance,
in a democracy of personal mobility....
[The freeway] is surely the structure
the archeologists of some future age
will study in seeking
to understand who we were.

—DAVID BRODSLY, 1981

We mass-produce everything
from public opinion to motor-car bodies;
and we mass-produce criminals too.

—HENRY TAYLOR FOWKES RHODES, 1937

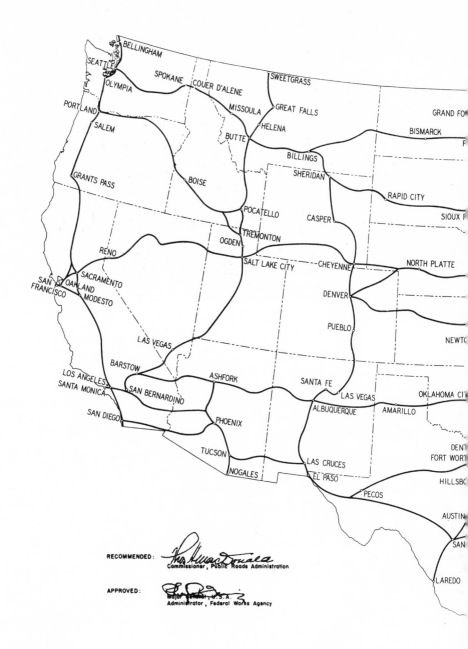

BELLINGHAM
SEATTLE
OLYMPIA
SPOKANE
COUER D'ALENE
SWEETGRASS
PORTLAND
SALEM
MISSOULA
GREAT FALLS
GRAND FO
BUTTE
HELENA
BISMARCK
BILLINGS
GRANTS PASS
BOISE
SHERIDAN
RAPID CITY
POCATELLO
CASPER
SIOUX
RENO
TREMONTON
OGDEN
SALT LAKE CITY
CHEYENNE
NORTH PLATTE
SACRAMENTO
SAN OAKLAND
FRANCISCO MODESTO
DENVER
LAS VEGAS
PUEBLO
NEWTO
BARSTOW
LOS ANGELES
SANTA MONICA
SAN BERNARDINO
ASHFORK
SANTA FE
LAS VEGAS
OKLAHOMA CI
SAN DIEGO
PHOENIX
ALBUQUERQUE
AMARILLO
TUCSON
DEN
FORT WORT
NOGALES
LAS CRUCES
EL PASO
HILLSBC
PECOS
AUSTIN
SAN
LAREDO

RECOMMENDED: _Thos. H. MacDonald_
Commissioner, Public Roads Administration

APPROVED: _[signature]_
Major General, U.S.A.
Administrator, Federal Works Agency

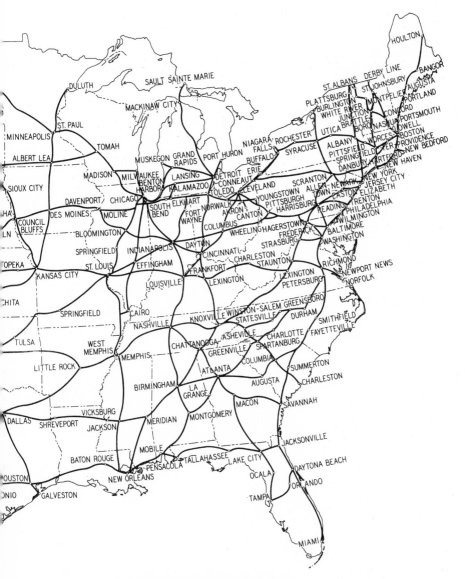

PUBLIC ROADS ADMINISTRATION
FEDERAL WORKS AGENCY

NATIONAL SYSTEM OF INTERSTATE HIGHWAYS

SELECTED BY JOINT ACTION OF THE SEVERAL STATE HIGHWAY DEPARTMENTS
AS MODIFIED AND APPROVED
BY THE ADMINISTRATOR, FEDERAL WORKS AGENCY
AUGUST 2, 1947

KILLER ON THE ROAD

Introduction

═ KILLER ON THE ROAD ═

In the mid-fifties, Congress transformed how the American nation traveled, lived, and worked. The Federal-Aid Highway Act of 1956 green-lighted the planet's largest public work: the 42,795-mile National System of Interstate and Defense Highways. The nation eagerly embraced its expressways, at least at the start. Nothing is more American than striking out for new horizons, so it seemed only appropriate that America should have the biggest, fastest, safest, most beautiful roads the world had ever seen.

Before the concrete was dry on the new roads, however, a specter began haunting them: the highway killer. He went by many names: the "Hitcher," the "Freeway Killer," the "Interstate Killer," the "Killer on the Road," the "I-5 Killer," the "Beltway Sniper." Some of these criminals were imagined, but many were real. Highway violence followed hard on the heels of interstate construction: the nation's murder rate shot up in the sixties and seventies. America became more violent and more mobile at the same time.

Were they linked? Did highways lead to highway violence? Yes and no. More highways meant more travel, more movement, more anonymity—all conducive to criminality. Highway users could become easy victims: stranded motorists, hitchhikers, drifters, and truck stop prostitutes were vulnerable to roving predators. But most killers are not predators, most predators don't roam the country, and highways have never been the main stage for the nation's bad actors. In the cultural unconscious, however, highways and violence quickly became entwined. Jim Morrison sang about a killer hitchhiker; slasher films dispatched hitchers by the score; Steven Spielberg's first feature film, *Duel*, centered on a faceless, murderous trucker. Add a steady stream of news stories about snipers on over-passes, snatchers at rest stops, drive-by shooters, drivers with road rage, and the conclusion is clear: the highway is full of dangers! If a song or book title contains the word *Interstate* or *Freeway*, expect mayhem, or at least some road-related blood-shed. If you're watching a movie in which the family car breaks down on the highway—extra points if it's in the rain, at night— you know what to think: *Don't get out of the car!* There's a psy-chokiller on the road.

By the eighties, when the interstate network was completed, it was considered a dangerous place—and not just because of car accidents. People feared hitchhiking, breakdowns, rest areas, truck stops, and aggressive drivers. There was a killer on the road all right, and regardless of how real he was, he had a choke hold on the American imagination. Today the high-way killer, like the train robber, the gangster, and the mobster before him, has entered the cast of American outlaws, and the freeway has taken its place among landscapes that easily lend themselves to nightmares.

The freeway killer's rise as a type paralleled the nation's increasing disillusionment with its highways. Expressways were originally considered not only safe and speedy, but beauti-ful: the nation's first limited-access divided highway, the Penn-sylvania Turnpike, was nicknamed the "Dreamway." People lined up for hours to drive on it. In the fifties, new interstates were featured in ads for cars, gasoline, tires, and more. Chevy ads featured a collection of divided highways, asking, "Which would you pick as America's finest road?" It's a startling contrast with car ads today, where vehicles glide down winding two-lanes, cruise down beaches, perch on rocky overlooks, bounce over cobblestones—go anywhere, in short, except down a divided highway.

Today the highways are not only seen as ugly, they are often depicted as downright vicious. "The road," writes James Kunstler, "is now like television, violent and tawdry." Critic Jane Holtz Kay described the "mechanical scythe of the highway" that "maimed whatever it touched." Even when not actively committing murder, the expressway has become a marker of social dysfunction: films from *Falling Down* to *Freeway* to *Crash* propose highways as analogs for cultural psychosis. Moviemakers can simply toss out an image of a freeway packed with cars to suggest a world gone mad. In the opening sequence of James Cameron's blockbuster *Terminator II*, a slow-motion shot of a busy interstate dissolves into a nuclear holocaust. Somehow, the film hints, the highway took us here. Sold to the nation as the safest, fastest, most beautiful route to the best of all possible worlds, our interstates weren't here for long before they were recast as highways to hell.

Why should this be? Why should one of our most impressive public works evoke in us feelings of fear and unease? Indeed, a few deranged individuals did use the highway system, and the anonymous landscapes it created, as a means to murder. But the response to those crimes went well beyond their actual danger to the population. The disproportionate fear of the killer on the road reveals cultural misgivings about highways and the values they represent.

If you're at all typical right now you're probably thinking one thing: *Cold War*. Of course it makes sense that the highway program would be linked to violence in the American mind, because the highways were part of the Cold War drive to heighten the nation's civil defenses. Atomic Armageddon can't be far from anyone's mind when looking at roads designed to evacuate cities and move military troops and tanks. You may even have heard that one mile in every five has to be straight so that airplanes can land on the interstate in a war emergency. I heard that story many times growing up, and even more times while working on this book. In fact, it's an urban legend—the Federal Highway Administration debunks it on its website. But it's part of the larger and more enduring myth about our interstate highways, which we'll dispense with right off: the myth that they were built for civil defense.

In 1954, President Eisenhower asked key members of his administration to begin formulating a "dramatic plan to get 50 billion dollars' worth of self-liquidating highways under construction." Although he was very fond of recounting how he had seen Germany's autobahns during the war and wanted Americans to have the same thing, Ike wasn't looking for a defense program; he was looking for a stimulus program. He and his economic advisors believed road-building would be an effective way to "prime the pump" of the economy and avoid recession. They were especially worried about this after Eisenhower, true to his campaign promise, ended the war in Korea—plunging the nation into an economic downturn. No one wanted this, particularly the Republicans, still smarting from the public perception that Herbert Hoover had done too little to fend off the Great Depression.

The highway program was thus first and foremost an attempt to counter recession. Its real purpose, as one of Eisenhower's advisors puts it, was "economic development . . . what the program could contribute to economic growth of industry and of agriculture and of our communities." In fact, "Defense" was only added to the interstate network's name after the highway bill failed to be approved the first time it went to Congress. In 1955, Congress declined to create a "National System of Interstate Highways." In 1956, it passed the bill creating the "National System of Interstate and Defense Highways." "The defense angle was a very persuasive part of the argument, you see," noted Senator Prescott Bush, a member of the Senate Public Works Committee during the Eisenhower era, in a 1967 interview. "*Very* persuasive." Frank Turner, executive secretary to the President's Advisory Committee on highways and later head of the Bureau of Highways, called defense in the highway program "an afterthought." But it was an afterthought with PR payoffs.

Defense was so much an afterthought that in the final highway bill, an earlier appropriation of $50 million for access roads to military installations was taken out. By the time the bill was passed, defense was so far from anyone's mind, no one even thought to ask the military to weigh in on highway standards. In 1960, four years into interstate construction, the Department of Defense would point out that the overpasses were being built too low for its purposes. By then, it would be too late to change.

It would be wrong, however, to say that the interstate highway program that unfolded over the next half century was nothing more than a calculated effort to ward off the ghost of Herbert Hoover. When Eisenhower proposed the highway program, there were inevitable arguments about how to fund it. But no one in Washington was against highways. Highways fostered mobility, and mobility represented prosperity, connection, growth: it was nothing less than the core of the American dream. "The entire economy of the United States," Eisenhower's highway advisor Lucius Clay declared, "is built on transportation."

Retired Army General Lucius Clay—former military governor of Germany, organizer of the Berlin Airlift, close friend to Eisenhower, and CEO of the Continental Can Company—was the man who helped the president shape the interstate program. Eisenhower had appointed Clay to be head of the President's Advisory Committee, a group tasked with drawing up a plan to fund and execute the highway program. Clay chose four more members: Stephen Bechtel, head of one of the nation's leading construction companies; William Roberts, CEO of Allis-Chalmers, a construction equipment manufacturer; Dave Beck, president of the Teamsters union; and Sloan Colt, head of Banker's Trust. It has frequently been noted that

*It was a stimulus program: the many exhibits created by the government
to publicize the interstate highway program stressed the economic benefits
of highways. Courtesy National Archives (30N-372-60-93).*

these four men represented the major interests that stood to
gain from massive government spending on highways: construction, trucking, and banks. It has also been pointed out that
Lucius Clay sat on the board of General Motors. Neither Clay
nor Eisenhower saw a conflict there. They shared the opinion
of Charles Wilson, the former head of GM who became Eisenhower's secretary of defense. Asked at his confirmation hearing whether his connection with GM presented a potential
political conflict of interest, Wilson declared, "I have always
believed what was good for the country is good for General
Motors and vice versa."

General Clay also knew what was good for the country: cars.
After he and his committee issued their report urging the creation of a federally funded highway program, Clay made the
rounds of Washington gatherings to tout the proposed pro-

gram. Speaking to groups of city planners, state officials, and mayors, General Clay told American leaders why building more highways was critical to the nation's future. It was simple: in order to grow its economy, the nation needed to grow its auto industry.

"The importance of the automobile to the American way of life has increased beyond measure," he explained. "It is really now our basic industry. Approximately 1 in 7 of our workers directly or indirectly build or service the automobile. Approximately 1 in 6 of our wholesale and retail establishments directly or indirectly service the automobile. Any leveling off in automobile use would certainly be disruptive to our economy."

Roads, it seemed, were essential for one major reason: to induce Americans to buy cars.

· · · · ·

As General Clay was speaking, a young man in Lincoln, Nebraska, was dreaming of hot rods. Like all American teenagers, Charles Starkweather was in love with cars. Cars meant a growing economy to Lucius Clay, and to people like Charlie they represented the personal side of that dream: a better life. A car could take you places. Charles Starkweather had hardly been out of Lincoln, but he dreamed of getting a car and hitting the road. Not a new car, of course; he couldn't afford that. But an old one he could tinker with, maybe even soup it up a little. One year later, James Dean would play Jim Stark, the drag-racing hero of *Rebel without a Cause*. Charles Starkweather loved that movie so much he started styling himself after Dean. Jim Stark would win his reputation and his girl by being the toughest driver on the road, and Charlie Starkweather wanted that too.

Charlie wasn't alone. Teenagers across the nation saw cars as a route to everything good: adulthood, self-determination, advancement, sex. But they weren't just rebelling. Adults also loved cars. Almost as soon as it was invented, the car became a key element in the American dream, and the open road soon joined it. Throughout the early twentieth century, highway boosters preached the doctrine of salvation by cement: better roads, they claimed, enriched leisure, enhanced public health, and promoted social cohesion. Highways spread the blessings of prosperity by making people and money more mobile. The architects of the interstate program didn't want roads to alleviate traffic: they wanted roads to make more of it.

It was all part of the economic orthodoxy just coming into fashion: endless growth. The era's economists had determined that increasing consumption was the only way to raise the average standard of living without any ugly socialist ideas like income equity. As Eisenhower's Treasury Secretary George Humphrey summarized the conventional wisdom for a group of governors in 1954, greater affluence for all did not require redistribution of wealth: you simply "make another pie and everybody has a bigger piece." The highway program was a way to enlarge the pie.

It was the economics of more. Selling more cars meant manufacturing more cars; manufacturing more cars meant creating more jobs; creating more jobs meant more people to buy more cars—and on and on it went, like a freeway leading off toward a distant horizon. There was little concern for what lay at the end; there was only the beauty of growth and the dedication to velocity for its own sake: a Manifest Destiny for modernity. It wasn't mere greed. To the barons of automobility, more cars meant more money for them, yes—but more cars also meant growth and success for everyone. It meant a nation of movers and shakers, an economy that was going places and people who were getting somewhere. *Getting ahead, moving up, riding high*: the very language of success in America is the language of movement and speed. Freeways with cars to fill them meant mobility—social as well as physical. "[T]he automobile," declared the Labor Department, "has aided wage earners . . . in breaking down barriers of community and class."

People like Charles Starkweather bought into this fantasy.

But they sometimes bumped up against an awful truth: the barriers of class and community could not be breached by everyone. For people at the very bottom of the economic ladder, the postwar years were a time when those barriers grew even higher. People like Charlie became even more isolated from the mainstream.

Eminent Harvard economist John Kenneth Galbraith saw it happening. In 1958, Galbraith published his enormously influential book *The Affluent Society*. In a chapter called "Inequality," Galbraith posed the question of why everyone—the left as well as the right—had turned so fiercely against the notion of sharing the wealth. The answer was economic growth. The average person in the fifties was a lot better off than his counterpart a few decades earlier, not because any revolution or regulation had redistributed income—in fact, inequality was greater than ever—but just because the economy was growing so much. There really was a bigger pie, as Secretary Humphrey promised, and everyone had a bigger piece.

Almost everyone. In fact, while the middle class was growing and the average standard of living was on the rise, the poor at the very bottom were worse off than ever. Their piece of the pie was shrinking fast, but few people cared. "Increasing aggregate output," wrote Galbraith, "leaves a self-perpetuating margin of poverty at the very base of the income pyramid. This goes largely unnoticed, because it is the fate of a voiceless minority." Eventually, this voiceless minority would come to be called the "underclass."

Although it was sold to the public as a program for jobs and civil defense, the interstate highway program was driven by the principle of growth. Some historians have called it the last big New Deal program. It might better be called the first corporate entitlement: a welfare program for corporations instead of people. It created construction jobs, but not enough jobs to make a difference, in part because rapidly improving construction equipment was continually reducing labor needs. The makers of that construction equipment, along with the makers of cement and steel and, of course, car and oil companies, were the real beneficiaries. There were trickle-down effects: those companies hired more people. Land values near the new roads skyrocketed; the need for highway engineers increased. But studies show that as many states began pouring half their capital outlays into roads, prices of goods and services were driven up. The large-scale economic effect of highway building was to drive up inflation and intensify economic upswings and downswings—exactly the opposite of what Ike had hoped. The highway bill would do little for the real economic losers.

This, too, was a kind of violence. Each outburst of panic about the killer on the road revealed barely disguised anxiety about what a commitment to mobility really meant. Was the nation being connected, or driven apart? Was its standard of living improving, or were some people being left behind in the race for material success? Was endless growth—with its dedication to the proposition that consuming equals happiness—really the road we wanted to take?

"We've built our lives on wheels," declared a 1955 Ford brochure supporting the highway program, "and we can't afford traffic jams." Mobility was a sign of the times, and there was anxiety about that. Many people feared that the nation was leaving behind its roots in close-knit communities and human connection and heading toward a new culture of materialism, selfishness, and anonymity, a world where you are what you drive, and where encounters between citizens were as likely to end in bloodshed as brotherhood. The highways came to represent the nation's ambivalence about having built its life on wheels.

And yet, who could resist it, the allure of the open road, the highway circulatory system pumping goods and people from one side of the nation to the other? If you grew up in rural America, as I did, you probably saw the interstate as a lifeline, a long gray ticket out of town. The fascination of the transcontinental road trip—like the siren song of the frontier—is an invitation to remake yourself anew. Hitchhike your way across the USA and at the other side, you can become a new person. If that's not utopia, what is?

Freeway as new world/freeway as world gone wrong. We remain schizophrenic about our interstates: we can't decide if they are delivering the American dream or destroying it. That's probably because they did some of both. Highways linked people together and drove them apart; created opportunities for urban development while hastening white flight from city centers; offered access to the nation's natural treasures while ramming concrete alleys over its landscapes; spawned a boom in franchises while destroying mom-and-pop stores; revitalized trucking and drove a stake in the heart of passenger rail. Roads are, as Ted Conover writes in *The Routes of Man*, "double-edged." While the dream of the open road means freedom, escape, and betterment, we know that, like so many dreams, it can easily morph into a nightmare. And we acknowledge that nightmare in the bogeyman of the freeway killer.

The first—and still the most famous—of those bogeymen was Charlie.

This new highway program
will affect our entire economic
and social structure. The
appearance of the new arteries
and their adjacent areas will
leave a permanent imprint on
our communities and people.
They will constitute the
framework within which
we must live.

—ROBERT MOSES, 1956

There will always be
differences in the inherited
sensitivities of children and
no amount of effort can quite
equalize opportunities.
In a less complex social order,
these differences do not
constitute serious threats
to the social interests.
In modern society, however,
slight differences in sensitivity
and environment may have
profound consequences. They
may make the difference
between the useful citizen
and the murderer.

—JAMES REINHARDT, 1960

The first stretch of interstate built in Nebraska, I-80 between Omaha and Lincoln, is nearly completed, shown here with three highway overpasses and two railroad overpasses built by Capital Bridge. Courtesy National Archives (30N-362-60-284).

≡ WHAT A MEAN WORLD THIS IS ≡

He won twenty dollars at the demolition derby the day before he killed his first victim—a gas station attendant—and celebrated by taking his fourteen-year-old girlfriend to the drive-in, heater running in his '49 Ford. His January 1958 murder spree was complicated by car trouble: a flat tire, a jammed transmission, a hand brake that wouldn't release. Between murders, he visited the mechanic for repairs, his girlfriend riding the Ford up the lift, holding a Pepsi and a shotgun. Eventually he would abandon his own car and steal a 1950 Ford hot rod with double antennas and big pipes, and then, even better, swap that for a rich man's Packard. That's the car he would be caught in, racing east across Wyoming on Highway 87, having killed eleven people, evaded Nebraska's National Guard, and led police on a multistate manhunt. Nineteen-year-old Charles Starkweather was America's original highway killer, and he remains its most celebrated, with classics like Terrence Malick's movie *Badlands* and Bruce Springsteen's song "Nebraska" based on his tale. Starkweather's homicidal spree was the first to be explicitly linked with America's burgeoning car culture, a trail of murders linked by automobiles and propelled by the killer's burning need to be on the road.

"Nobody has to tell me what a mean world this is," Starkweather said from jail, and he seemed just the man to prove it. Causeless, rootless, remorseless: Starkweather was new to America. "He is like nothing I have ever seen," Robert McClung, a gas station employee, said at the trial. But if Americans had never seen Starkweather, they had imagined him. He was a creature the fifties forged: an angry young rebel against everything the nation held dear—family, community, education, productivity, God. He was, in the lingo of the time, a JD, a juvenile delinquent disgusted by the adult world. In the movies he was Jim Stark, James Dean's tortured alias in *Rebel without a Cause*. Starkweather, like so many teens, idolized Dean. He wore secondhand jeans and leather jackets, combed his hair into a slick pompadour like Dean's. He spent hours practicing the star's cigarette-dangling sneer in front of a mirror, becoming the real-life emblem of the cultural anxiety Dean evoked—a nation's fear for its youth and, by extension, its future.

The week after he was captured in Wyoming, Starkweather was written up in the national magazines. In *U.S. News & World Report*, he shared the page with an article about signage for the new interstate highway system. The accompanying picture showed a test directional sign:

Metropolis
Utopia
2 Miles

Starkweather's violent spree intruded on a nation paving its way to Utopia. The interstate highway construction getting going as Starkweather took to the road was the biggest, most tangible sign of America's commitment to a new self-evident truth: that the nation's well-being depended on growth, and that growth depended on cars. But it was in the car-centered culture of America's juvenile delinquents where that dream first showed its dark side: mobility, rootlessness, lack of human

*The Federal Highway Administration still occasionally uses the
"Exit: Metropolis Utopia" signs that were first used as test signs in
Greenbelt, Maryland, just as Starkweather went on his spree.*

connection. Starkweather briefly became a symbol for the
nation's fear of the road it was going down—though it wasn't
enough to make anyone hit the brakes.

· · · · ·

Charles Starkweather was born in Lincoln, Nebraska, in
November 1938. He was the third of seven kids, all but one
of them boys. When he was three, his family moved to what
Charles called a "shabby" house on the city's northeast side.
They were an unexceptional clan. His father, Guy, was a car-
penter and handyman who worked off and on due to various
ailments; for a short time in 1950, while he suffered from a bad

back, the family was on welfare. After that, Guy's wife, Helen, found work as a waitress. Neighbors thought they were fine. Guy Starkweather drank, and he had a temper, but so did a lot of men then. On the stand at his son's trial, he admitted to once pushing Charles into a window. Charles hit him first, he said.

In photographs, Guy Starkweather has a slick, skinny mustache and a smirk, his hat always cocked at a rakish angle. Helen, on the other hand, looks timid and sallow, her eyes alert like a gopher's. In the most famous photo of the two of them, Helen's saddle-shoed feet are pressed tightly together below her girlish skirt. Guy has his dog's collar in one hand and his wife's two hands in the other. Three years after Charles's murderous spree, Helen Starkweather would file divorce papers against Guy on the grounds of extreme cruelty. Today we would focus on these suggestions of family dysfunction as a hint about what went wrong in Charles, but in the fifties, they barely made the paper. His childhood looked bafflingly normal.

After his arrest, Charles did what most convicted killers do: he deflected blame for his actions. From prison, he constructed a story to explain his rage toward the world. Other kids teased him, he said, for his bowed legs and his red hair. It all began on his first day of kindergarten, when students got to stand and tell the class what they had done that summer. In his half-illiterate, half-brilliant style, Charles wrote that he "sat listening to them in silence as they tolded about them selves going swimg, shows, fishing, camping and some tolded about going to other states to vist their relatives." When his turn came and he walked to the front of the room, kids began to giggle at his bowed legs. His nervousness showed:

> I was talking very quiet and I guess the other kids couldn't hear me because I was interrupted by Mrs. Mott, "speak a little louder Charlie, so everyone can hear you,"—so I spoked louder and as I did my pronunciation of words got mixed up and all at once the whole class bursted into laughter. I goggled around at the kids laughing and I tooked a gripped of my self. I began

to speak again my voice was smerying faint and cracked, the kids bursted into laughter again, I flinch, startle, flaccid, lacking in firmness, then I was competely flabbergast as my words became flat as I started to speak again I sadden they had no regard for my feelings, I swallowed dryly, glanced toward Mrs. Matt exspecting her to help me but she was observing me with unspoken admiration of my silence, then as I started to moved my lips in motion to speak Mrs. Matt said, "you may set down if you like Charlie."

The account is almost Joycean—and little of it seems to be true. Charles's first teacher, whose name was not Mott or Matt, could not remember a single incident where other kids picked on or teased him. But Charles insisted that other kids' cruelty explained everything. "Why did I become rebellious against the world and its human race?" he wrote. "'Cause that first day in school I was being made fun at, picked on, laughed at." Eleven people dead: it's a lot to blame on kindergarteners.

In fact, no one considered Charles unusual. His grades were not great, and he repeated the third grade, but IQ tests put him at or just below average. He had a tendency to get into fights, but boys were boys back then. He was never considered a psychiatric problem or referred to the school counselor. "There were others much worse than Charles," one teacher recalled.

Still, somehow, during childhood Charles Starkweather built up an overwhelming resentment of people who had more than he had. He was sensitive to his "shabby" home and to his mother's job as a waitress. He always shopped for his clothes in used clothing stores, because in those places, what people thought of him didn't matter. "One thing sure," he said, "I never give nobody much a chance to be dirty to me if I didn't have to." Even his descriptions of bullying eventually circle back to a sense of social inferiority: the other kids had gone to "shows," gone camping, visited other states—things Charles and his family never did.

The Starkweathers were downwardly mobile—at exactly the

moment when most of the nation's trajectory was up. The post-war years were boom time in America. The nation's production of goods and services doubled in the decade between 1946 and 1956, and median and mean family income doubled between 1949 and 1973. Driven by the GI bill, home ownership was on the rise. After years of pent-up demand, Americans were shopping like mad: appliances, televisions, vacations—much of it with newly popular credit cards. Mostly they were buying cars. In 1955, Detroit would ship 8 million of them—a new record. It was all part of the postwar promise: people would drive their cars right into the growing middle class.

The vision was clear to people like Alfred P. Sloan, chairman of the board of the biggest, richest corporation in the world: General Motors. In the twenties, Sloan foresaw the future of the auto industry, and it was not Henry Ford's model of mass-producing inexpensive, long-running, no-frills cars for everyone. The future of the auto industry was in constant change: in getting consumers to want the latest style of automobile, and in convincing them that the car they drove telegraphed their status to the world.

Sloan gave carte blanche to his chief designer, Harley Earle, to create a vision of affluence to which American consumers would aspire. Earle's look—widely copied by the other automakers—was about physical speed, but it also meant upward mobility. "Going places" financially meant trading up automotively: from a Chevy to a Pontiac to a Buick to a Cadillac. "If you earned it," Cadillac ads proclaimed, "why hesitate?" Oldsmobile promoted a concept called Oldsmobility: "an agile way to travel that's in a class by itself!" Chrysler advertised "the Forward Look of Motion." The American dream now had wheels.

Charles Starkweather wanted a car of his own, but he couldn't afford one. His family was left out of the nation's headlong rush toward social betterment, and he knew it. His parents couldn't even give him spending money for clothes or dates. Eventually, he did the only thing he could do: he got a part-time job hauling garbage with his brother Rodney. He hated it. He had to get up early, and he came home stinking of trash. Most of all, he hated the rich people whose garbage he had to handle. He treated them with a sullen arrogance. Rodney recalled that Charles would often shout "Go to hell!" from the truck at strangers. "Nobody knowd better than to say nothin' to me when is 'a heavin' their goddamn garbage," he declared.

In 1954, at sixteen, Charles was diagnosed with severe myopia. For years, he had been unable to see the chalkboard in his classrooms. His family decided to give him a fresh start, moving him to a new school for ninth grade. He was put in a class for slow learners.

At the new school, he met Bob Von Busch, another "tough," who became his best friend. Bob later recalled their antics: beer runs to Kansas, hanging out at the drag races, stealing cars for joyrides, chaining the rear end of a cop car—*American Graffiti*-style—to a drive-in.

"He could be mean as hell, cruel," Bob said of Starkweather years later. "If he saw some poor guy on the street who was bigger than he was, better looking, or better dressed he'd try to take the poor bastard down to his size. But I didn't think too much about it at the time. We were all a little like that then."

Before long, the two boys cemented their friendship by going in on the purchase of a 1941 Ford.

· · · · ·

In 1955, Congress held hearings on the highway bill proposed by General Clay's committee. The number the committee wanted the federal government to spend on roads—$101 billion—boggled the mind. Clay's report insisted the outlay was necessary: the nation was growing, its economy was growing, and its highways must match them in growth. "The relationship is, of course, reciprocal," the report declared: "an adequate highway network will facilitate the expansion of the economy which, in turn, will facilitate the raising of revenues to finance the construction of highways."

The highway promoters were unabashed in their equation: prosperity required more cars on the road. Francis du Pont— the former head of the Bureau of Public Roads whose family owned a 25 percent stake in General Motors—testified before the House Public Works Committee in March.

"[I]s it not true that the highway system needs of the United States of America are almost without limit," he was asked, "and will they not be almost without limit on and on?"

"I hope so," du Pont replied.

Nebraska was ready. State engineers already had plans underway for a limited-access highway across the state. Nebraska governor Victor Anderson spearheaded a regional Governor's Conference on the Interstate Highway System in Denver that June. There, leaders of the ten states met with bankers, heads of contracting companies, and highway commissioners to discuss Ike's proposed bill. These people knew a good thing when they saw it. Federal money for road building would guarantee a long-term gravy train for the construction industry, for cement and asphalt and steel suppliers, for bridge builders and people who built earthmovers. Together, the business leaders and the governors hammered out a joint statement urging Congress "to proceed expeditiously with the enactment of the pending road program."

That summer, as the highway bill languished in committees, Charles Starkweather completed the ninth grade and dropped out of school. He quit hauling garbage and found another job, baling newsprint and loading trucks at the warehouse of the Newspaper Union. He made twenty-five dollars a week. But he was not a stellar worker. He had to be told things multiple times and frequently fell asleep on the job. He gashed his head on a baling machine, requiring stitches. His boss speculated that he might be mentally retarded.

The one thing Charles was good at was working on his hot rod. With his father to cosign on the loan, he had traded up from the co-owned car with Bob. He bought a used 1949 Ford sedan, and like so many industrious teenagers of the era, he worked on it constantly. He frequently charged auto parts to his company, having the cost deducted from his paycheck. When his expenses surpassed what he was paid, his boss halted the practice. To Charles, this seemed unfair. Everything at the Newspaper Union was unfair. Other workers were praised and promoted, but he was not. He especially resented the "college boys" his boss hired: he claimed he would train them, then watch as they advanced and he didn't. To Charles, this proved that he was doomed to a marginal place. No one gave him half a chance. His Newspaper Union superiors, he griped, had him "numbered for the bottom."

It was not an unreasonable way to feel. Lincoln in the 1950s was, like most small American cities, a deeply class-conscious town. It was sharply divided between the neat upper-middle-class neighborhoods on the city's south side and the slummy areas on the north. The University of Nebraska at Lincoln sat right in the middle, surrounded by architecturally splendid fraternity houses and facing the tower of the State Capitol, as if emphasizing that education and connections were the route to money and power. The Lincoln newspapers breathlessly reported the goings-on of local people who mattered: Junior League benefits; University Club lectures; the engagements, farewell parties, vacations, and country club parties of Lincoln's high society. On Sundays, when the two papers issued a joint edition, the society pages expanded. "Patio parties, swimming parties, dinner dances and picnics were on Saturday's schedule for Lincolnites," reported a typical Sunday column of July 1956. Even on weekdays, pictures of local socialites took up as much space as world events.

It was a starkly divided world, no less for the young than for the adults. On the one hand, there were the pool parties and prom dresses and engagements of the well-connected younger set. And on the other hand, there were the hot rods and blue jeans and bad attitudes of the delinquents and rebels without a cause. It was clear to Charles Starkweather which camp he was in, and it wasn't entirely by choice.

"They say, this is a wonderful world to live in," he wrote from death row, "but I don't believe I ever did really live in a wonderful world. I haven't ever eaten in a high class restaurant, never seen the New York Yankees play, or been to Los Angeles or New York City, or other places that books and magazines say are wonderful places to be at, there hadn't been a chance for me to have the opportunity or privilege, for the best things in life."

• • • • •

"**H**uge Highway Bill Is Signed," reported the *Lincoln Star* in June of 1956; "Work for 630,000 Persons Foreseen." Congress had passed the Federal-Aid Highway Act, and it was being touted not only as a Cold War necessity, but as a welcome boost to employment in a nation that feared economic slowdown. The business world knew better. "The Boom Is Just Beginning!" cried *Business Week*'s headline. But the magazine's editors weren't talking about a jobs boom. It was a boom for the builders of construction machinery, for the makers of asphalt, cement, and steel. In fact, the magazine cheerfully declared, the highway bill would mainly benefit the materials and equipment industries. Road-building machines had grown so efficient, no new workers need be hired. The present workforce would suffice for the entire interstate program.

It was all good news for Lauer Ward, the owner of two prominent Lincoln businesses, Capital Bridge and Capital Steel. He had just weathered a national steel strike. Now, the strike was over, and with passage of the highway bill, Lincoln immediately announced plans for a big project: rebuilding the 10th Street rail viaduct. The new overpass would connect downtown Lincoln to the proposed Interstate 80 route, slated to pass north of town. The viaduct's location was practically in the backyard of Capital Bridge, and it was no surprise when Ward's company got the contract to build it.

Lauer Ward went by his middle name. His first name, Chester, he shared with his father, Chester K. Ward, who founded

Capital Bridge and Steel as one company in 1925. Lauer Ward had grown up in Lincoln and had done everything by the book. He went to the University of Nebraska, becoming a member of Sigma Alpha Epsilon. There, he met Clara Olsen, a Delta Gamma, whom he married. Lauer Ward attended Harvard Law, then served as an officer in the Army Air Forces during World War II. After that, he returned to Lincoln to take over his father's company, now broken into two separate companies: one that built bridges and one that cast steel.

The Wards were prominent members of Lincoln society: Lauer Ward was a friend of Governor Anderson. He sat on the boards of several banks, was a member of the Rotary Club and the University Club, and served as vice president of the local Humane Society. Clara Ward was active in a variety of civic causes and the Junior League, and she had once been vice president of the University of Nebraska Alumni Association. They were members of Holy Trinity Episcopal Church, and they socialized at the country club, just two blocks from their stately white brick home on Lincoln's elegant south side. They were the kind of people whose parties were written about in the local society pages.

For the Wards, Eisenhower's new roads bill could not have been better. The new interstate standards called for grade separations of all roadways and train lines crossing the expressways. This meant the interstates would need bridges—ninety-six of them on the Omaha-Lincoln leg of I-80 alone—using the kind of precast steel girders made by Capital Steel. Of the $42.5 million spent on this section, nearly a third would go toward building its bridges.

Although he was not given to showy gestures, in 1956 Lauer Ward bought a new Packard for Clara. At a list price of over $4,000, it was a true luxury car, with a V-8 engine, power steering, and power brakes. Its model name was the Patrician.

· · · · ·

C harles Starkweather also had a good year in 1956: he got his first girlfriend. His pal Bob had begun dating Barbara Fugate, and he introduced Charles to Barbara's little sister, Caril Ann. Caril and her family lived in the Belmont section of Lincoln, a slummy neighborhood of shacklike houses north of the Cornhusker Highway. Caril and Barbara's mother had divorced their father and remarried Marion Bartlett, a night watchman at a trucking company. The girls had a two-and-a-half-year-old half-sister, Betty Jean. The family's nondescript five-room rental house was covered in asphalt shingles shaped to look like brick. It sat in an unkempt, debris-strewn yard, with an outhouse and a crumbling chicken coop out back. There were no doors between the rooms and no phone. Marion Bartlett had only recently installed indoor plumbing.

Charles and Caril hit it off right away. They often doubledated with Bob and Barbara, going to drive-in movies or restaurants in Charles's Ford. Ill-educated but confident, thirteen-year-old Caril was a good match for Starkweather. She looked grown up for her age, and talked and swore like an adult. She knew how to drive, although she didn't have a license. Her sophistication was largely a matter of attitude: after her arrest, it was reported that she didn't know the United States had fought a war in Korea and couldn't recognize Harry Truman in a photo. Before their fugitive trip, she had never been out of Nebraska and had barely been out of Lincoln. But to Charles, she seemed worldly and smart.

With Caril, Charles found an escape from the feelings of social inferiority that tormented him. Her family was even poorer than the Starkweathers. She didn't look down on Charles, but loved him for who he was—red hair, bowed legs, and all. She had so little that even the shabby presents he could afford were exciting to her: a record player, a radio, cheap jewelry, and stuffed toys. Asked later about the things in Caril's tiny room, Charles proudly replied, "If it's there, I gave it to her."

According to Charles, they decided to run away together. With Caril, he would escape a world that had him numbered for the bottom. "When we would go together there would be no 'uppity' kids from big houses whose old man was a doctor or a president of a bank," he said. "We'd make people the way we wanted to make them. They wouldn't love us but that didn't matter 'cause we thought enough of each other to last as long as we would last, and after that it didn't matter. Anyhow, the people we got through with couldn't hate us."

In other words, as he said on another occasion, "dead people are all on the same level."

• • • • •

In 1957, the state issued contracts for its first section of I-80: the leg from Omaha to Lincoln. One of the first six contracts went to Capital Bridge. It was clear there were more to come. That fall, the Wards enrolled their son Michael in the top-notch East Coast prep school Choate. He was fourteen, the same age as Caril Ann Fugate.

As people like the Wards prepared for the big boom, however, the nation slid into recession. Charles Starkweather lost his job at the Newspaper Union. His boss was planning to fire him, but Charles beat him to the punch by quitting. Then Guy Starkweather got angry that Charles was letting Caril drive his car without a license. They fought, and Guy kicked his son out of the house. Charles moved in with the newly married Bob and Barbara for a while, then got his own room in their rooming house. On North 10th Street, not far from where the new via-duct would be built, it meant he was closer to Caril. He looked for a new job, but couldn't find one. Finally, he started hauling garbage again. He made forty-two dollars a week, less than half the average household income in Nebraska. Periodically, he failed to pay his rent and the landlady padlocked his door.

At those times, he often stayed at the local Crest filling station on the Cornhusker Highway, not far from Caril's house. He bummed cigarette money from its employees and hung around talking about hot rods. He would sleep in his car, and the all-night attendants would wake him up in time for his garbage shift. In spite of their kindness to him, sometime in November 1957, Charles resolved to rob the gas station. "I just got fed up with havin' nothin' and bein' nobody," he said.

On the last day of November, Charles took Caril to the Capitol Beach racetrack, where he liked to enter the "demolition race": it wasn't yet called the demolition derby. Driving a battered Chevy, he won the twenty-dollar purse. To celebrate, he and Caril went out for dinner, then to the Cornhusker Drive-In for a double feature. He drove Caril home in time for her eleven o'clock curfew, collected a 12-gauge shotgun he had borrowed, and, at three a.m., drove out to the Crest station.

On duty was Robert Colvert, a twenty-one-year-old navy veteran with a pregnant wife at home. Leaving his car out front, Charles went in and bought a pack of cigarettes from Colvert. He returned to his car, then went back and bought a pack of gum. Finally, in his car, he tied a red bandanna over his face and went into the station a third time, this time with the gun. Colvert readily gave him all the money in the cash register, just over a hundred dollars, but when Charles asked him to open the safe, he said he didn't have the combination: he hadn't been working there long enough. Charles believed him. Marching him outside, he told Colvert to get in the Ford and drive. Charles climbed into the passenger seat, and still holding the gun on Colvert, directed him to Superior Street, a lonely side street where local teens liked to go parking. He ordered the coatless Colvert out of the car. As Colvert walked away, he shot him once in the upper body, knocking him down, then again, point-blank in the back of his head. Police found Robert Colvert's body the next day lying on the dirt road, telephone poles receding silently into the distance.

Lincoln was shocked at the murder. But since the filling station was out on the highway that went from Omaha to points west, the police assumed the killer must be a transient. They canvassed pawnshops, to see if any out-of-towners had recently purchased a shotgun. Meanwhile, Starkweather tried to cover his tracks with amateurish obviousness. He paid off his surprised landlady, gave his Ford a new paint job with quick-drying paint, and went to a used clothing store and bought a bunch of clothes, paying the bill in stolen change. None of these things raised a red flag. Someone at the Crest station told the police about Charles's visit, but couldn't remember his name. Charles Starkweather wouldn't even be suspected of Colvert's murder until he confessed to it after his arrest.

For a while, Charles and Caril enjoyed their newfound prosperity. They went to movies and restaurants and bought holiday gifts. They even made a point of going to the Crest station to look at a stuffed dog. But the money went quickly, and to make things worse, Charles was fired from his garbage-collecting job for laziness. Before long, he fell behind on his rent and was once again locked out. He started sleeping in the unheated garage where he kept his car. It was time to run away. But there was a problem, he said later: "People started gettin' in our way."

• • • • •

On January 21, 1958, Charles borrowed a .22 rifle from his brother Rodney and went over to Caril's family home. It's unclear whether he had murder on his mind. He claimed he and Marion Bartlett planned to go hunting. He took some discarded carpet samples he had found at a junkyard. Caril's mother had said she would like to have them.

Caril's mother and stepfather did not like Charles. They saw him as a go-nowhere proposition for Caril, a perpetually underemployed hoodlum with a bad attitude besides. They might be poor, but Charles was worse: a juvenile delinquent like the ones you read about in the papers. To make matters worse, Caril had been gaining weight, and the family began to worry she might be pregnant. Charles only deepened their suspicions when he began to talk of marrying her.

When he got to the house on Belmont Street on January 21, Charles claimed, he got into a fight with the family. According

"People started gettin' in our way." Charles and Caril, photographed by his landlady, before the killings. Courtesy of the Lincoln Journal Star.

to him, they yelled at him and physically threw him out. He
went to a nearby grocery store and called the trucking company
where Caril's stepfather Marion worked, saying Mr. Bartlett
was sick and wouldn't be in for a few days. Then he went back
to the Bartletts.

What happened in the sad little shack on Belmont has
never been entirely clear. Charles gave at least seven different
"confessions." In some versions, the family attacked him and
he killed them all in self-defense before Caril got home. In others, he walked in on a fight between Caril and her family and
took her side by killing them. In another version, he claimed
he didn't even murder them all: he shot Marion Bartlett, but
Caril finished off her mother with a knife and beat her baby
sister to death.

What's known is that Marion Bartlett was shot in the head
with the .22. His wife Velda Bartlett was shot in the face, bludgeoned with the butt of the gun, and stabbed several times.
Two-year-old Betty Jean was stabbed in the throat, then bludgeoned with the butt of a rifle. The bodies were wrapped like
mummies in blankets, rugs, and paper, and secured with rope.
Caril's mother was shoved down the toilet in the old outhouse.
Her half-sister was put in a box and left on the seat. Her stepfather was dragged through the yard and stashed in the chicken
coop. Charles claimed that he did all this disposing of the bodies while Caril sat on the couch, watching television. Caril said
she came home and found Charles there; he told her the family
was being held hostage, and that if she didn't do as he said, he
would kill them.

Charles and Caril stayed together in the Bartlett house
for six days after the murders, eating junk food, watching TV,
playing gin rummy, and reading comic books. They had sex.
Charlie practiced knife-throwing; Caril spent one afternoon
cutting out paper dolls. She fended off relatives, telling them
that the family was sick in bed, and later put a note on the door
that read "Stay a way Every Body is sick with The Flue—Miss
Bartlett." She later claimed that she did these things to keep

Charles from killing her kidnapped family. Charles described these days as "the most wonderful time I ever had."

After repeated requests from relatives worried by the family's disappearance, the police visited the Belmont house the night of January 25, four days after the murders. Caril came to the door in her bathrobe and told them everything was fine. The police, unwilling to be dragged into what looked like a domestic dispute, left. The next day Charles returned the gun—missing a butt plate where he'd bludgeoned Velda Bartlett—to his brother Rodney, and Rodney showed it to their father Guy. Guy Starkweather, suspecting some kind of foul play, called the police and asked them to arrest his son. The police didn't take this request very seriously; Guy, they noted, had been drinking. Finally Caril's grandmother visited and was told by Caril to go away, because "Mommy's life is in danger if you don't." The grandmother convinced the police to send some officers back to the house with her. When they got there, no one answered the door. One police officer broke in, but the house seemed to be in order, and no one was inside. Charles and Caril, frightened by the grandmother's persistence, had already fled.

On Monday afternoon, six days after the murders, Charles's best friend Bob Von Busch and his brother Rodney took matters into their own hands and searched the Bartlett premises. After looking in the outhouse where the bodies had been stashed, they called the police. An alert was issued:

Pick up for investigation, murder, Charles R. Starkweather. May live at 3024 N St., nineteen years old. Also pick up Caril A. Fugate, 924 Belmont. Starkweather will be driving a 1949 Ford, black color, license 2-15628. This is a sedan, no grille, and is painted red where the grille was, and has no hub caps.

• • • • •

The flight of Charles and Caril was complicated by car trouble. First, the Ford had a flat tire. Then the spare had a bent rim. By the time they collected more spare tires from Charles's garage, the transmission was grinding. They stopped at the nearest service station to have it packed with sawdust—a common practice in the fifties to quiet noisy gears. Caril sat in the car, her stepfather's loaded shotgun on her lap, and drank a Pepsi while the Ford went up on the lift.

For some reason, they did not have the bent tire rim fixed there but continued on to Tate's, another garage, where they replaced it. They bought ammunition at the station and hamburgers at the adjoining diner. Then they drove to the farm of seventy-year-old August Meyer, a family friend of the Starkweathers who often let Charles hunt on his property. Meyer lived outside the tiny farm town of Bennet, about six miles southeast of Lincoln.

Bennet today looks much as it did then: a tiny town—population 544, according to the sign at its edge—with a few storefronts and a grain elevator clustered along the banks of a sluggish river. In 1958, the road out to Bennet from Lincoln had just been paved. August Meyer's farm sat on the edge of the small town. As Charles and Caril made their way up the muddy, slushy two-track, the Ford got stuck. They hiked the rest of the way up to Meyer's house. When they got there, Meyer came out, and Charles asked to borrow some horses to pull out his car. Then—he later said in self-defense—he shot Meyer in the head. He dragged the old man's body into a nearby washhouse and covered it with a blanket. He and Caril rifled through Meyer's house for anything useful. They collected some socks, gloves, a sweatshirt, a hat, a pump rifle, some snacks, and less than a hundred dollars in cash. They found a spade and went back to dig out the Ford.

As soon as they freed the car and got it going, it slid into a ditch. In trying to get it out, Charles stripped the reverse gear. A farmer who lived nearby saw them and stopped. He had a cable, and he attached it to his car and pulled them out. Charles gave him two dollars for his trouble.

The pair then drove up another lane toward the Meyer

house. Charles peeked in the window at Meyer's body and saw the blanket on it had slipped. Fearing someone had been there, they fled. They drove back to Tate's service station and bought shells for the .22 and a map of Kansas, hoping to throw police off their track. Then, with that odd indecisiveness, they went back to Meyer's farm, where they got stuck again. They abandoned the car and began walking along the road, each of them carrying a gun. The unlucky teenagers who happened to drive by were Robert Jensen Jr. and his girlfriend, Carol King. Starkweather later reported that Jensen stopped and considered whether or not to pick them up. But then he recognized Charles.

"You have a Ford, right? A '49?" he reportedly said. He too was a Ford man. His was a 1950 model, with double antennas, white sidewall tires, and loud "pipes." It was a hot-rod car, but seventeen-year-old Bob Jensen was no hoodlum. He and his sixteen-year-old girlfriend Carol King were the perfect opposites of Starkweather and Fugate: good students, popular at school and attached to their families. Carol King was a cheerleader and a majorette, and Bob Jensen was class president and a former football player. They were engaged. Their yearbook photos—she in a lace-trimmed Peter Pan collar, he in a plaid, button-down shirt—appeared in almost every newspaper story on the crimes. They look mature and already a little staid, each smiling slightly, as if contemplating the day when they would trade in Bob's hot rod for a station wagon.

Their bodies were found the next day in a storm cellar, a dank cryptlike hole on Meyer's property that was all that remained of an old school. The teens appeared to have been marched down there and executed. Bob had been shot six times around his left ear, from behind. Carol had been shot in the head from behind. Her body was lying on top of Bob's, partially undressed, and she had been stabbed multiple times in the vagina with a stiletto-type weapon that was never found. Newspaper accounts referred to this as "an unnatural sexual attack." Later, Charles confessed he had tried to sexually assault King but it was too cold. Then he withdrew that confession, insisting he had only said it to protect Caril. She was the one who had actually killed King, when he left her guarding the girl. He claimed he hadn't even seen it happen.

When Jensen and King were found dead, the story of the crime spree went national. The killing of a working-class family in a poor neighborhood of Lincoln was hardly news outside eastern Nebraska, but a pair of model teenagers murdered by their delinquent counterparts was headline stuff. *Hunt Teens in 6 Slayings*, screamed the *Chicago Tribune*'s inch-high headline. Jensen and King were widely described as "popular"; Starkweather now became the "brutal killer of 6." The story hit home in a nation already panicked over juvenile delinquency. If America needed proof that the kids were not all right, here it was, in a photograph of the fugitives pinched from the Bartlett house by a reporter. It was the perfect foil to the clean-cut school photos of Robert Jensen and Carol King: the blue-jeaned Charles and Caril sprawled on a settee, she clutching a cheap white purse, he with cigarette dangling—James Dean–style—and a smirk.

· · · · ·

This was not the first time America had fretted over its youth, nor would it be the last. But the Eisenhower-era panic was wide-ranging and intense, because it linked up with larger, deeper anxieties about the sweeping changes overtaking American life.

Historians today doubt there was any measurable increase in juvenile crime during the fifties: the flames of panic were fanned by the media and Hollywood. The FBI helped too: it issued reports claiming that delinquency had spiked 70 percent since 1948. In 1954, at televised congressional hearings on juvenile crime and comic books, teachers, ministers, doctors, police officers, social workers, legislators, and teenagers all offered theories about this "steadily mounting problem of nationwide proportions." By 1955, an estimated two hundred bills relating to juvenile delinquency were bouncing around Congress. Books rolled out regularly with titles like *Juvenile in Delinquent Society, 1,000,000 Delinquents, Youth in Danger,* and *The Shook-Up Generation.* Popular magazines like *Life, Look, Time,* and *Newsweek* ran lurid tales of teens gone wrong.

As the nation wrung its hands, analysts tried to point fingers. Slums, broken homes, working mothers, community breakdown, immigration, gangs, insufficient social services, and bad schools were all blamed for teen waywardness. TV and movie violence were denounced. Comic books, particularly crime and horror comics, came under special scrutiny. From today's vantage point, it looks a lot like cultural McCarthyism. The fifties are famous today for their postwar reembrace of traditional values. Overhyped fears about rebellious youth fit right in with that picture: the men in gray flannel suits hating Elvis, drag racing, and Dean. But to see the delinquency panic as merely conservative backlash is to miss out on its true nature. There was a surprising amount of introspection and cultural questioning in the nation's fears for its youth.

At its root, America's concern for its kids reflected widespread dismay at the lifestyle taking shape in the postwar years. This was partly class anxiety, as the GI bill and prosperity threw open the doors of the middle class to a massive influx of hopefuls. How could the old standards of behavior be maintained if the traditional elites were no longer running the show? But delinquency anxiety also reflected real cultural misgiving: what was this new world America was building? Politics were militaristic and society was materialistic. If the kids were on the wrong path, wasn't it the adults who had led them there? As a Yale professor wrote in the *New Republic* in 1960, "juvenile delinquency in America is largely a reflection of institutions and values which typify our way of life."

One of those values was mobility. The *Saturday Evening Post*'s five-part 1955 series "The Shame of America" began its list of sweeping social changes with "increased mobility [that] results primarily from the invention of the automobile and from the demands of our economy for a working population which can migrate easily from place to place." Or as Benjamin Fine put it in *1,000,000 Delinquents*, "When a child thinks of himself as a transient, he is much less inclined to be governed by what society thinks of his behavior, and has a harder time finding constructive outlets for his energy." Fine called the phenomenon "rootlessness." In *Youth in Danger*, Robert Hendrickson blamed the "new mobility of our population" for leaving families to "drift." Mobility was frequently invoked to explain why California's delinquency rates were so high: more of the state's residents were recent transplants.

The new mobility ranked high on every list of causes for the teen crime wave. But this put the nation in an odd position. Mobility was the very ideal the postwar nation was embracing—not least in the construction of a nationwide system of express highways. Linked as it was to social mobility, physical mobility—even as its dark side was being gleaned—was fast becoming national dogma.

Hollywood understood this contradiction best, and moviemakers mined it to good effect. In the more than sixty delinquency-themed movies made in the fifties, mobility is both problem and solution. The delinquent may be a sign of social breakdown—a threat to old ideals of family and community—but he's also a hero, an icon of a new era of speed, power, glamour, and freedom. James Dean embodied that doubleness brilliantly—the angry rebel, the new hero.

"What can you do when you have to be a man?" anguished Jim Stark asks his father in *Rebel without a Cause*. His father has no answer. The older generation—conformist, distant, hypocritical—can't offer the teens a decent model for how to be adults. The only thing for the kids to do is retreat to their car-centered world, where manliness is proved behind the wheel. Mobility signified the breakdown—Jim's family moves every time he gets into trouble—and it also provided the only relief, letting the hero prove his worth to the girl he loves. And it propelled Dean into immortality in September of 1955, when he slammed his Porsche 550 Spyder into the side of a 1950 Ford Tudor two weeks before *Rebel*'s release. Americans feared what Dean represented, and they made him a hero and an icon, too. Danger was part of the allure.

•   •   •   •   •

In Lincoln, delinquency was a problem no less than anywhere else. One person who took it to heart was Lauer Ward. On January 28, he had a meeting with Governor Victor Anderson. The interstate program was underway, working east from Sarpy County to the outskirts of Omaha, and already a freeway revolt was forming in the city. People from working-class communities on the eastern edge of town were joining together to resist the taking of their homes. A public hearing was scheduled for the next day. There was also the problem of getting money released for the 10th Street viaduct. Furthermore, there was talk at the federal Department of Labor about setting minimum wage rates for state contractors working on interstate jobs. The prevailing wage rate the labor secretary wanted was much higher than the wage Nebraska firms like Ward's paid. The governor needed to take a stand against the Washington busybodies.

But by the time Ward met with Governor Anderson, he was distracted from his highway concerns by the unfolding crimes in Lincoln. The morning papers had reported the bodies discovered at the Bartlett home. By the afternoon, August Meyer's body had been found in Bennet, and by the day's final editions, the bodies of Jensen and King had been found in the storm cellar. All the stories reported that Starkweather and Fugate were being sought for questioning. Six murders and two teens on the run: Lauer Ward was visibly disturbed when he and Governor Anderson met at 5:30. Caril Ann Fugate was the age of his own son, Mike. What was happening to America's youth? The company president and the governor looked at the papers and puzzled over how kids could go so wrong. What Lauer Ward couldn't know was that as he talked to his old friend, those very teens were already terrorizing his own home.

• • • • •

After killing King and Jensen, Starkweather had taken Bob Jensen's Ford and driven about a hundred miles west on Highway 6. But then, for some reason, he turned around. He later claimed Jensen's car was running badly and he wanted another one. But there were cars to steal outside of Lincoln. Returning to Lincoln was illogical, but what he did next was bizarre. He drove to Lincoln's toniest neighborhood and spent the day in the home of one of city's most prominent families: the Wards.

No one has ever figured out exactly why Charles and Caril chose the Ward household to victimize. Charles later claimed he had picked it at random. In other comments, he said Caril picked out the house. But his garbage route boss told police that people had seen Charles shoveling snow for the Wards. Other people suggested he sometimes did odd jobs for the Wards' maid. She may have even invited him in to warm up and have a bite to eat. Perhaps that was when he first got a look at the "best things in life."

Irving Junior High, which Charles Starkweather had attended, was just a couple blocks from the Wards' home. It was a nice school on the swank side of town: Charles was removed by his family—or kicked out, stories differ—after eighth grade. Before going away to Choate, Michael Ward had also attended Irving. He was four years younger than Starkweather; it's possible the two of them overlapped at a school where, undoubtedly, the younger boy fit in better. Charles may have known who the Wards were; he may even have harbored a secret resentment of them. It's tempting to think he was thinking of Michael Ward when he complained about "'uppity' kids from big houses whose old man was a doctor or a president of a bank."

But even if Charles didn't know the family's name, what he

did know was that if he was numbered for the bottom, the people who lived in that house were marked for the top. The Wards' sprawling white Colonial—bay window, sun porch on the side—was a far cry from the Starkweathers' "shabby" old house or the Bartletts' "slummy" shack. It sat in the elegant Country Club section of Lincoln where Charles had collected garbage, two blocks from the club's gated entrance. The house had a big, well-landscaped lawn and a separate garage out back. After getting a couple hours of sleep on the street, Charles and Caril pulled Bob Jensen's car partly into the Wards' rear garage. Charles, holding a rifle, knocked on the kitchen door, and Lillian Fencl, the Wards' fifty-one-year-old deaf maid, answered it.

Once again, a clear narrative of what happened has never been possible, because Charles's and Caril's accounts differ. They both agree that Lauer Ward was already at work when they arrived. They took Clara Ward and Lillian Fencl hostage, then spent the day hanging around the house. Caril took a nap,

Charles hated "uppity kids from big houses whose old man was a doctor or a president of a bank." The Ward home today looks much as it did in 1958. Photo by the author.

and Charles asked Clara Ward to make him breakfast. He asked for pancakes, then changed his mind and asked for waffles. At around lunchtime, Clara went upstairs to "change her shoes." After forty-five minutes, Charles went up to see what was taking so long. He claimed she emerged from one of the bedrooms with a .22 and shot at him. He dodged the bullet and, when she tried to run past him, threw a knife into her back. He dragged her into the bedroom and tied her up, leaving her bound and bleeding, but alive. Back downstairs, he and Caril guarded Fencl. When the newspaper arrived in the late afternoon, they cut out its front-page pictures of themselves and the Bartletts. The pictures, found on them after their arrests, cast doubt on Caril's claims that she didn't know her family was dead.

When Lauer Ward was due home, Charles waited by the kitchen door. As usual, he claimed there was a scuffle, reporting that he shot Ward as he was attempting to open the front door and flee. He then took Lillian Fencl upstairs and tied her up in a bedroom, leaving Caril to stand guard over her while he rifled through the house for food, money, and fresh clothing. He sent Caril to get some new clothes, and she picked out a suede Western jacket from Clara Ward's closet. Both women, Charles claimed, were alive when he left them, implying that Caril was the women's real killer. At one point, he took a polygraph that suggested he believed Clara Ward was alive when he left her house.

Caril, however, claimed that Charles had killed Clara Ward by stabbing her in the throat and later stabbed the bound Lillian Fencl to death while Caril stood watch at the window. Neither Charles's nor Caril's version of the events in the Ward house makes complete sense. Lauer Ward was discovered dead just inside the living room, still wearing his coat. He had been shot in the throat and the temple, and stabbed between the shoulder blades after he fell. Clara Ward was found wearing only a nightgown and lying on the floor beneath two beds that had been pulled together as if to hide her. She was bound and gagged and had been stabbed once in the back and many times in the chest and throat. Lillian Fencl, gagged and tied to a bed in another bedroom, had been stabbed many times in the chest, stomach, arms, and legs. These stabbings, like the sexual assault of Carol King, were done with a heavy, stiletto-like knife that was never found.

Charles and Caril pulled Bob Jensen's Ford the rest of the way into the garage. They made their getaway in Clara Ward's Packard Patrician.

• • • • •

When the bodies of the Wards and Fencl were discovered on the morning of January 29, Nebraska panicked. The license plate number of the Packard was broadcast over and over. State troopers, sheriffs, and deputies sped to Lincoln. Governor Victor Anderson, shaken by his friend's murder, called out the National Guard, "all the experienced combat men we can get," and posted troops at the National Bank of Commerce. Schoolkids were organized into groups to be walked home: "Come out, Charlie!" they yelled. But for grown-ups it was not fun and games. Hotels filled up with employees frightened to go home. Some home owners left their cars in open garages, keys in the ignition, in case the pair showed up looking for a vehicle. Others stockpiled ammunition and weapons. Men with guns stood watch as children left school; gangs of vigilantes roamed the streets. Local sheriff Merle Karnopp began assembling a posse by collecting men at bars and giving them guns.

Lincoln's mayor, Bennett Martin, told television reporters the triple murder was "the most terrible thing that's ever happened in Lincoln"—apparently forgetting the triple murder of the Bartletts reported just one day earlier. He offered a five-hundred-dollar reward for information leading to Starkweather's arrest. Clearly, the game had changed. No longer were the murder victims slum-dwellers or rural teens. Starkweather had struck out at the city's powerful, a couple who seemed to symbolize the nation's aspirations.

41

The Ward killings unleashed the era's ready reserve of Cold War anxiety. People were especially on edge in January 1958: three months earlier, the Soviets had launched *Sputnik*, the world's first satellite, sparking panic that communists were winning the arms race. The Soviets' beeping sphere provoked national hand-wringing over whether America, blinded by materialism, had gone soft. "It is not very reassuring to be told that next year we will put a better satellite in the air," declared Senate minority leader Lyndon Johnson. "Perhaps it will even have chrome trim and automatic windshield wipers." The nation's panic escalated when the administration rushed a U.S. satellite project into testing. The American satellite exploded just above the launching pad in December.

Pictures of National Guardsmen patrolling the streets of Lincoln evoked the fear of a Soviet invasion. The *Washington Post* promptly labeled the crime spree a "chain-reaction of death." But images of armed guards escorting children to and from school also echoed the pictures that had recently been coming out of Little Rock, where President Eisenhower had sent the 101st Airborne to enforce a desegregation order against defiant Arkansas governor Orval Faubus. Communists in space, black students in Southern schools: the nation was tightly wound, expecting at any moment to have to take up arms to defend what it saw as its way of life. Whether the national menace turned out to be Russian nukes, nine black high school students, or two teenagers with shotguns, it would be fought. The irony was that, just as Lincoln woke up to the threat of Starkweather, Starkweather was finally gone.

· · · · ·

In *On the Road*, published in 1957, Sal Paradise and Dean Moriarty drive a rich man's Cadillac east all night across Nebraska's Highway 30. After the murders at the Ward home, Starkweather and Fugate finally got on the road, reversing the beatniks' trajectory, fleeing west across Nebraska's plains.

They were headed to Washington, where Charles's older brother was a chef. They drove all night, taking Highway 34 to Grand Island, where they picked up State Route 2, a lonely highway cutting diagonally through the widely spaced towns of Nebraska's barren Sand Hills.

It was the farthest either of them had ever been from home. When asked about their journey in his prison statements, Charles repeatedly asked for a map so he could *show* the police and lawyers where he went, like an excited vacationer back from his first trip abroad. He recounted details for them: he got gas in Grand Island; around Mullen he nearly ran off the road and had to stop and sleep. They drove through Broken Bow, Dunning, and Alliance: Caril circled the towns in pencil on their map. At Crawford they switched to Highway 20. At Fort Robinson, they bought nine bottles of soda pop, before taking, as Charles recalled, "all those winding roads through the mountains."

Charles gave such a complete account of their flight that when I visited Lincoln, I was able to follow the pair's exact route. The Sand Hills appear to have changed little; if anything, they probably have fewer people now than they did then. State Route 2 rolls through one tiny, near-defunct town after another, paralleling the train track, down which coal trains from Wyoming rumble at regular ten-minute intervals. Between the current two-lane highway and the train track sits the old SR 2, abandoned and crumbling away, probably the very road Starkweather drove on. Highway 20 has been straightened quite a bit since the fifties, so that as Nebraska gives way to Wyoming, you aren't driving on "winding roads through the mountains." In fact, you aren't driving through mountains at all. The ridges outside Fort Robinson are the rather undramatic escarpment that marks the northern edge of the High Plains. It looks nothing like the Rockies, or the Cascades, where Charles and Caril were supposedly heading. It doesn't even look like the Poconos. But to a couple kids who'd grown up in flat-as-a-pancake Lincoln, the pine-covered ridges must have seemed mountainous indeed.

It was morning when the pair crossed the Wyoming state line. As they neared the small town of Douglas, they heard on the radio that the Wards had been found, and an alert had gone out on the Packard. Charles decided it was time to get a new car. West of Douglas on Highway 87, near a place called Ayers Natural Bridge, he saw a Buick parked by the side of the road. Merle Collison, a traveling shoe salesman from Montana, was asleep in the front seat.

An oil company lease agent named Joe Sprinkle drove by a few minutes later. He saw the Packard and the Buick by the side of the road, and thinking there had been an accident, he pulled over. As he approached the Buick, he saw a girl crying in the backseat. A young man got out of the driver's side. Sprinkle asked if he could help. Starkweather pointed a rifle at him and told him, "Help me release the emergency brake or I'll kill you." Charles had shot Collison through the driver's side window, then found he couldn't release the hand brake. For a hot-rodder, he didn't have much luck with cars.

Upon seeing the dead man in the Buick's front seat, Sprinkle decided to take matters in hand. He grabbed Charles's gun, and the two of them began to wrestle for it. That's when deputy sheriff William Romer drove by. As soon as he stopped, Caril jumped out of the Buick and ran toward the police car, screaming for help. The sheriff later testified that she told him she had been held hostage and that Starkweather "was going to take me to Washington and kill me." She also told the sheriff that she had seen all nine murders in Nebraska.

As soon as the sheriff arrived, Charles ran to the Packard and took off, going east toward Douglas. Romer radioed for assistance. Before long, the Packard was being pursued by Douglas chief of police Robert Ainslie and county sheriff Earl Heflin. They chased Starkweather into Douglas, where he lost time maneuvering through traffic on the town's main street. Continuing east out of town, Ainslie drove and Heflin fired at the Packard's tires as it raced toward Nebraska. Finally he landed a shot in the rear window. Glass exploded into the car, and a shard hit Charles near the ear. Thinking he'd been shot, he stopped the Packard in the middle of the road and gave up quietly. In a widely repeated comment, Sheriff Heflin sneered: "He thought he was bleeding to death. That's the kind of yellow SOB he is."

Newspapers gleefully jumped on the bandwagon, now cutting the captive Starkweather down to size. He was rarely mentioned without a diminutive adjective: "runty," "bantamweight," "pint-sized." Editors at the venerable voice of Midwestern conservatism, the *Chicago Tribune*, stuffed as much invective as they could into a single headline: "'Mad Dog' Swaggering No-Good to Kin; Bowlegged, Pigeontoed."

Charles and Caril quickly signed papers allowing them to be extradited back to Nebraska. Both of them were afraid to fly, so Nebraska police drove to Wyoming to get them. On the way home, Starkweather told Lincoln sheriff Merle Karnopp: "I always wanted to be a criminal but not this big a one." The letter he wrote to his parents from the Wyoming jail had less swagger: "ism sorry for what i did in a lot of ways cause i know i hurt everybody, and you and mon did all you could to rise me up right," he wrote. "But dad i'm not sorry for what i did cause for the first time me and Caril have more fun, she help me a lot, but if she comes back don't hate her she had not a thing to do with the Killing all we wanted to do is get out of town."

· · · · ·

The thrilling capture of a dreaded fugitive made headlines across the nation. The following week, *Life*, *Time*, and *Newsweek* all ran photo spreads on the killings. Starkweather's capture shared top billing with the successful launch, on January 31, of *Explorer*, America's first satellite.

The newspapers and magazines breathlessly reporting on Starkweather and Fugate were also offering up a vision of the nation's interstate highways. The "greatest construction job in history," Caterpillar ads declared, was underway. The company ran ads in *Time* and *Newsweek* offering readers a free booklet showing "all the routes of the magnificent Interstate-Defense System." Among articles describing Starkweather's "souped-up" Ford, his obsession with "hot rods," and his mad flight down America's highways, the Portland Cement Association declared that "concrete is preferred for the 41,000-mile Interstate System." The Asphalt Institute was pushing a booklet called "The Better Way to Better Roads," urging Americans to "See that your Interstate Highways are paved the heavy-duty ASPHALT way." Nebraska newspapers also reported that the Labor Department had set wage rates for interstate construction at an average of sixty cents an hour more than those set by the Nebraska Highway Department. Governor Anderson was refusing to comply.

The nation's response to Starkweather was practically a referendum on automobility and all that it implied. It surfaced all the concerns—mobility, community breakdown, a rootless and restless generation—that kept the nation fearful for its future. The fear was focused on America's youth, but people knew kids weren't the only ones to blame. The *Lincoln Star* ran a series on the problem of delinquency. "Could these crimes have been prevented?" asked reporter Nancy Benjamin. "Are we, as a community, facing up to the problem of juvenile delinquency?" The overarching issue, the series concluded, was a breakdown of community. Charles Starkweather was the direct result of Lincoln becoming a "big city," part of the asphalt jungle.

Across the nation, people scrutinized society for what went wrong. "The Starkweather case is another grim reminder of America's need to make a more intelligent effort to solve its social problems," a reader from Bethesda, Maryland, wrote to the *Washington Post*. "Atomic destruction is not the only threat we face. Within our own society there are sicknesses and weaknesses that should be diagnosed and cured at an early stage." The writer concluded that the nation's values were lopsided: "The sight of the uselessly large and elaborate cars on our roads often makes me think: The *things* are getting better; the *people* are getting worse."

Helen Starkweather also saw her son in the context of the nation's struggles. At his trial she testified that she had raised "six problems and one catastrophe." Later, she regretted the remark, and dictated an open letter to the *Lincoln Star.* "I did not mean that I had raised six problems in the definition the dictionary gives to the word 'problem,'" she insisted in a letter that shares her son's difficulty with words.

> What I meant was, I had problems to be met. Every mother and father has. . . . At the pace this old world is set today, one cannot deny there are numerous problems that children and youth find hard to cope with. What with the atomic bomb, the speed of our planes being faster than sound, Sputnik, and our world is coming to, so we should see what our young folks are up against.

As his trial proceeded, Charles did little to help himself. He snoozed, acted defiant, and refused to play along with his attorneys' insanity defense. He was hostile toward his lawyers and friendly to the prosecutors, who presented him as the cold-hearted killer he'd decided he wanted to be. In May 1958, after two weeks of testimony, a jury took less than a day to convict Charles Starkweather of murder in the first degree for the killing of Robert Jensen. The recommended sentence was death. Some sources report that Guy Starkweather remarked, "The Lord giveth, and the Lord taketh away." Others report that he told his wife and his son Rodney, "We ought to go someplace and eat a big, fat steak."

In October, three months after her fifteenth birthday, Caril Fugate went on trial for murder. To the delight of the media, Charles Starkweather took the stand to testify against her. Caril rested a hand on her attorney's arm as Charles told the

"I always wanted to be a criminal, but not this big a one." Lincoln looks on
as Charles goes into the courthouse one last time, to be sentenced to death.
Courtesy of the Lincoln Journal Star.

court that his previous statements exonerating her had been
"hogwash." Under oath he declared that she had never been
tied up or bound, that she had passed up frequent opportunities
to escape. She had been in the room when he killed her family,
had watched TV while he stuffed her dead mother down the
privy, had held a gun on Robert Jensen and taken the money
from his wallet. She had argued against giving themselves up,
and at one point had even suggested they kill the café workers
at Tate's service station, because their hamburgers tasted "like
dog meat." Her lawyer put Caril on the stand to try to limit the
damage, but it did the opposite: she was a bad witness, icy and
often hostile or confused by questioning. In November 1958,
after one day of debate, the jury convicted her of first-degree
murder, recommending a sentence of life in prison. The teenager broke down and sobbed when the verdict was read.

In March 1959, Sunday newspapers across the nation carried a *Parade* magazine with a cover proclaiming: "Mass Murderer Charles Starkweather Writes His Own Story." The story—heavily corrected and edited from his actual text—is a string of clichés slathered with Starkweather's unstinting self-pity. It recounts his normal home life, his abuse at the hands of vicious kindergarten bullies, and his continued suffering as an adolescent (he gave everyone in the class valentines, but not everyone gave one to him). It winds up with a rote statement of regret—"Today, my feelings are of great sorrow and remorse for the people I killed. . . . I pray that God will be forgiving of what has been done"—and a homily aimed at youth: "I would tell them to go to school, to go to Sunday school, to go to church . . . to obey their parents and guardians, and stay away from bad influences, and never undertake anything that you don't understand."

America had undertaken something it didn't understand, but there was no stopping it. The nation was being remade in the name of automobility and the limitless economic growth it promised. Charles Starkweather's violent acting out suggested the disconnection that was the dark side of mobility, and how it might play out for the frustrated and voiceless minority left out of the promised boom. But the nation was in love with movement. It was in love with Elvis Presley's swinging suits and hangdog hair, and with the speed lines and raked tailfins of its cars. It was in love with its new Boeing 707 passenger jets and the rockets that launched its satellites. And it was in love with its interstate highways, roads like I-80, which Lauer Ward helped launch in Nebraska, a ribbon of Portland Cement that would eventually bypass all those small towns that Caril Ann Fugate circled on the map as she and Charles Starkweather passed through, headed toward some dimly imagined Utopia of their own.

• • • • •

In a string of appeals for new trials and clemency, Stark-weather managed to delay his execution several times. In May 1959, he found an unlikely ally in the fight: Caril Ann Fugate, who hoped he would aid her appeal by recanting his testimony against her. On May 21, with Starkweather scheduled for execution the next day, she wrote a desperate letter to President Eisenhower begging for the stay of execution that the new Nebraska governor would not grant Charles.

"I have been denied by Governor Brooks a request to see him," she wrote, "and see if he will tell the truth in front of a minister or someone else who would be fair before he is executed." The president declined to get involved. "The Starkweather case," wrote his special counsel, "is entirely a state matter." Fugate would serve eighteen years of her life sentence, until its commutation allowed her parole in 1976. She moved to Michigan, got a job, and occasionally launched attempts to exonerate herself.

Charles Starkweather maintained his attitude of wounded self-pity to the end. Asked if he regretted throwing his life away, he replied, "I throwed away nothin' cause I didn't have nothin'." And on the eve of his execution, when prison officials asked him if he wanted to donate his eyes to an eye bank, he snapped, "Why should I? Nobody ever gave me anything."

On the evening of June 24, 1959, gangs of Bennet teens cruised past the Lincoln prison and idled on the road outside, blasting their car radios and sitting on their hoods. Inside, Charles Starkweather, wearing jeans and a chambray shirt, swaggering like Dean to the last, was strapped into the electric chair at 12:05 a.m. and issued three charges of 2,200 volts each. The headlines were somber. "Mass Killer Goes to Chair in Nebraska," read the *Chicago Tribune*. "Murderer of 11 Goes Calmly to His Death," declared the *Los Angeles Times*. In the *New York Times* he was "slayer of 11," in the *Washington Post*, "Killer of 11." No one called him bantamweight, pint-sized, runty, or even a youth. After eleven deaths, it was the twelfth—his own—that finally made a man of him.

The nation continued building its roads. Very soon, battles would begin over them. But it was all celebration, five months after Starkweather's death, when the first segment of Nebraska's I-80—6.4 miles near Gretna, with overpasses built by Capital Bridge—opened to traffic.

"Without pressing too hard, and doing a few loopy-loops around freeways and bypasses,
I managed to think up some method for following through with this act," Ed Kemper
told police of his first highway murders. Here are his hunting grounds: the newly

Americans are living in the midst of a miracle. A giant nationwide engineering project—the Interstate Highway System—is altering and circumventing geography on an unprecedented scale.

—NATIONAL GEOGRAPHIC, 1968

As the Woodstock generation, female no less than male, has taken to the nation's roads, armed mostly with trust and innocence and a desire to get somewhere else, the old order of highway violence has been stood on its head.

—NEWSWEEK, 1973

built Ashby Avenue on-ramp on I-80 in Berkeley, where he picked up hitchhikers Mary Ann Pesce and Anita Luchessa. Photo by Kemper's employer, the California Division of Highways. Courtesy National Archives (406G-2-13-65-367).

≡ FORKLIFT ≡

His mother called him Guy. His friends in the police force called him Big Ed. His buddies at the Highway Division called him Forklift. In the end, he was more of a bulldozer, a massive machine carving its way through a once-bucolic California town. As the seventies dawned, an excess of madness bubbled up in the sleepy coastal community of Santa Cruz. An auto mechanic turned homicidally anti-auto. A would-be highway engineer who heard voices telling him to kill. And Forklift, a nice guy, one of the boys, given another nickname by the town's residents: the Chopper.

His journey began in 1963, the year America went mad. The United States was increasingly embroiled in a baffling war in Vietnam, the civil rights movement was turning violent in town after Southern town, and in November, Lee Harvey Oswald assassinated President Kennedy as his motorcade crept through Dallas. Then Oswald himself was assassinated on live television by Jack Ruby. Later that week, as the murder played over and over on the nation's small screens—the crowd of nondescript cops, the diminutive Oswald crumpling, his face distended into Edvard Munch's *The Scream*—fourteen-year-old Edmund Emil Kemper III of Helena, Montana, stole his mother's car, drove himself to a depot, and took a bus to his father's home in Van Nuys, California. He too had reached a boiling point.

Ed Kemper was a disturbed young man. According to his sisters, he chopped the heads off their dolls, killed the family cats, and liked to play a game where he pretended to die in the gas chamber. He had a habit of staring that made the neighborhood kids nervous. It didn't help that he was huge for his age, a giant of a boy with a brooding look. His parents had divorced in 1961. Kemper's story was that his father, Ed Junior, was a John Wayne–like war hero who had gone on secret suicide missions in the Special Forces, and his mother, Clarnell, was a domineering man-hater. Frustrated with her husband's inability to complete college and get a decent, middle-class job after the war, she hounded him until he left. Once he was gone, she took out her frustration on her strange, sullen son.

Unfortunately for young Ed, his father's new wife didn't like his hulking, strange presence either. So after the boy had spent a few weeks with them, Ed Kemper Jr. took his son Ed III on a holiday visit to the home of the first Ed Kemper in tiny North Fork, California. At the end of the holiday, the father went back to Van Nuys—leaving young Ed behind. The teenage boy was distraught. He didn't want to live with his grandparents out in the middle of nowhere. The abandonment was made worse by the fact that it was Ed's father, the boy's idol, who had done it. Nobody wanted him, it seemed. Young Ed brooded for less than a year. At age 15, Ed Kemper III stood watching his grandmother as she sat at the kitchen table correcting proofs of a story she had written for *Boys' Life*. Then he lifted his .22 hunting rifle to his eye and shot her in the back of the head. He went outside, waited by the side of the garage for his grandfather to come home, and killed him too. "I just wondered how it would feel to shoot Grandma," he told police when they asked him why he had done it. "'Mad-at-World' Youth Kills His Grandparents," reported the local newspaper, right under the breaking news "Cute Little Girl's Kissing Santa Claus."

Ed Kemper, mad at world, looked a lot like a fifties juvenile delinquent, an angry young man like Charlie Starkweather venting his frustration on anyone who crossed his path. Committed to Atascadero, a state hospital for the criminally insane, he would emerge to remake himself entirely. The hostile, thwarted rebel would morph into the latest model of madman to haunt the American highway: the methodical killer on the road, depicted in magazines, movies, and a Doors song, threatened in police warnings, rumored on college campuses where idealistic young people were trying to build a better world, one that included the freedom of untrammeled mobility.

In the sixties, young people had taken to the road in great numbers, thumbing their way along the nation's new interstate highways. By the late seventies, all that would change. The killer on the road, a small danger amplified to a mythic threat, would change the nation's relationship to its car culture. His increasing hold on the national psyche paralleled the nation's transition from loving its new roads to hating them. From beautiful, safe dreamways, the freeways came to be seen as destructive atrocities imposed on the landscape by a money-grubbing highway machine. And as the highways came to be seen as concrete monsters, hitchhiking increasingly came to be seen as foolishly inviting ruin from monsters in human form.

· · · · ·

The nation's romance with its highways ended before the honeymoon was over. After the initial exuberance, the reality of having created a self-perpetuating highway juggernaut set in quickly. In 1960, Congress began investigating the program for waste and fraud. Critics pointed out that the highway trust fund—which socked away federal gas tax revenues solely for building roads—had spawned an unstoppable highway lobby, what one historian called "a virtual Möbius strip of money." This wide-ranging consortium of road builders, equipment manufacturers, state highway officials, automakers, and oil companies—they came to be called the "road gang"—seemed dedicated to paving the entire nation. Highwaymen had built a soulless machine, eerily reminiscent of the military-industrial complex Eisenhower warned against on his way out of office. In the sixties, activists began talking about "busting" the highway trust fund: letting some of the money banked by the federal gas tax be used for mass transit projects, rather than being reserved for roads alone. Even the staid *Reader's Digest* took a stand, publishing an article called "Let's Put the Brakes on the Highway Lobby!" in 1969.

Part of the impulse came from the growing environmental movement. Highways were beginning to feel like an assault on the nation's landscapes: they were leveling mountains, infringing on rivers, mowing down forests, and increasing air pollution by encouraging driving. The situation was especially dire in California, the state the rest of the nation looked to when it wanted to see the future. Thousand-year-old redwoods had been felled, valuable farmland had been asphalted, and a granite cliff-face in Yosemite had been blasted through. When, in 1963, California highway engineers released a plan to drop twenty-two nuclear bombs to vaporize the Bristol Mountains and clear a path for I-40, that only proved to critics what the interstate program really was: war on nature. Three years later, author Richard Lillard wrote that "As 1970 draws near, and the Age of Superhighways is at hand, many Californians see as a new menace the white serpentine tentacles of concrete that wind around communities and smother the environment. Eden has become the world's biggest concrete asphalt desert." Another denunciation of California's auto-centric development, William Bronson's *How to Kill a Golden State*, described the interstate network as "a monument to materialism, concrete proof that speed and dollars are the highest values in our culture."

The moral implications were important. It wasn't just that highways were ugly: they were damaging to the human soul. Around the time of the first Earth Day in 1970, a tidal wave of anti-interstate books hit bookstores. Their titles say it all: *Superhighway—Superhoax, The Road to Ruin, The Pavers and the Paved, Highways to Nowhere, Dead End, Autokind vs. Mankind.* The authors weren't just concerned about the destruction of communities and ruination of the landscape. They were worried about the highway system's effect on the humans who used it. "We human beings are sensitive organisms," wrote John Robinson in *Highways and Our Environment* (1971), "and consciously or not, we react to our surroundings." When those surroundings were a highway seen from behind the wheel, the effect was to deaden the driver to human connection.

The notion that cars had the power to unleash primitive, antisocial urges had been around since the dawn of the auto era, and it bloomed again in the seventies. As Ronald Buel put it in *Dead End*: "We are a violent people. . . . The auto falls solidly within this tradition. It keeps people from treating other people as human beings. One thinks of passing the car in front of you, or beating the other car to a parking place, instead of passing the *person* in front of you or fighting the *person* for a parking place. The auto prevents casual contact with others unlike oneself. And because we don't understand the humanity of others, there are fewer limits to our aggressive tendencies."

There was one exception to this understanding of the highway. One group of people was attempting to use the highway system to foster human connection, rather than separation: hitchhikers. Standing by the side of the road in bell bottoms and fringed vests, guitars slung over their shoulders, long hair blowing in the wind, America's countercultural youth had found a glorious new way to roam the nation: depending on the kindness of strangers. Strangers who included people like Ed.

• • • • •

In 1969, Ed Kemper was released from Atascadero. During his four years of incarceration, the United States had changed dramatically. Americans' support for the war in Vietnam, nearly universal when Kemper was sent away, had evaporated. After the president's murder, there had been more assassinations: Malcolm X, Martin Luther King Jr., Robert Kennedy. Radical groups were advocating violent upheaval: the Black Panthers, the Weathermen, Students for a Democratic Society. And many of the nation's urban ghettos had erupted in violence: Watts in 1965, Detroit and Newark in 1967, Washington, DC, in 1968. If the world had taken a turn toward violence in 1963, it was roaring down that road at full speed six years later.

Against the recommendations of his doctors, Kemper was paroled into his mother's custody. Clarnell had divorced a third time and taken a job as an administrative assistant at the new University of California campus in Santa Cruz. Ed moved into her home in Aptos, a Santa Cruz suburb.

Kemper, a boy with serious aggressive tendencies, had spent his formative teen years incarcerated with violent offenders and psychopaths. It hadn't done his mental health much good. Sexually, he was still a child, strongly attracted to women, yet terrified of them. He was socially inept. He had little formal education and slim hope of getting a good job. But he wanted, as his mother might put it, to make something of himself. He had been a model prisoner, working his way up to administering psychological tests to other inmates. While in custody, he had even earned a Junior Chamber of Commerce pin that he wore proudly on his lapel.

His dream was to be a member of the California Highway Patrol. He applied to both the Berkeley police department and the state troopers. His mother tried to help him by campaigning to get his juvenile record expunged. His record would ultimately be sealed, but it didn't matter: even without his murderous history, his massive size—he had topped out at six feet nine inches tall and 280 pounds—disqualified him. The only work Kemper could find was manual labor on farms in the Watsonville area outside Santa Cruz. He claimed this disappointed his mother: like his father, he was failing to get ahead. He and his mother fought bitterly about it, sometimes screaming at each other loud enough for the neighbors to hear. Finally, Kemper managed to land a job as a flagman with the California Division of Highways. With a steady and fairly respectable job, he got his own apartment in Alameda, a Bay Area city just south of Oakland.

He bought a car. His choice of model was significant: a Ford Galaxie. The model's new "Thunderjet" engine made it a popular choice for police departments, and Kemper fixed it up like a police car, installing a radio transmitter and a microphone on the dash. He bought a motorcycle too. If he couldn't be a cop, he could look like one. He even hung out with cops at a Santa Cruz bar called the Jury Room. "Big Ed," as his police friends called him, was clean-cut and respectful, a far cry from a lot of young people in town.

Santa Cruz, an idyllic coastal resort boasting beach, redwood forests, and dramatic mountains, was undergoing some growing pains of its own. It had long been a sleepy retirement and weekend community, but, in the late sixties, everything was changing. The new campus, opened in 1965, attracted a new breed of college student—longhairs who went to class barefoot and organized teach-ins to protest the Vietnam War. The town's mellow lifestyle appealed to other unconventional types too. Hippies and surfers flocked to the area. Witches and Satanists established themselves in the hills outside of town. Communes were founded. An alternative bookstore called the Hip Pocket opened downtown, while a cheap café called the Catalyst served up coffee, beer, and music to the hippie crowd. Santa Cruz had become a magnet for what was coming to be known as the counterculture.

In choosing to hang out with cops, Ed Kemper had chosen sides in a town sharply divided between "straights" and "freaks." To the older, long-term residents, Santa Cruz's new hippies were an "undesirable transient element." In the summer of 1970, the city attempted to reduce their numbers by limiting their transience: prompted by several conservative council members, town legislators considered enacting an antihitchhiking ordinance. Noisy young longhairs stormed a city council meeting, chanting "Sieg heil!" and "Power to the people!" The hippies saw the proposed ban as an outright attack on their way of life. Hitching was not only central to their low-budget, freewheeling lifestyle, it was the perfect expression of countercultural ideals. It was a way of expressing trust in one's fellow man. It was living in the moment instead of obeying a rigid schedule. And it was ecological and antimaterialist, because hitchers didn't need to buy cars. In short, it was "a beautiful, groovy way to travel," as one nineteen-year-old girl told *Newsweek* in 1969. Frequent news articles on the burgeoning phenomenon all cited the hippie commitment to using highways for impromptu human connection. As one hitcher put it to the *Santa Cruz Sentinel* in 1971: "Mostly you just feel how much people need each other and how much they take care of each other."

The straight world may not have thrilled to the grooviness of it all, but many in it were uncomfortable limiting personal freedom, and the Santa Cruz ban didn't pass. Then, in October 1970, the town experienced another tense moment between the straight world and the freaks. A prominent local eye surgeon, Dr. Carl Ohta, was found dead in his swimming pool, along with his wife, his two sons, his secretary, and the family cat. All of them, down to the cat, had been bound with the doctor's trademark silk scarves and shot, execution style. The doctor's house was aflame and its driveways blocked with his own expensive cars. Under the windshield wiper of the Rolls Royce, police found a note declaring that World War III had begun. "I and my comrades from this day forth will fight until death for freedom against anything or anyone who does not support natural life on this planet," it read. "Materialism must die or mankind will."

The conclusion was clear: hippie eco-freaks had murdered the doctor and his family. The town erupted in hostility toward its longhairs. Gun sales skyrocketed and bomb threats poured into hippie headquarters, the Catalyst. Frightened hippie informants told police about John Linley Frazier, an unstable young man who lived in a shack not far from the Ohta residence and often talked about murdering "materialists." A former auto mechanic, he had quit his job and stopped driving when a religious experience—probably drug-fueled—had convinced him that cars were destroying the environment. Police staked out the shack and arrested Frazier within a week. He was tried in early 1971 and sentenced to death for the murders. (The sentence was commuted to life in prison in 1972 when California called a halt to capital punishment.) At his trial, friends testified that he had frequently talked of a "revolution" in which people would have to either change their ways or be killed.

"It came down to the people who were in favor of nature against the people who were putting down blacktop and buying things," one of his friends recalled.

Hippies helped put Frazier in jail, but many were somewhat sympathetic to his cause. The antimaterialist counterculture was antiblacktop. Some in the straight world pointed out that this was in direct conflict with their enthusiasm for hitchhiking. But the hitchhiking kids didn't see a contradiction. Sharing rides reduced the number of cars on the road, thus limiting the need for new pavement. And it changed the nature of the highway, from a place you moved through encased in a private cocoon to a place where strangers met each other and bonds between people were created. Chance encounters on the nation's roadways could lead to just about anything.

·····

Ed Kemper was interested in chance encounters. He spent his free time in 1970 and 1971 cruising the Bay Area's highways. From Alameda, where his apartment was, north to Oakland and Berkeley. Or south, down the Nimitz Freeway, to San Jose, then southwest to Santa Cruz. He could get on the new interstate, I-80, zooming east out of Oakland, and he could link up to the still-in-progress I-5, connecting LA and San Diego to Sacramento and points north. In 1971, he had an accident on his motorcycle: another driver ran a red light and knocked him down. He received a $15,000 settlement and had a cast on his arm for the next two years. He had to spend a lot of time at his mother's place, recuperating. This led to more fights. When things got unpleasant, Kemper would get in his car and just go. And wherever he went, he picked up hitchhikers.

On May 7, 1972, Ed Kemper piloted his Galaxie onto I-80 in Berkeley. The Ashby Avenue on-ramp was a popular spot for hitchers wanting to go into San Francisco. Sure enough, he saw two young women there with a sign indicating their destination: Stanford. Kemper slowed to a halt and invited them in.

Mary Ann Pesce and Anita Luchessa, roommates at Fresno State College, had been visiting friends in Berkeley. They planned to see a pal at Stanford before heading back to school. They could have gotten a ride from someone they knew, but they wanted to hitch; it would be an adventure. They were both pretty and well dressed; they seemed like nice, middle-class girls. This was important to Kemper: he only picked up hitchers, he explained later, "if they were young, reasonably good-looking, not necessarily well-to-do, but say, of a better class of people than the scroungy, messy, dirty, smelly, hippy types I wasn't at all interested in. I suppose they would have been more convenient, but that wasn't my purpose."

Kemper asked the young women a few questions and quickly ascertained that they didn't know their way around the area. He drove around in a few confusing twists and turns, then, instead of taking the Bay Bridge west to San Francisco, he drove south, to Alameda. He stopped for gas there and went to the restroom, where he looked for Stanford on a map. It was to the south. He went back to the car and drove east.

"I took them the other way, out on 680, which would come in on the rural highway," he told police later. "I told them a story about how I was working for the Division of Highways. They were impressed with my radio transmitter, and they thought I was a secret agent or something. I kept telling them that I wasn't a policeman . . . and they'd give each other little looks."

Clearly enjoying being taken for the cop he longed to be,

Kemper drove to a secluded area near Livermore. Then he stopped the car and showed the young women his gun; he had borrowed it from one of his superiors at the Highway Division. He told the girls that he was taking them back to his home in Alameda, implying that he planned to rape them. He told Luchessa to get in the trunk and Pesce to hide in the backseat. Mary Ann Pesce immediately began to talk with him, calmly offering that he might just want to talk about his problems. Kemper, a veteran of five years of state-funded psychotherapy, was not going to be swayed so easily, but he did say later that he really liked her.

"I was really quite struck by her personality and her looks," he told police, "and there was just almost a reverence there."

Kemper handcuffed Pesce—a cop friend had given him a badge and a pair of handcuffs—and locked Luchessa in the trunk. He returned to the backseat and Pesce. He had what he called "this nifty idea about suffocating her." He tried to suffocate her with a plastic bag; then he tried to choke her with a bathrobe tie. She struggled too much, so he got out a knife and stabbed her many times, finally slashing her throat. As he was killing her, he said, "there was absolutely no contact with improper areas." He reported that her last word was to call out her friend's name: "Anita."

Once he felt sure Pesce was dead, Kemper went to the trunk and confronted the terrified Luchessa. He stabbed her so many times he later professed amazement at how long she lived. Finally, she stopped fending him off. He drove the bodies back to his apartment in Alameda, took them inside, dismembered them, and took Polaroid pictures. Later, he buried the bodies in the mountains near Santa Cruz. He kept the heads for a while, until they began to rot, then he threw them over the edge of a cliffside roadway into a ravine. He spent hours going over every item in the young women's bags and wallets. He was thrilled to find that his instinct about them was correct. Pesce's ID showed that she was from Camarillo, a well-off bedroom community north of LA. She was even a member of the Bear

Valley Ski Patrol. He drove up the Ventura Freeway to look at her home and was delighted when it turned out to be in an affluent, "country club" neighborhood. Sometimes, he told police, he went back to Mary Ann Pesce's burial site, "to be near her . . . because I loved her and wanted her."

Despite that "love," Kemper didn't feel bad for killing the two young women. After all, they shouldn't have been hitchhiking. At eighteen, the two of them "weren't much more than children," he acknowledged, "but I felt that they were old enough to know better than to do the things they were doing . . . out there hitchhiking, when they had no reason or need to. They were flaunting in my face the fact that they could do any damn thing they wanted, and that society is as screwed up as it is. So that wasn't a prime reason for them being dead. It was just something that would get me a little uptight, the thought of that, them feeling so safe in a society where I didn't feel safe."

• • • • •

Hitchhiking was not invented by the counterculture. For many decades after the introduction of the automobile, hitching rides was perfectly mainstream. In the days when few people owned cars, giving a ride to someone who needed one was simply the decent thing to do. During the Depression, a lift was a means of helping out the less fortunate. And once the war broke out, picking up hitchhikers became nothing less than patriotic duty, since soldiers often thumbed their way to or from their bases. Emily Post even sanctioned the practice for young women who had jobs in the defense industry—though she suggested drivers and hitchers restrict their conversations to impersonal topics, like the weather.

"What'd you say we're supposed to be doing?" Claudette Colbert asks Clark Gable in Frank Capra's 1934 comedy *It Happened One Night*. "Hitchhiking," he replies, and after launching into a pedantic lecture on thumbing technique, he promptly fails to thumb down a ride. The famous scene that follows, in which Colbert flashes a leg to bring a car to a screeching halt, is typical of Hollywood's pre-seventies embrace of hitching. Hitchhiking is a narrative device, throwing together characters like Joel McCrea and Veronica Lake in the 1941 Preston Sturges comedy *Sullivan's Travels*, or even a "meet cute," as when Jean Arthur gets a ride from John Wayne in *Lady Takes a Chance* (1943). Character actors as varied as Elvis Presley, Debbie Reynolds, and Cher can all be found hitching in postwar films, and as late as 1973, *Breezy* director Clint Eastwood set up a May/December romance by having flower child Breezy (Kay Lenz) hitch a ride with the middle-aged William Holden. Before she meets him, however, Breezy finds herself in the car with a lecherous creep. She jumps out of his car at a stop sign. "Freaks!" she exclaims as the car roars off. "Another typical day in the life of Miss Dumb-Dumb."

Antihitchhiking campaigns began around the time the interstate highway system did. In the late fifties, the Automobile Association of America launched a campaign called "Thumbs Down on Thumbers." It aimed at dissuading drivers from picking up hitchers by suggesting they might be dangerous felons or con artists. The FBI—impelled in part by J. Edgar Hoover's hatred for student activists who were hitching to civil rights and antiwar demonstrations—joined the campaign, issuing scary statistics and creating a poster titled "Death in Disguise" that featured an ominous hitchhiker. "Is he a happy vacationer or an escaping criminal," the poster asked, "a pleasant companion or a sex maniac—a friendly traveler or a vicious murderer?" The *Saturday Evening Post* had the answer in 1957: "The Hitchhiker You Pick Up May Be a Dangerous Criminal!" The magazine reported that "Drivers have had their heads bashed in with stones, have been dismembered and have been disemboweled by strangers they picked up on the highways." The problem was hitchers, though, not highways: the same issue included a feature impatiently assessing progress on the interstate highway program called "Where Are Those Superhighways?"

In spite of early scare campaigns, hitchhiking continued to

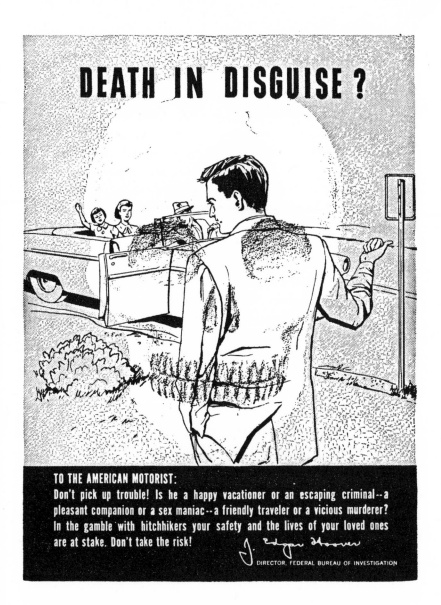

An early FBI antihitchhiking campaign. The FBI disseminated scary facts
about hitchers in part because J. Edgar Hoover hated that student activists
were hitchhiking to civil rights marches. Courtesy FBI.

grow in popularity. In the sixties, articles published in magazines as varied as *Life, Harper's*, the *National Review, Newsweek*, and *Scholastic* all viewed thumbing in a positive light. A 1966 *Sports Illustrated* feature was typical: it recounted fun stories about hitching, described as "a valid ticket to adventure for uncountable thousands every year." Author Janet Graham—a practiced hitcher—even included a perky list of "Tips to Girl Hikers." They included "Take a companion—or a hatpin"; "Be neat but not gaudy—no low-cut blouses"; "If he's tipsy or wolfish, say you are heading elsewhere"; and "Learn in five languages: 'I'm going to throw up.'"

Part of why the practice persisted was that early campaigns against hitching presented the hitchhiker as the threat. Early hitch-horror films like Felix Feist's *The Devil Thumbs a Ride* (1947) and Ida Lupino's *The Hitch-Hiker* (1953) cast the hitchhiker as villain, a story line that continued even in later films like Roger Corman's *The Hitcher*, made in 1986 and remade in 2007. In these films, the hitchhiker never has a backstory; he simply looms into sight by the side of the road and opens his campaign of torment. As a result, these films don't feel true to social reality: the motiveless hitcher is simply a force of evil, a near-supernatural harbinger of death like Javier Bardem's affectless Anton Chigurh in *No Country for Old Men*. Played with sadistic relish by Rutger Hauer in *The Hitcher*, the killer-hitchhiker even has a totemic name: "John Ryder."

The Hitcher was partly inspired by Jim Morrison's song "Riders on the Storm," from the 1971 Doors album *L.A. Woman*. Morrison's lyrics—whispered and sung at the same time for added effect—describe a hitchhiking murderer and warn the driver not to give him a ride, but here, too, the image feels like a metaphor. Morrison was not writing a public service message about picking up hitchers: to be a rider on the storm is simply to be a person on the turbulent journey through life, with the hitchhiker standing in for any bogeymen who can ruin the trip. (The metaphor is played out even further in Morrison's obscure 1969 art film *HWY: An American Pastoral*, where he himself plays the murderous hitcher.) The hitcher-killer felt no more real than the zombies, werewolves, or aliens who stalked the nation's dreams. And in fact, the real danger of hitchhiking was almost never to the driver; it was to the hitcher.

• • • • •

Once he started again, Ed Kemper couldn't stop killing. Four months after murdering Mary Ann Pesce and Anita Luchessa, in September of 1972, he was once again cruising Berkeley. Near a bus stop, fifteen-year-old Aiko Koo, an aspiring dancer, was holding up a sign with the letters "SF." She was on her way to a dance class in San Francisco and had grown tired of waiting for the bus. Kemper passed her, then did a U-turn to pick her up. She climbed right in without asking him any questions.

"There was absolutely no problem," he said later. "Apparently she was not an accomplished hitchhiker."

Koo, the daughter of an absent Korean father and a Latvian mother, lived in Berkeley with her mother and her grandparents. Her mother worked at the university to afford dance classes and private school tuition for Aiko. The young girl was talented, ambitious, and hardworking. She talked openly to Kemper about the fact that her father was not around. Ever on the lookout for class clues, he deduced from her speech and appearance that she came from "a home of meager means." One clear sign, he said, was that "there was no family car. The only transportation that she had was a bus to and from where she would go."

Koo knew which freeway ramp she wanted Kemper to take, so in order to get to a more remote area, he pretended to miss it, then drove on and off the freeway a few times. Finally, as they neared the Coast Highway that led to Santa Cruz, he pulled out a .357 Magnum—another gun borrowed from a friend at the Highway Division—and informed Koo she was being abducted. She begged him not to kill her. He told her he only wanted to talk, but that in order to get her to his mother's house without the neighbors getting suspicious, he would have to tie her up and tape her mouth. She consented. Kemper then attempted to smother her, and failing that, strangled her with the muffler she was wearing. At some point, he said, he raped her. When she was dead, he put her in his trunk and drove to a beer joint. After drinking a couple beers, he went out to his car, opened up the trunk, and looked at her body, doing, as he put it later, "one of those triumphant things . . . admiring my work and admiring her beauty, and I might say, admiring my catch like a fisherman." Then he drove to Aptos and, with the dead teenager in his trunk, sat and pleasantly chatted with his mother. Later, he took the body home and dismembered it.

Two days later, with Aiko Koo's head in his trunk, he drove to Fresno for a psychiatric examination. Based on the interview, the psychiatrists determined that Kemper was no longer a threat to society and that his juvenile murder record should be sealed.

• • • • •

By late 1972, the Santa Cruz County sheriff's department was beginning to notice a disturbing increase in the number of reported violent crimes. Rape was on the rise, and murders, though rarer, were trickling in. In July 1971, Linda Zuniga had disappeared while hitchhiking to her parents' home in Watsonville, a lower-middle-class community of mostly Hispanic residents. Her wallet had been found off Highway 1. Zuniga was a student at Cabrillo College, a junior college known for helping students transfer into the UC system. She was an adult, and police don't go looking for adult missing persons unless foul play is indicated. After one brief news item, the story died.

In August of 1972, hikers found a head on Loma Prieta mountain outside Santa Cruz. It was identified as the head of Mary Ann Pesce, murdered by Kemper three months earlier. In September, a fifty-five-year-old loner who lived in Santa Cruz, Lawrence White, was found bludgeoned to death along Highway 9. The next month, another Cabrillo College student, twenty-four-year-old Mary Guilfoyle, disappeared while hitchhiking to an employment agency in Santa Cruz. Her husband reported her missing, but again, since she was an adult, there was little police could do. Then in November, in nearby Los Gatos, a Catholic priest was stabbed to death in his confessional. The murder of a priest in his own church made headlines, but no one really thought the crime was related to the other murders. Newspapers, however, began reporting that Santa Cruz County was "a high-crime area." A November 1972 story in the *Sentinel* reported that the county's crime rate was the nation's seventh-highest—worse, the paper noted, than Detroit's.

With the exception of Mary Ann Pesce, Ed Kemper had killed none of these victims. But he was ready to kill again. On January 8, 1973, his record newly expunged, Kemper legally bought a .22 automatic pistol and cruised the UC Santa Cruz campus. His mother had gotten him an "A" parking sticker, reserved for students and employees of the college, so it was easy to get riders. No one thought twice about getting into a car bearing a university decal and driven by a polite, clean-cut young man. That night, he picked up three different hitchhiking women and took them all where they were going. "There were too many people standing around that possibly knew them when they got in," he explained.

But there was no one standing around when he picked up Cynthia Schall, a Cabrillo College student who had a babysitting job in downtown Santa Cruz. She was hitching on Mission Avenue, the road that led to Highway 1 out toward Aptos and her school. When Kemper pulled out his gun, she got scared, and he played his usual game of cat-and-mouse, telling her he simply wanted to talk, but he needed her to get in the trunk. Once he got her in the trunk, he shot her in the head and was surprised at how quickly she died. He took her back to Aptos, and this time he took the body into his mother's home. The next day, with his mother at work, he dismembered Schall's corpse with his Division of Highways axe. He got rid of her torso at the dump and threw the arms and legs over a cliff down the coast, but he buried the head in his mother's backyard. Kemper made a big joke of this later, claiming he had buried Schall's head face-up because his mother "always liked people to look up to her." In fact keeping the head close was largely pragmatic. Schall was the first woman he had shot; he needed to keep the head around until it decomposed so he could retrieve the bullet.

Schall's arms and legs washed up on a beach a couple days later; her torso was discovered in a lagoon near Santa Cruz. But the discovery was soon overshadowed by another mass murder: a mother and her two sons, residents of a cabin outside Santa Cruz, were found stabbed and shot on January 25. The next morning, two more people, friends of the dead mother, were found shot to death in their home not far away. The murders were said to have something to do with drugs, which made the "straight" community feel better.

On February 5, Ed Kemper got into a big fight with his mother. He told her he was going to a movie. "I said, the first girl that's halfway decent that I pick up, I'm gonna blow her brains out," he told police later.

He drove to the University of California campus. It was raining. The first girl he saw was Rosalind Thorpe, and she was halfway decent. Even in the rain, she hesitated before getting in, but then she saw his university decal and hopped in the front seat. As they drove on, chatting amicably, Kemper saw Alice Liu by the side of the road, a beautiful girl in nice clothes. Kemper figured it was having Rosalind in the car that got him Alice.

"From some of her I.D., college friends, stable background, and all that, I imagine she was a cautious hitchhiker," he said, "and we appeared to be a couple, and with that A tag on there . . . So she didn't hesitate at all about getting in."

This time, Kemper was still in a funk from his fight with his mother, so he made short work of the killing. He got past the campus guard and to the point where the road tops a hill and Santa Cruz can be seen below. Pointing out the beauty of the view, he reached down for his gun and with no warning, shot Rosalind Thorpe in the side of the head. She slumped against the passenger side window. Quickly, being careful not to hit the brakes, which might cause someone behind him to take notice, Kemper reached around toward the backseat and shot Alice Liu several times. She slid down in the seat, unconscious, but she was making a little sighing sound that bothered Kemper. Still, he couldn't stop and do anything about it in town, so he cruised on through Santa Cruz, one dead girl and one dying girl in his car.

Once he was safely out of town, Kemper stopped and shot Alice Liu again, point-blank in the side of the head. He moved both girls into the trunk and drove to his mother's house, stopping for gas on the way. Once there, he chatted with his mother for a while, as usual, then said he needed to go out for cigarettes. He went out to his car, opened the trunk, and beheaded both bodies. The next day, he took Alice's body into his mother's house and had sex with it. Then he put the body, wrapped in a blanket, back in the trunk in broad daylight and drove to Alameda to dispose of both young women. Late that night, he rolled the bodies off the edge of the Eden Canyon Road near I-580 and then drove to Pacifica, on the ocean, to throw their heads and hands over a cliff called Devil's Slide.

With the disappearance of Thorpe and Liu, public hysteria swept the town. These weren't part-time junior college students; these were nice, middle-class coeds on a flagship University of California campus. Both, however, were known to hitchhike. People began speculating about links between the murders. The killer was called "the Butcher" or "the Chopper." Panic increased the following week when some target shooters in the woods near the campus came across a skeletonized female body. Dental records showed that it was Mary Guilfoyle, the Cabrillo College hitchhiker who had disappeared on her way to the employment agency.

Hitchhiking was clearly the problem. The sheriff's office issued a press release warning female college students against it. "Ten rapes, eight assaults with intent to commit rape, three incidents of indecent exposure, two kidnappings, and one incident of sex perversion," it read. "That's 23 cases in 1972 in the unincorporated area of Santa Cruz county—all connected with hitchhiking." The police math was bad, but local newspapers began printing stories with titles like "Women Hitchhikers—Why Do They Do It?" The local underground newspaper ran a banner ad declaring "Women, it is no longer safe to hitchhike in this community." The sheriff shifted the blame to the women themselves: "When women hitchhike," he declared, "they are asking for a lot more than a ride."

Some groups tried to establish rules that would make the practice safer. An organization called Women Against Rape, or W.A.R., posted rape hotline phone numbers in public telephone booths and offered a list of hitchhiking suggestions like "Never hitch at night," "Don't sit in the rear of a two-door car," "If the driver starts talking about sex, change the subject immediately," and "Accept rides from people most like yourself—age, sex, ethnic and social background." The university also weighed in, warning female students to stay in at night, or failing that, to hitchhike in pairs. It suggested they only take rides from cars with university parking decals.

Writing about the murders in 1974, author Ward Damio declared it was "impossible not to think of the victims of Edmund Kemper while reading these instructions. . . . How many of these rules did they break?" The answer is practically none. Kemper was roughly the same age as his victims, with a similar ethnic and social background. He easily killed women who were hitching in pairs, he never propositioned his victims or gave any hint that he was a sex fiend, and he had a university parking decal.

• • • • •

"The old order of highway violence has been stood on its head," declared *Newsweek* in February 1973. "Instead of the driver fearing the pickup, it is now the hitchhiker herself who runs by far the greater risk of being robbed, assaulted, abducted, murdered—or, most likely of all, raped." The magazine declared violence against hitchers "a new and still unofficial category of crime." That year, the *Hitchhiker's Field Manual* noted: "At first, the driver was the victim of most hitchhiking crimes, but in the past few years the tables have turned, and most violence is directed toward the solicitor." Author Paul DiMaggio downplayed the threat, however, pointing out that with more thumbers on the road, there were bound to be more crimes against them.

But the media had embraced the cause. *Reader's Digest*, early to the antihitching movement, had declared in 1970 that "police across the country indicate that the one common factor in many unsolved cases involving people found sexually molested and murdered along rural roads is that they 'liked to hitchhike.'" By mid-1973, other voices were joining the chorus. Articles like "Hitchhiking Really Isn't Cool!" (*Seventeen*), "Hitchhiking: The Deadly New Odds" (*Good Housekeeping*), and "Hitchhiking: Too Often the Last Ride" (*Reader's Digest*) declared the practice unsafe. Police in San Diego began handing hitchers a pamphlet titled "Hitchhiking: Easy, Fun, Deadly."

Santa Cruz was quickly becoming exhibit A in the antihitching campaign. *Reader's Digest* reported crime waves in Santa Cruz, Ann Arbor, Boston, Boulder, Berkeley, and San Diego, declaring, "In the case of a girl who hitchhikes, the odds against her reaching her destination unmolested are today literally no better than if she played Russian roulette." Police regularly claimed there was little they could do about "highway violence." "Why should we waste our time?" one detective told the magazine. "Most juries figure that if the kid put out her thumb, she was asking for it."

· · · · ·

A s student volunteers in Santa Cruz organized search parties for Alice Liu and Rosalind Thorpe, another seemingly random murder occurred in the town. On the morning
of February 13, 1973, a retired fisherman working in his gar-
den was shot and killed by a man in a Chevy station wagon. A
neighbor who saw the whole thing called the police and gave
them a thorough description. Within hours, Herbert William
Mullin was under arrest. Two days later, he was charged with
the retired man's murder, as well as the unsolved "drug" murders. Later, he would also be charged with killing the Los Gatos
priest, the drifter on Highway 9, Mary Guilfoyle, the Cabrillo
College hitchhiker, and four teenagers camped out in a forest
lean-to outside of town. Herbert Mullin was responsible for
much of the violence that had been haunting Santa Cruz—but
not all of it.

Raised in a conservative Santa Cruz home by deeply religious parents, Mullin had bounced back and forth between the
straight and hippie worlds for a long time. He had completed
Cabrillo College's two-year program in civil highway technology, then switched to San Jose State to study Eastern religions
instead. He started dropping acid and registered as a conscien-
tious objector, but later reverted to conservatism and attempted
to join the marines. He was rejected because he had been committed to mental hospitals multiple times. Back in Santa Cruz,
he slid further and further into an insanity some said was
drug-induced. His family, deeply concerned, attempted to find
a place where he could receive long-term care, but under bud-
get cuts enacted by Governor Ronald Reagan, who had been
elected in 1967, mental hospitals across the state were closing.
There was no room for someone semifunctional like Mullin.
Living on his own, Mullin went off his meds. He told police that
the voice of his father came to him periodically, ordering him to
commit murder in order to avert an earthquake that would kill
thousands. In October 1972, he began to obey.

Mullin's trial took place in July 1973. Prosecution and defense agreed that Mullin had committed the murders and

that he was patently crazy. But the prosecution asserted that, crazy or not, he should be considered legally sane. Ultimately, the jury agreed. Mullin was convicted and sentenced to life in prison. It was some relief, but not total relief. Police didn't believe that Mullin was responsible for any of the "Butcher murders." The man they called "the Chopper" was still at large.

· · · · ·

The day after Mullin's arrest, two of Kemper's fellow Division of Highways workers stumbled upon two headless bodies in the woods just off I-580 in Alameda County. Five days later, the bodies were identified as Rosalind Thorpe and Alice Liu. District attorney Pete Chang declared that Santa Cruz must be "the murder capital of the world." A week later, over a thousand students and friends turned up on the UC Santa Cruz campus to attend a memorial service for the two young women.

Ed Kemper had reached his breaking point. He was convinced he would be caught at any moment. In fact, police had already come to his house and taken his gun—they had been alerted to the fact that a convicted felon had bought a firearm. Kemper explained that his youth record had been expunged, but they confiscated the gun anyway, while they determined whether he could legally own it. To Kemper it seemed sinister. Perhaps they knew something. Perhaps they were just waiting to arrest him. He was certain he was going to be caught soon, but it wasn't the prospect of being jailed that tormented him. It was the thought of his mother finding out what he had done. There was only one way to prevent that: he would have to kill her.

At close to midnight on April 24, 1973, Officer Andrew Crain at the Santa Cruz Police Department got what he thought was a prank call. Someone in Pueblo, Colorado, wanted to talk to the officer investigating the coed killings. At first the caller wouldn't give his name, but then he said he was Big Ed Kemper. Crain knew Big Ed. He told Kemper to call back; the detective assigned to the coed murders was home in bed. Kemper called back a couple hours later, collect, and another officer refused to accept the charges. Kemper called again at five a.m., rambling and begging the Santa Cruz cops to send someone to the Pueblo phone booth where he was and take him into custody. He gave the address and described the car he was driving. He rattled off its license plate number. Finally, an officer said they would send someone over.

"I wish to shit you would, really," Kemper replied, "'cause I have over 200 rounds of ammo in the trunk and three guns. I don't even want to go near it." He told them he had been taking No-Doz and driving nonstop for two days straight, that there were eight dead people involved. The officers asked him to describe some of the victims. He described Rosalind Thorpe and Alice Liu. Then he told them that the last two victims had been his mother and one of her friends. The bodies were still in the house in Aptos. The police officers asked for the address. Kemper gave it to them, helpfully spelling the street name.

"You see, what I'm saying is, there is a break somewhere," he rambled. "I can't tell you what's wrong with me, you know. But I had this big thought, you know, everybody thinks everything is cool, and then I pick up and split and say fuck it, I'm just going to drive until I can't drive anymore, and then I'm just going to open up, you know? Driving all the way out here, I'm reading about some clown out in Idaho doing it, some guy out in L.A. doing it, Jesus Christ, you know!" Santa Cruz police kept him rambling on until finally, to Kemper's relief, some Pueblo officers arrived to arrest him.

Once in custody, Kemper continued to confess, eagerly and thoroughly. He described each of the murders in graphic detail, down to the dismemberment and disposal of the bodies. He remembered everything his victims were wearing and described all the little effects—rings, wallets, ID cards—that he kept for as long as he dared. He speculated at length on his motives. He told police he had finally gotten around to what he had always wanted to do: killing his mother. He described bashing her head in with a hammer while she lay sleeping. He told

His mother called him Guy. His coworkers at the Division of Highways called him Forklift. And the citizens of Santa Cruz called him The Chopper. Giant Ed Kemper was docile as a kitten once arrested. Associated Press photo.

them he had beheaded her, because "what's good for my victims is good for my mother." He said he had cut out her larynx and put it down the garbage disposal, but the contraption had spit it out: "This seemed appropriate," he reportedly said, "as much as she'd bitched and screamed and yelled at me over the years." This lurid detail seems likely to be an embellishment for law enforcement's benefit. Kemper had always liked cops.

Kemper was brought back to Santa Cruz, and he led police to several of his victims' bodies. District Attorney Chang told the press that Big Ed blamed the murders on his victims. He never would have acted out his fantasies, he said, if it hadn't been for "the availability of naive girls who were hitchhiking."

· · · · ·

To the road builders and highwaymen, the freeway meant economic growth founded on mobility. To the hippies, the freeway fulfilled a different fantasy: that the open road could lead to connection, community, and "finding yourself." It provided a space in which they could act on their antimaterialist ideals—by sharing others' cars rather than owning them—or at least engage in an informal economy, trading "gas, grass, or ass" for a ride. It was a stage for acting out human trust and easy exchanges with others. And, experienced in tandem with strangers, it was a place where they connected with the landscape and the nation.

Throughout the seventies, crackdowns and attempts to criminalize hitchhiking were understood by the counterculture as "a means of harassing long-hairs," to borrow words from the *Hitchhiker's Field Manual*. Women were somewhat at risk of rape or worse, but the guidelines issued to help women stay safe were a sign of how invested youth were in maintaining their reinterpretation of automobility as a means of connection, not isolation. When hitchhiking died out, that reinterpretation died as well.

An article in *Mother Jones* in 1976 was already proclaiming the end of an era. In "A Half Dozen Ways Things Were Better," author Bruce Morgan contrasted the openness and political engagement of 1969 with the present. One of the ways in which the past was superior to the present was that "hitchhiking was a cinch."

"In a time with so many claiming to be kin, hitchhiking represented a real-life test of those abstract linkages," Morgan wrote. "Lately people have gotten into protecting their own space, and that is bad news indeed for those who want to share it."

· · · · ·

With Forklift behind bars, the highways continued to get a bad rap. Hitchhiker murders were publicized throughout the seventies. As Kemper was on his killing spree, seven hitchhiking women disappeared near Santa Rosa, California; their murders have never been solved. Twenty-seven young boys—many of them picked up while hitching—were killed by Dean Corll in Houston and Pasadena in the early seventies. Six hitchhiking teenagers were murdered in three New Jersey counties in 1974, leading police in Dover County to start taking "young girl" hitchhikers into custody for their own safety. Donald Henry Gaskins, arrested and convicted in 1976, stalked Southern roads for hitchhikers and transients. As the decade progressed, Boston, Minneapolis, Boulder, Miami, and Los Angeles all reported outbreaks of crime against hitchers. As the theme song to the 1977 exploitation film went, "when you go thumbing a ride, you can never tell when you'll *Hitch Hike to Hell!*"

How dangerous was hitchhiking in reality? There are almost no studies of the question. The one actual piece of research was a study commissioned by the California Highway Patrol in 1974. *California Crimes and Accidents Associated with Hitchhiking* determined that hitching was a factor in only 0.63 percent of reported crimes. Statistically, it was hardly more dangerous than walking down the street. Nevertheless, public fear continued to grow. By the end of the seventies, hitchhiking was largely considered a foolhardy act. In 1979, when Rutgers University women's groups protested the campus police practice of handing women who were walking alone at night a card that read "If I were a rapist, you'd be in trouble," the cops stopped handing out the cards—except to women seen hitchhiking. Of course, women weren't the only potential victims. As cops in New Jersey were trying to scare hitchhiking women, young men soliciting rides in Orange County, California, were being stalked by the first person to be branded the "Freeway Killer" by the media. The "Freeway Killer," in fact, turned out to be three different men—Patrick Kearney, Randy Kraft, and William Bonin—all of whom used Southern California's interstates to find murder victims. As with Herbert Mullin and Ed Kemper in Santa Cruz, police had a hard time sorting out whose victims were whose.

Ed Kemper went on trial in November 1973. The courtroom was packed, many of its seats filled with young women the age of Kemper's victims, prompting the judge to order bailiffs to kick some spectators out. "I'd be much happier if this room weren't full of teenage girls," he noted dryly. But perhaps the teenagers sensed that they were seeing the end of an era. Big Ed might be locked up for life, but the open road would never be the same.

Kemper's lengthy confessions made things easy on the prosecution at his trial. Even his attorney's attempt to have him declared insane lacked vigor. The jury took only five hours to find Forklift guilty—a verdict his own lawyer called "reasonable enough." Kemper, sentenced to life in prison, spent years trying to have himself lobotomized to end his homicidal urges.

Kemper and his fellow hitchhiker-killers didn't just murder young women. They helped kill a vision of the freeway as a place for new forms of human connection. They were aided in that murder by the public's general unease about the world the highways were making. As freeways dismembered the landscape, it became easy to believe they were haunted by malevolent murderers like "the Chopper." Today, hitchhiking is unthinkable for most people. Not long ago, I was driving in the Midwest with my daughter. Accelerating down an interstate on-ramp, we passed a scruffy bearded man in jeans and a work shirt, a cardboard sign in his hand.

"Is that a *hitchhiker*?" my daughter cried. "I've never seen one before!"

From the late seventies onward, the highway was increasingly seen as a place of isolation, hostility, and danger. Travelers took to the road with a new sense of vigilance. But when children began disappearing in Atlanta, the nation would begin to see something city-dwellers had been facing for two decades. Highways were more than a place where the violent could find victims. They themselves were becoming murderers, and their victims were entire communities.

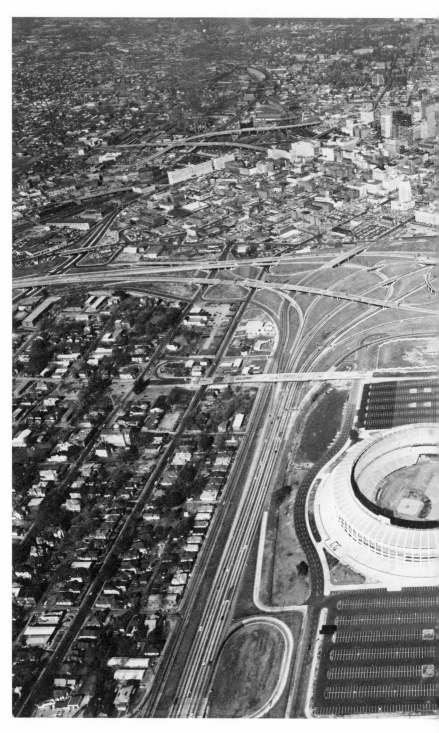

Highway construction and urban renewal transformed the nation's cities. In Atlanta one-third of the city's housing stock—the vast majority occupied by poor blacks—was demolished for freeways and urban renewal projects, including the stadium shown here. Courtesy National Archives (406G-5-42-66-124).

*Every major city from Boston
to Los Angeles is festooned,
draped—or is it strangled?—
with ribbons of concrete.*

—*NEW YORK TIMES*, 1966

*The War on Black Children
takes many forms. Homicide
is only one aspect of the
violence waged against the
most defenseless segment of
our society by individuals,
institutions, and the economic
reality of black life in America.*

—*BLACK ENTERPRISE*, 1981

≡ THE CRUELEST BLOW ≡

I n October of 1979, Eula Birdsong was sitting in the balmy Southern fall sun when Yusef Bell ran by. Nine-year-old Yusef was a nice boy, smart and friendly and respectful to elderly folks like her—not at all like a lot of the young hoodlums around Mechanicsville, the shabby Atlanta neighborhood where they lived. Eula often asked Yusef to do favors for her, and today she asked him to go to the store and get her some Bruton snuff. She offered him seventeen cents for the job. Yusef agreed, and headed out to the Reese Grocery Store on McDaniel Street.

The Bell family had moved in upstairs from Eula not long ago. The mother, Camille, was struggling to make ends meet and wound up in public housing. But she worked hard to protect her kids from the malign influences of the ghetto. All four of the Bell kids were good students, but Yusef was the star, a student at the local gifted program with an almost encyclopedic memory. People in the neighborhood liked to quiz him just for the fun of hearing him rattle off answers. He seemed destined to make something of himself, to get out of the shabby McDaniel-Glenn projects where he lived.

But Yusef Bell never came back from the Reese Grocery Store with Eula's snuff. Eighteen days later, his strangled body was found in the crawl space of an abandoned school not far from his home. People in the neighborhood were shocked. He had been such a promising boy. At his funeral service, Reverend Timothy McDonald of Ebenezer Baptist Church, where Martin Luther King Jr. once preached, declared Yusef's death a tragedy for the community: "His potential to liberate his people was blighted out."

Blighted out. It was an odd phrase. Blight was a word heard a lot in the seventies, but it was always used for cities, as in "urban blight." Yusef had been killed by a person; someone had placed human hands around his small neck and squeezed it until he stopped breathing. That was murder, not blight.

And yet, there was a connection, felt at first by the black community and later by the whole nation. Beginning in the 1960s, urban highways had been used to drive a radical program of urban renewal aimed at eliminating blight. But what they did was produce more of it. They dispersed poor communities, helped jobs, businesses, and middle-class residents flee the center city, and turned formerly stable neighborhoods into dangerous ghettos. The highway program divided the nation's cities into zones separating white from black, affluent from poor, hope-filled from hopeless, allowing the well-off to ignore the poorest sections as they slid into squalor and despair. It devalued the lives of the urban poor. Children like Yusef Bell became easy prey for a killer partly because of decisions made by urban planners and highway engineers with little thought for the effect they might have on kids' lives. So in that sense, Yusef was indeed blighted out. The blighting had begun more than a decade before he was born.

· · · · ·

Shortly after the 1956 highway bill passed, the *Saturday Evening Post* published an encomium on the coming interstate network. "A happy by-product of all these expressway developments," it declared, "is that they invariably do an excellent job of slum clearance as they knife through the poorer sections of the city." Buying highway right-of-way in low-rent neighborhoods would save the government money. But even more, planners saw it as beneficial. The knife metaphor says a lot about how planners saw interstates: as weapons in a war against slums. Robert Moses put it most famously in his graphic description of building urban expressways: "When you operate in an overbuilt metropolis, you have to hack your way through with a meat ax."

When the highway bill passed in 1956, the consensus among city planners and politicians was that swinging the meat ax would save America's cities. Highways would untangle snarled traffic in central business districts, stemming the exodus of retailers to the suburbs. They would separate dank manufacturing areas from leafy residential enclaves, promoting a more wholesome and orderly way of life. And they would plow through the city's poorest, shabbiest residential areas, eliminating urban blight. To the planners, using highways to "knife through the poorer sections" was not violence, but surgery. And there was little doubt about who needed that surgery: African American migration into urban centers during the world wars had changed the racial makeup of cities. For planners, "urban blight" was often synonymous with "black neighborhood."

In its first decade, the interstate highway program destroyed some 330,000 urban housing units across the nation, the majority of them occupied by minorities and the poor. After that the pace picked up. No one knows the exact number, but estimates are that the highway program displaced around a million Americans. Black neighborhoods bore the brunt of it. Highway programs wiped out Paradise Valley, the Detroit neighborhood that gave birth to Motown. They bulldozed Overtown, the heart of black Miami, and North Claiborne Avenue, a vibrant African American commercial boulevard in New Orleans, home to the nation's largest stand of live oak trees. In Boston, New York, Charlotte, Nashville, Montgomery, Birmingham, Columbus, St. Paul, and Los Angeles, black communities were lost to the freeway. Expressways were used not only to clear out communities the planners dubbed "slums," but to isolate and contain the black neighborhoods that remained.

"When the American people, through their Congress, voted a little while ago for a twenty-six-billion-dollar highway program," declared Lewis Mumford, "the most charitable thing to assume about this action is that they hadn't the faintest notion of what they were doing." The renowned urban theorist was convinced that highways wouldn't just destroy black neighborhoods; they would blight city centers. His remarks at a 1957 urban planning conference in Hartford, Connecticut, launched a small wave of antifreeway sentiment. Critics pointed out that highways simply choked central business districts with traffic they had no capacity to handle. This would just speed up the exodus of businesses and middle-class residents who had already been heading for "streetcar suburbs" for decades. As the *New York Times* put it: "Autos are strangling cities coast to coast."

Strangling, knifing, choking: this assault on cities was not Eisenhower's vision for the highway program. In fact, historians often claim the president was surprised to discover that freeways were being built in cities at all. In his biography *Eisenhower: The President,* Stephen Ambrose claims that the revelation came in July of 1959, when the president's motorcade was stuck in a Washington traffic jam. When an aide told him interstate construction was to blame, a surprised Ike protested that couldn't be: the interstates were not meant to enter city centers.

Parts of Ambrose's biography have been challenged lately, and this story, too, has to be doubted. By mid-1959, Eisenhower already knew that the interstates were plowing into downtowns: earlier that year, he had assigned an advisor to review the program's role in urban areas. He chose General John Stewart Bragdon, a former West Point classmate, to draw up a report. In June, a month before Ambrose's traffic jam supposedly happened, Bragdon handed the president a memorandum recommending that the Bureau of Public Roads reroute expressways around central cities. At Eisenhower's request, Bragdon spent almost a year preparing a report on how to do it. He presented it to Ike in April 1960. Wielding seventeen charts and stacks of documentation, General Bragdon recommended linking transportation to comprehensive land-use planning, developing multimodal mass transit, and allowing states to collect tolls on high-traffic highways—in short, everything progressive planners advocate today.

Poor Bragdon: his report was doomed. Bertram Tallamy, the federal highway administrator, was also at the meeting. Tallamy was an Eisenhower appointee and a road builder's road builder. His father and grandfather had been contractors. His mentor was autocratic highway builder Robert Moses, the man known for reshaping New York City with highways. Former chairman of the three-person commission that oversaw the building of the New York Thruway, Tallamy had learned a key lesson from Moses: never brook opposition. He came to Bragdon's presentation armed only with one thing: a copy of the Yellow Book.

The Yellow Book was created by the Bureau of Public Roads in 1955, after the highway bill failed in Congress. Officially titled *General Location of National System of Interstate Highways Including All Additional Routes at Urban Areas*, the booklet contained almost no text: just maps of one hundred American cities with interstate highways bisecting and ringing their cores. Today it's generally acknowledged that highways are bad for cities, but in 1955, every city wanted them. And the Yellow Book offered them up, showing members of Congress exactly what goodies they could take home to their districts if they passed a highway bill. After it was distributed, every representative opposed to the bill, save one, switched sides and voted for highways.

At the April 1960 meeting, Eisenhower testily declared he had never seen the Yellow Book before that day. Now his aides were saying that the Yellow Book had sold the interstate pro-

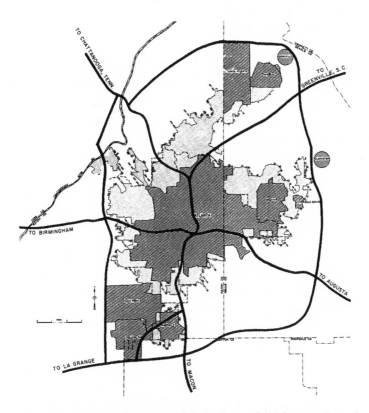

On page after page in what was called the "Yellow Book," highway engineers drafted a plan to drive freeways through every urban center in the nation. Few were able to stop the building of "white men's roads through black men's bedrooms." U.S. Government Printing Office, 1955.

gram in Congress. Was this true? Tallamy assured him that the Yellow Book had been on the desk of every congressional representative when the 1956 highway bill was passed. Like it or not, urban freeways were what Congress had been promised. Eisenhower said he was disappointed, but his hands were tied. A few weeks later, he dissolved Bragdon's highway advisor position and reassigned his old friend to a nice out-of-the-way post on the Civil Aeronautics Board. The strangling of cities would proceed as planned.

What's amazing, looking at the Yellow Book today, is how casual it appears, how easily the highway engineers knifed through urban America. The interstates are not numbered or named. There are no explanations. There's just city after city with heavy black lines scrawled over its core: it looks like highway engineers took Sharpies to an atlas of American cities. And yet, in most cases, the routes are amazingly accurate, as if the planners' black pens had the alchemy to turn ink into pavement. Atlanta, for instance, is ringed in by an oval: the beltway, I-285, known today as the Perimeter. Bisecting the Perimeter is a swooping line from southwest to northeast: the I-75/I-85 Downtown Connector. And knifing east across Atlanta's midline, from Birmingham toward Augusta, is the highway now known as I-20. I-20 would play a key role in Atlantans' understanding of why, in the late seventies, their children began to disappear.

• • • • •

The interstate program's transformation of America unfolded with great speed, but in Atlanta it was especially dramatic. By the early sixties, four interstate highways were converging on its downtown in a thirty-two-lane interchange—the largest in the South. Large parts of the city's black neighborhoods—Mechanicsville, Vine City, Buttermilk Bottoms—were mowed down. About one-third of the city's existing housing stock was demolished by the highway program and urban renewal; 67,000 residents were displaced, 95 percent of them black. Most were renters, and so went uncompensated. Many had a hard time finding new housing. Priced out of the freeway-accessible middle-class suburbs, they were forced into a smaller and smaller area in the center city. Thousands ended up in the unsavory public housing projects the city was building at the same time. The fifties, sixties, and seventies saw the rapid construction of bland complexes with ironically sunny names: Perry Homes, Harris Homes, Bowen Homes, Hollywood

Courts, East Lake Meadows. By the eighties, Atlanta would lead the nation in public housing units per capita. Twelve percent of its population would be tenants of the Atlanta Housing Authority. Many of them ended up there when they were displaced by city projects.

It was a one-two punch: first highways, then urban renewal. The highways cleared the way to build projects and pack people into them, then isolated the resulting neighborhoods. In a town where planners had once infamously attempted to build a wall dividing black and white neighborhoods, the freeway served as a de facto wall. "The downtown portion of the city's highway system," wrote one planning professor, "was configured to eliminate portions of poor black neighborhoods on the east side of downtown, creating a buffer between the central business district and the remnants of the neighborhoods."

One area isolated by the downtown freeway was the Auburn Avenue neighborhood. "Sweet Auburn" was declared "the richest negro street in the world" by *Forbes* in 1956. It was the address of the *Atlanta Daily World*, one of the nation's oldest black newspapers; the Odd Fellows building, home to more than 120 black-owned businesses; WERD, the city's first black-owned radio station; and clubs like the Royal Peacock and the Top Hat, frequented by the likes of B. B. King, Ma Rainey, Ray Charles, and Aretha Franklin. It was the street on which Martin Luther King Jr. was born. But in the early sixties the city insisted on moving I-75/I-85, originally planned for the largely unused railroad right-of-way, to the eastern edge of the central business district. Completed in 1964, the so-called Downtown Connector plowed through the black neighborhoods of Mechanicsville and Summerhill, bisecting Auburn Avenue and mowing down a block of buildings just blocks from Ebenezer Baptist Church, where Reverend King and his father both preached. A decade later, a city-commissioned study by the Georgia Institute of Technology College of Architecture reported that the "once vibrant Auburn Avenue street life has essentially disappeared, business activity has declined, and

*"Sweet Auburn," once called the "richest Negro street in the world,"
today remains blighted by the freeway. Photo by the author.*

many historic and other structures stand deteriorating and underutilized." The area, the architects said, might easily be called "a slum."

. . . . .

C amille Bell never wanted her children to grow up in the slums. Her father was an engineer. Her mother taught high school science. Bell was a National Merit Scholar who went to college in Tennessee, and then quit college to come to the South and work for civil rights with the Student Nonviolent Coordinating Committee. It was the sixties, a time of immense hope and passion, when it seemed the nation was really changing. Atlanta, for instance, had proven that a Southern city could desegregate peacefully in 1961, when nine black children were enrolled in four previously all-white schools downtown. This wasn't Little Rock: there were no riots, no National Guard. Atlanta proudly called itself "the city too busy to hate."

In the sixties, though, local wags dubbed it the "city too busy moving to hate." By the time Camille Bell arrived in Atlanta, its center was rapidly being abandoned by the middle class. Throughout the decade, 40 percent of Atlanta's white population decamped for the leafy suburban enclaves outside the city limits. And it wasn't just white flight: middle-class blacks moved out as well, to an inner ring of neighborhoods on the city's fringe.

Workers in the downtown neighborhoods lost jobs as offices, shops, and factories also migrated to the suburbs. Nineteen suburban office parks sprang up just outside the Perimeter beltway in the sixties alone. Huge corporate office parks like Perimeter Center and shopping malls like the Cumberland Galleria mushroomed near freeway interchanges. They were surrounded by seas of asphalt and poorly serviced by bus, meaning carless city residents couldn't get to jobs there. And downtown, once highway construction cleared residents out of the way, a new city-within-a-city began to rise. The redeveloped central business district, a shining temple to commerce, was made possible by clearing a roughly twenty-square-block section of "blight": the old railroad right-of-way and the former Vine City neighborhood. Skyscrapers shot up like weeds: Peachtree Center in 1961, the Hyatt Regency Atlanta in 1967. The economy boomed outside the beltway and a new white-collar paradise was rising in the city center, but in the old neighborhoods unemployment skyrocketed.

Atlanta's transformation was not unique; across the nation, urban renewal and expressway construction were doling out misery in the urban cores. Something had to give, and in the summer of 1966 it did. Urban riots broke out across the nation. The press called them "ghetto insurrections." Atlanta's happened in Summerhill, one of the city's oldest African American neighborhoods, settled by freed slaves during Reconstruction. An eclectic community of roughly 12,500 blacks, Jews, and Greeks had occupied the area, but by 1966, all but a small remnant were gone. The majority of its buildings had been razed. The original plan was to create public housing there, but when developers expressed concern about letting poor people live so close to their "new" downtown, the land was reallocated to construction of a stadium for the South's first major league baseball and football teams.

As riots go, it was tame. The mayor climbed onto a police car to address the crowd, but protesters rocked it until he fell off. "When they first cleared the land up there," explained one protester, "they told us they'd put up housing, and then they put up the stadium." The next summer, another riot broke out in the black neighborhood of Dixie Hills. This time, four people were shot by police. *Time* magazine pointed out that more than six hundred cheap apartments had been built in Dixie Hills in the previous decade. "Rats and roaches infest every building," the magazine declared, "plumbing is erratic, owners refuse to make repairs or even plant grass in the dusty, barren areas between buildings. Trash and garbage have been collected irregularly, gaping holes in the streets have gone unrepaired, and recreational facilities have been nonexistent. Most serious, more than half of the younger men are unemployed."

Riots spread across the nation. In Detroit that summer, rioting killed forty-three people and burned down much of the urban core. Michigan's governor, George Romney, a former automotive executive, declared that urban renewal and freeway construction were partly to blame. The Motor City never recovered from its freeway revolt. Cities such as Newark, Chicago, and Washington, DC, also suffered riots in the late sixties that were sparked in part by the highway program— "white men's roads through black men's bedrooms"—and urban renewal, or as the black community renamed it, "negro removal." By 1968, even the *Saturday Evening Post* decried the "racial double standard" in the interstate highway program.

In his 1970 book *Highways to Nowhere*, cultural critic Richard Hébert profiled the damage highways were inflicting on a number of cities, including Atlanta. The city had grown, he said, but "blacks found themselves receiving at best the crumbs of the new progress" because the best jobs had left the center. Without transit, the black population was trapped in a decaying downtown. "While highways and automobiles may not be destroying the urban cores of the nation single-handedly," Hébert concluded, "they most certainly are dealing them the cruelest blow."

In 1969, Federal Highway Administrator Frank Turner submitted to Congress a list of sixteen cities—including Atlanta—where popular protests were blocking interstate construction. The bland reasons he gave for freeway opposition— "displacements," "effect on community"—ignored the racial implications. By the first Earth Day in April 1970, freeway revolts were underway in cities from Boston to New Orleans, Miami to Portland, Oregon. All of them included accusations of racial injustice. But the media tended to ignore this part of the story. Stripped of its background as part of the civil rights movement, the freeway revolt ended up sounding like a bunch of not-in-my-backyard whiners throwing a wrench in the wheel of public works. Today it's rarely remembered that the battle against the freeway juggernaut for the soul of the American city was also a new chapter in the nation's history of racial conflict, a chapter where Jim Crow stepped behind the curtain and emerged in a new guise: infrastructure.

· · · · ·

C amille Bell was right at the center of that battle. Her first local employer, the Atlanta branch of the Student Non-violent Coordinating Committee, was active in organizing the community to fight displacements. In 1967, she got married and began to work in an employment office. There, she saw the men coming in desperate for work because so many jobs had fled the inner city. The process didn't slow down. Between 1970 and 1980, the population of many counties surrounding Atlanta doubled, while the city itself lost residents. By 1973, Atlanta's technically desegregated public schools were 90 percent black, and they were some of the nation's worst. Even a 1974 technical report commissioned by Central Atlanta Progress, the down-town development nonprofit, warned of the "extreme separa-tion" suburbanization and urban renewal were creating.

In 1978, Camille Bell and her husband divorced. Her young-est child, Tonia, was two. Bell quit her job at the employment agency to stay home with the kids. But then her family—like so many in the city—was displaced. In the Bells' case, the cause was transit construction: after much public debate, the city was building a light rail system. The Metropolitan Atlanta Rapid Transit Authority was a well-intentioned attempt to counter-act some of the transportation racism the interstate program had wrought. But Atlanta sprawls over four counties, and two of them, the white counties of Cobb and Gwinnett, had refused to be part of MARTA. They were afraid "urban youths" would gain access to their affluent utopias. A former commissioner in Cobb County even joked that he'd like to "stock the Chattahoochee"— the river separating the city from its suburbs—"with piranha."

When the transit project condemned the Bell family's home, they moved into McDaniel-Glenn, a public housing project a few blocks south of I-20 and just west of the new stadium that had displaced the Summerhill neighborhood. Camille Bell tried to counter the ghetto's influence by encouraging her kids to work hard in school, and by enrolling them in gifted programs. But McDaniel-Glenn was a grimy place, notorious for drug-dealing and violence. As the crow flies, it was about a mile from Atlanta's new central business district. But even without the monster freeway interchange that stood between them, the two downtowns would still have been worlds apart.

• • • • •

By the time the Bells moved into McDaniel-Glenn, the transformation of Atlanta from a sleepy Southern backwater to a shining beacon of commercialism was complete. Over the course of a decade, downtown Atlanta had built a whole new skyline: in addition to the Peachtree Center and the new Hilton, there was the Omni International, a complex containing a hotel, restaurants, stores, theaters, arcade, ice rink, and indoor amusement park. Nearby was Colony Square—offices, hotel, retail, ice rink. In 1976, the city completed a huge trade show complex, the World Congress Center, obliterating the black neighborhood of Lightning. The new Atlanta was focused on offices, conventions, and upscale retail: new commerce for the "New South." Architecture critic Ada Louis Huxtable called it "Instant City."

"Atlanta has become now a kind of perpetual Renaissance City," crowed a developer in 1975, "a robust and eclectically composed great merchant city with a cosmopolitan variousness and panache, a Twentieth-Century rendition of Medician Florence with mellow magnolia-soft inflection." The new downtown, enthused this rhapsodist of real estate, held "heroic mirror towers surging up one after another into the sky like huge shouts of expectancy—a kind of architectural New World Symphony assembling in the air before our eyes."

These heroic towers—many of them designed by glitzy Atlanta starchitect John Portman—were walled-off urban fortresses designed to barricade the prosperous business district from the adjacent black neighborhoods. Portman's Peachtree Center set a new standard in enclave architecture. Its lower levels looked inward, onto a lobby that replaced both public plaza and park—it contained a half-acre indoor lake. Peachtree Center and the other downtown buildings were connected to each other with pedestrian skyways suspended above street level. Portman explained that this was to make sure "everything is within reach of the pedestrian"—the assumption being that the city's streets and sidewalks were no place for a person to walk.

All of these facilities were clearly marked off as private space, presenting imposing faces of concrete, steel, and tinted glass to the street. Entrances were optimized for automobiles. The Peachtree Center and the Omni complex banned anyone under eighteen without adult supervision. Guards were even stationed at the Peachtree Center's dramatic glass elevators to prevent joyriding. The *New York Times* saw the point, noting when the Omni opened in 1976 that "the suburban couple can ice skate, dine, go to a movie, meditate, get chased by a witch, shop, get their hair done, and drink on a lily pad without once going out of doors where the undesirables might be." Add to that the fact that they could zoom past the dangerous inner city neighborhoods on the freeway, park their car in an underground garage, and take an elevator directly into the lobby, and you can understand how this was a world that barely noticed when, just one mile away, young Yusef Bell was "blighted out," his broken body stashed in an abandoned school for more than two weeks.

· · · · ·

Camille Bell buried her son. Her ex-husband did not come to the funeral. Camille was not told that police had earlier interviewed him and his girlfriend in connection with Yusef's death. Yusef's father thought the boy would be found alive, but his girlfriend disagreed. She told police about a psychic vision she had experienced, in which Yusef was buried beneath concrete.

Bell thought the police showed a surprising lack of interest in her murdered son. Heartsick in the months following Yusef's death, she began to notice something odd in the black community. Children, primarily adolescent boys, had been vanishing with what seemed like astonishing regularity. Edward Smith, 14, had gone missing after leaving the Greenbriar Skating Rink. Alfred Evans, 13, took a bus to a movie theater downtown and was never seen alive again. Both their bodies were found a few months before Yusef's. Milton Harvey, 14, had ridden off on his bike and been found dead in a vacant lot in September. And after Yusef's death, child murder began to seem like a regular occurrence. Angel Lenair disappeared on the way to a friend's house and was found dead in a vacant lot in March 1980. Jeffery Mathis, 11, went to get cigarettes for his mother that same month and never came home. Christopher Richardson, 12, disappeared on his way to a recreation center pool. Latonya Wilson, 7, went missing from her bedroom in the Hillcrest Apartments in Dixie Hills. Eric Middlebrooks, 14, left home on his bike and was found dead the next morning behind the Hope-U-Like-It Bar, just across the I-20 interchange from his home.

Newspapers called them "ghetto kids." They lived in the city's housing projects, or in the low-rent homes nearby vacated by whites. Their families were often unstable and struggling to make ends meet. Most of the kids worked odd jobs, running errands, collecting cans, carrying groceries, or hawking air fresheners at shopping plazas. They played in the same blighted places where their bodies were found: in empty lots, beneath highway overpasses, in the parking lots of low-end shopping plazas or the basements of abandoned buildings.

Police saw nothing unusual. Violence was on the rise throughout the United States, and in Atlanta things were even worse: the city had 231 homicides in 1979, making it the murder capital of the nation. State troopers had been dispatched by the governor to help the overwhelmed Atlanta Metro Police. But Camille Bell felt in her soul that these deaths were not just inner city business as usual.

July 1980 was a tense month nationwide. The hostage crisis in Iran dragged on. Americans distracted themselves by obsessing over who shot J.R. The GOP convention was held in Detroit: the Michigan governor's black Lincoln was stolen as he attended it. The first major urban riots since the sixties erupted in Miami when six police officers were acquitted of bludgeoning a black insurance salesman to death because he failed to pull over while speeding. The Florida National Guard barricaded the Liberty City projects to contain the rioting. In Atlanta, temperatures reached record highs. And Anthony Bernard Carter, age 9, was found stabbed to death on a grassy bank behind a warehouse.

Camille Bell and some other mothers met. Fed up, they formed the Committee to Stop Children's Murders. They held a press conference and declared there was a clear pattern to what was going on: poor black children were being killed. They demanded that police dedicate more resources to the murders and consider that they might be connected.

Under pressure, Atlanta public safety commissioner Lee Brown announced the formation of a task force to investigate the cases full-time. Less than two weeks later, Earl Lee Terrell was kicked out of a city swimming pool for roughhousing. The ten-year-old, a round-faced boy with prominent ears and wide, expressive eyes, sat on a bench outside, waiting for his sister. Then he left. A woman later said she saw him standing on a corner near Jonesboro Road, crying. That was the last time anyone could report seeing Earl Lee Terrell alive. His name was added to the list of missing and murdered children. Still, police insisted that the deaths might not be linked. If there was a pattern, they declared, it wasn't that the children were poor and black; it was that their bodies were all found just south of I-20.

Then, on August 21, 1980, the body of Clifford Jones was found beside a dumpster at the Hollywood Plaza Shopping Center near the Perry Homes housing project. The thirteen-year-old had gone out to collect aluminum cans and ended up strangled and left out with the trash. For the first time, the slayings made the front page of the *Atlanta Constitution.* Jones was found near the ghetto, but he was not a ghetto kid. He wasn't even from Atlanta. He had been visiting his grandmother, who lived in a house on Lookout Avenue. And he was the first child to disappear north of I-20.

The *Atlanta Constitution* published a map showing where murdered children had been found. "Link Hinted in Slayings of Children," the paper declared. A homicide commander protested that the Jones murder was not related to the others. "The finding of the body north of I-20 destroys the pattern," he told reporters.

Less than a month later, on September 14, 1980, eleven-year-old Darron Glass left a church bus at the corner of Glenwood and Second Avenues, near the notorious East Lake Meadows housing project, where he lived. Although fairly new—it was built in 1970—East Lake Meadows quickly developed a crime rate eighteen times the national average, becoming known as "Little Vietnam." Alfred Evans, one of the first murdered children to be found, lived in East Lake Meadows as well. Darron Glass was last seen walking down Memorial Drive. His body has never been found.

Around this time, Camille Bell took a ride with Chet Dettlinger and showed him the place where Yusef disappeared on his way to the grocery store. Dettlinger was plotting the kids' addresses, their last known whereabouts, and the places where their bodies were found on a map. He had a theory about the murders. By the time Darron Glass went missing, Chet Dettlinger was convinced that "geography had become a parameter in and of itself."

Dettlinger, a former Atlanta cop turned private investigator, was earning Atlanta Metro's ire by investigating the murders on his own and offering the press his conclusions. They centered on a map, which the chain-smoking, straight-talking ex-cop was frequently seen wielding on the news. Dettlinger spent a lot of time taking journalists on what he called his "tour of death," a drive over twelve interconnected roads that he claimed composed the killer's route. His subsequent book *The List*, nominated for a Pulitzer Prize, excoriates the police task force for ignoring the geographic links between the cases. The route was the key, he kept saying. There was a pattern, a logic, to the killings, and if people would just look at the map, they'd be able to figure it out.

The problem with Dettlinger's map was that it didn't really explain anything. It helped make the case that many of the killings were connected, but it didn't offer any rationale for senseless child murders. It didn't paint a picture of the killer or elucidate why kids were vulnerable to him. Dettlinger, too, was focusing on the roads rather than on the world the roads had made.

• • • • •

In early October, Charles Stephens vanished from the projects on Pryor Circle in southwest Atlanta. Then, on October 13, 1980, an explosion at a day-care facility in the Bowen Homes project killed four children and one adult. It was difficult not to see the explosion as related to the mounting murders, even as city officials declared it an accident. Mayor Maynard Jackson was heckled when he tried to address the Bowen Homes community. Jackson, a patrician African American from Atlanta's established black elite, was the city's first black mayor, and he was sensitive to accusations that he was out of touch with the urban underclass. After the Bowen Homes explosion, he raised the reward for information leading to Atlanta's child murderer from $10,000 to $50,000, then to $100,000.

Nevertheless, hysteria and paranoia were sweeping through the black community. Bizarre theories arose: the Ku Klux Klan was killing black kids in retaliation for two highly publicized murders of whites by blacks in Atlanta the year before. The police were involved, with or without the Klan's help. Satanists were snatching the kids and killing them in cult rituals. The FBI was behind it. The CIA was behind it. The most bizarre theory blamed the Atlanta-based Centers for Disease Control: its scientists were said to be murdering young black boys to harvest interferon, a cancer-fighting chemical, from their penises.

It didn't help that the nation was in one of its periodic swings to the right. Many in the African American community felt alienated by the conservative rhetoric of Ronald Reagan, who would be elected president that November. Some claimed a pattern of violence against blacks was afoot in the nation. Civil rights leader Vernon Jordon had been shot and wounded in Indiana in May. Black men were being shot and killed in Buffalo, New York. A string of unsolved murders of blacks haunted Salt Lake City. The Ku Klux Klan was resurgent: in October, an episode of the television news show 20/20 recounted the Atlanta murders in the context of increased Klan activity.

To the black community, it felt like things had been heading this way for a long time. The very real triumphs of the civil rights movement—school desegregation, the Voting Rights Act, the death of Jim Crow laws—were being undermined by programs replacing overt discrimination with covert bias: white flight, slum clearance, a transportation system centered on the car. The interstate program became a symbol for this new, insidious kind of racism, prejudice disguised as planning, something as simple as building roads instead of trains.

Atlanta's white community was also frightened, though for different reasons. It was less afraid of the killer than of what would happen when he was found. What if the Klan really was involved, or worse, the police? Or what if the killer simply looked like the serial killers who had been arrested in recent years: David Berkowitz, Ted Bundy, John Wayne Gacy? They were all white men. Newspaper columns and people on the street frequently voiced the fear that Atlanta could too easily become "another Miami," descending into chaos and racial enmity when it had worked so hard to be a model of the New South.

On a bright Saturday in late October, the black community organized its first neighborhood search. About three hundred volunteers gathered in the most blighted part of Dixie Hills, the area where the 1967 riot had led *Time* magazine to detail the miseries of substandard housing and unemployment. The volunteers began walking the streets, sifting through vacant lots. After only two hours, they came across a small pile of bones and a clump of hair gripped in a blue barrette. It was all that was left of Latonya Wilson, who had gone missing on that very street. After four months outside, her body gave no indication of how she had died.

· · · · ·

Nineteen eighty wound down. Aaron Jackson, 9, who lived near the Thomasville Heights Projects, disappeared from Memorial Drive's Moreland Plaza Shopping Center on November first. Ronald Reagan was elected president three days later. The day after the election, the attorney general authorized the FBI to participate in Atlanta's investigation. And the killings continued, one every three weeks or so. Patrick Rogers, 16, of Thomasville Heights, also last seen at Moreland Plaza, where he often bagged groceries. Lubie Geter, 14, last seen hawking car air fresheners at the Stewart-Lakeland Shopping Plaza on Route 166. Terry Pue, 15, a resident of the Hollywood Courts project: he had visited his sister in East Lake Meadows, then spent the night hanging out at a fast-food joint on Memorial Drive. He was last sighted trading in bottles at a shopping center nearby. The victims all came from the central city, but their bodies were turning up farther and farther out toward the city's edges, as if following the city's more affluent residents to the suburban fringe.

From their offices in an abandoned Lincoln-Mercury showroom, the task force fielded tips from out-of-town psychics, neighbors with dubious eyesight, former mental patients with grudges, and a man who claimed to be getting messages from God through the static on his TV. FBI agents assigned to Atlanta compiled regular memos for headquarters outlining progress in each case. Some cases were stalled. In several, a parent was the key suspect. Others had possible connections to drugs or "street rivalries." The agents expressed frustration. "In most of these cases," a late December memo said, "investigation has been conducted solely in black ghetto areas, where the police are 'the enemy' and non-cooperation is the rule. In these areas, people move constantly from location to location and in some cases, it has been necessary to conduct fugitive-type investigations to locate witnesses."

Camille Bell, like many in the black community, was angered by the ongoing suspicion of parents and the constant suggestion that "ghetto parents" failed to supervise their kids. "It takes a lot to get people concerned about a child out of the ghettos," she told the *New York Times* in January. "The feeling of the middle class, who cops and bureaucrats tend to be, is 'these people don't care about their children, so why should I?' But a lot of these ghetto people care deeply. Their kids are about the only things they have in the world."

In February 1981, twelve-year-old Patrick Baltazar asked his father for some money so he could go to the downtown Omni complex to play video games in the Galaxy 3 arcade. It was the last time anyone saw him alive.

The Omni was popular with Atlanta's kids, particularly the ones it was designed to exclude. Several of the victims frequented the place. Symbolic of Atlanta's new image as economic powerhouse and capital of the New South, it was a place that evoked the good life, a life of fashionable clothing and upscale food and kid-friendly entertainment. James Baldwin, sent to Atlanta to report on the child murders for *Playboy*, found the Omni fascinating: "One enters through a galaxy of shopwindows selling clothes that your momma and your papa can't buy. . . . among the establishments on the ground level,

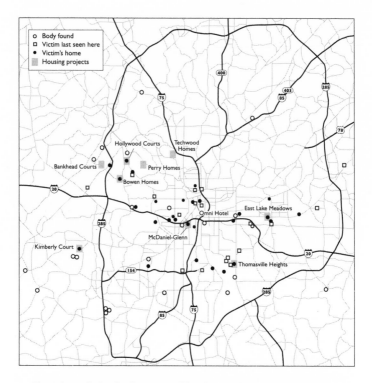

The Atlanta kids who disappeared lived in neighborhoods transformed by freeway development. They were last seen in the vicinity of twelve main arteries. Their bodies were found in vacant lots, freeway right-of-ways, and abandoned buildings. Map drawn by Bill Nelson.

there is a 'French' baker and a pinball, video-game arcade . . . In the center of all this is a tremendous open ice-skating rink (since closed) and at the opposite end of the floor, facing the arcade, is the movie house." The entire complex, he concludes, is "nothing less than a magnet for children and for those who prey on children."

Sometime after arriving at the Omni, Patrick Baltazar disappeared. His father, a dishwasher, spent hours driving the city streets, looking for his son. The boy was found a week later, his body discarded behind Corporate Square, an office complex between the Buford Highway and I-85.

• • • • •

March 1981 was a watershed. Curtis Walker, 13, a Bowen Homes resident who had vanished on February 19, was found strangled. Four more young men, ages 13 to 23, disappeared, bringing the count—depending on which murders and disappearances you counted—to more than twenty. Newspapers revealed that the police were finding trace evidence on the bodies. After that, the bodies stopped showing up in vacant lots. Instead, they began to be found in the city's rivers, the Chattahoochee and the South. The police took to staking out bridges.

Frank Sinatra and Sammy Davis Jr. shared the stage in a benefit concert at the Civic Center to raise money for the investigation. Atlanta's upper crust dressed up and paid a hundred dollars a head to attend the benefit auction and dinner afterward at the Peachtree Plaza Hotel. Outside the inner sanctum of the new downtown, volunteers convened every Saturday to search a different neighborhood for bodies. The residents of Techwood Homes, the nation's oldest public housing project, organized "bat patrols," in which groups armed with baseball bats—and the occasional gun—patrolled the project. When police turned up to arrest some of the leaders on weapons charges, they were surrounded by a jeering, hostile crowd. The day of the first patrol, a twenty-one-year-old man disappeared from Techwood Homes.

Camille Bell went on the road, traveling from city to city and appearing on television, in churches—wherever people were willing to hear about Atlanta's lost children. She and two other mothers traveled to Harlem and joined a candlelight vigil that drew a crowd of over ten thousand. They met with church leaders and New York City officials to discuss how to keep Atlanta's tragedy from spreading to other cities. "This kind of thing is a sign of our times," Bell said. "It's not a black-white issue; it's a people issue. If you don't know who your neighbor is, you're part of the problem." In Baltimore, she told an audience at a memorial mass that anonymity in the central cities was partly to blame. "We don't know who lives around us," she said.

In Washington, Mayor Marion Barry declared the killings part of a national swing toward racism. "A certain mood exists in this country, encouraged by the leadership," he declared, "that it is all right to do anything to black people." Barry was widely criticized for the comment, but it had some sting. The newly elected President Reagan hurried to sign a bill authorizing federal aid to Atlanta.

The murders had become a national spectacle. And in the anguished city, residents increasingly got the uncomfortable feeling that Atlanta itself was taking the rap. "In many ways, it's unfair," Andrew Young, the frontrunner in the upcoming Atlanta mayoral race, told the *Washington Post*. "Nobody questioned the competence of the New York City police or New York City's leaders during the Son of Sam murders. . . . Somehow Atlanta is on trial in this thing."

Part of what was going on was that hordes of reporters had descended upon Atlanta, and in the absence of suspects, they began to look at the city itself. Sociologists, child psychologists, and activists were trotted out to bemoan a variety of urban ills—all of which could be tied to the highway program. Kids, they said, were more at risk of victimization when they lived in "inward-looking, cold, impersonal and inhuman" public housing projects. They were more vulnerable in neighborhoods that lacked stability. Overcrowding and lack of privacy in the ever-smaller space allotted the ghetto forced kids to lead "public lives" that also made them easy prey. No one connected these things to two decades of highway construction and urban renewal. But newspapers did report that the police saw a pattern in "the placement of the bodies in secluded areas off major highways" and "the proximity of highways to sites where a number of the children were last seen."

Outside Atlanta, it was easy to feel that the city—combining the South's toxic racial history with the woes of a modern metropolis—must somehow have created this mess. Atlanta itself, wrote reporter Steve Oney in the *Atlanta Weekly*, entered "a period marked by both self-promotion and guilt, a period of municipal schizophrenia that made life seem surreal." Police tried to downplay the murders by expressing doubt that they were connected, as if dozens of child homicides in a single city didn't indicate something deeply amiss, no matter how many killers were involved. Public safety campaigns subtly tried to shift the blame to parents: "Do you know where your children are *right now?*" demanded an electric-lit sign in front of the Civic Center every night.

Many of the city's children were gripped with fear for the person they called "the Snatcher" or simply "the Man." A curfew was instituted for kids under fifteen. Children were sent to school carrying bats, knives, and sticks to defend themselves. None of it was likely to help: the murdered children had mostly vanished in broad daylight, and only one body showed any sign of struggle. In the few cases where disappeared kids were seen going off with someone, they were witnessed willingly climbing into a car. Clearly, "the Snatcher" was someone known to the victims. Or someone who made them an offer they couldn't refuse.

· · · · ·

Camille Bell took her three remaining children on a trip to Newark in April 1981. The official count was now twenty-two children missing or dead. Bell gave an exclusive interview to Harry Webber, a reporter for the *Baltimore Afro-American*. Feeling obliged to prove that the missing children—including Yusef—were not uneducated "hustlers" or delinquents, she had Jonathan, 12, Marie, 9, and Tonia, 4, demonstrate their intelligence for the reporter. Jonathan quoted a lengthy section of Martin Luther King Jr.'s "I Have a Dream" speech. Marie recited a poem by Paul Lawrence Dunbar. Tonia sang a Christmas song. It's an excruciating scene to imagine. *My children are worth protecting*, it seems calculated to say. Would Bell have felt that message so necessary if she hadn't lived through two decades where poor urban blacks were considered synonymous with "blight," something to be paved over without a thought?

That April, three young men disappeared, and in May, two more. And then, suddenly, it was over. Or was it? In early June, newspapers reported that the police had a suspect: twenty-two-year-old Wayne Bertram Williams, a self-described music promoter who lived with his parents in Dixie Hills, the neighborhood where the 1967 riot broke out. The Williams home was along the route identified by Chet Dettlinger and within a few miles of where many of the victims lived. Williams came to the task force's attention when police staking out a bridge on the Chattahoochee heard a loud splash and discovered him driving slowly over the river. He was questioned, but was not arrested. Two days later, the body of the twenty-eighth victim, twenty-seven-year-old Nathaniel Cater, was pulled from the water downstream of the bridge. Police began heavy surveillance of Williams. On June 3, he was detained for twelve hours and questioned.

Then came a slow-motion spectacle, in which the city's attention was riveted on Wayne Williams, a man not charged with any crime. The media and the police staked out his house. Police claimed they didn't have enough evidence to indict him. Then newspapers revealed that fibers found on some of the bodies matched fibers taken from the Williams home. They reported that the FBI wanted to arrest Williams immediately, but local police wanted more evidence.

Throughout all of it, Williams behaved like either an innocent man or an outrageously arrogant killer. He agreed to polygraphs. He told easily traceable lies. After his questioning, he called a press conference. He and his lawyer tried to get a gag order forbidding the media from publishing his name, address, or photograph. Fed up with police tailing him everywhere, he drove to the home of public safety commissioner Lee Brown, where he sat in his car and blew the horn.

On Sunday, June 21, Williams was finally arrested and charged with one count of homicide in the death of Nathaniel

Cater. He was ultimately indicted for only two of the murders. The district attorney said he still believed as many as eight to ten killers might be involved in Atlanta's child murders. About half the cases, he told reporters, were probably not related. Nonetheless, a few days later, the FBI began recalling agents from Atlanta, as if the entire ordeal were over. The business community was no less eager to get past the nightmare. The president of Central Atlanta Progress, the downtown business owners' group, announced that "a blanket of calm has spread over Atlanta after a very turbulent period." The city promptly began a PR campaign to repair its damaged reputation. "Let's pull together, Atlanta," the billboards chided.

Criminologists agree that it's highly doubtful one person committed all the murders on the task force list. Serial killers tend to be specific in the type of victim they choose, and while their modus operandi can change with circumstances, it usually doesn't vary wildly. The murder victims on the Atlanta list ranged in age from seven to twenty-eight. Two were girls. Sexual assault had occurred in some of the cases, but not all of them. Some victims were shot; some were stabbed. Others were bludgeoned, smothered, or strangled. Stranglings were carried out by hand and by rope. One boy fell from an overpass. For a few, cause of death could not be determined. For victims found in the river, drowning could not be ruled out.

What is clear is that many of the kids knew other murdered kids. Freelance investigator Chet Dettlinger determined that every kid on the list knew at least one other kid on the list, and many knew more than that. Patrick Rogers knew seventeen of the other murdered children. It's not as surprising as it seems. The kids lived in the same projects, hustled in the same shopping plazas, attended the same beleaguered schools, hung out at the same arcades and fast-food joints. They all came from a very tightly defined part of town—the part spreading south from I-20, with one finger stretching north toward Perry Homes. It was the area circumscribed by I-20 in the north, I-285 (the Perimeter) in the west, and to the east, the Downtown Connector: the same exact area shaded on planners' maps as that slated for highway development and urban renewal.

· · · · ·

In early 1982, Wayne Williams was tried for two murders. The evidence against him was circumstantial. The trial was allowed to proceed in a way that seemed obviously stacked against him. Three weeks in, the judge ruled that prosecutors could use evidence from ten other murders—murders with which Williams was never charged—to establish a "pattern" of killings to strengthen their case.

The black community continually expressed reservations about the trial—even though the judge and most of the jury were black. Chet Dettlinger and Camille Bell actually provided

Wayne Williams leaving the Fulton County Jail en route to his trial. A spoiled child with inflated self-esteem, he made a good suspect. But many in the community, including some of the victims' families, doubted he could have committed all the murders. Associated Press photo / Gary Gardiner.

help to the defense. But Wayne Williams was an excellent suspect. The spoiled only child of older parents—they called him "the miracle child"—he had been convinced he was a prodigy without ever being asked to exert himself. He had dreams of being a broadcast journalist, and his parents had gone bankrupt trying to underwrite his low-power radio station. Then he began promoting himself as a hotshot talent scout—though he never actually scouted a single talent. He had talked a lot about how he was forming a band to be called Gemini. And he had distributed flyers announcing his search for musical talent at the Omni and in several of the housing projects and shopping centers where victims lived or hung out. In many people's eyes, this added the missing piece of the puzzle. It now made sense that the murdered kids would have gone with him. He had offered them the very thing they wanted most: a way out of the slums.

After being questioned by police, Williams had called a press conference and distributed copies of his "résumé," a fantasy-fueled list of accomplishments. He claimed that he had attended Georgia State (he had dropped out), that he had flown F-4 fighter planes (he later explained that he meant he had been given a ride in one), and that he was "heavily involved with various media" (he was a photographic stringer for a couple local television news outlets). Clearly, he suffered from delusions of grandeur, and the number of lies he told to both police and the press suggested there was something pathological in his addiction to untruth.

Williams fit the serial killer mold in a number of other ways too. Like many serial killers, he was a law enforcement buff, with a police scanner and lights in his car. He had even once been fined for impersonating a police officer. Killers frequently insert themselves into the case at several points, and Williams had done this: witnesses testified to seeing him at one of the funerals, and he had shown up at one of the crime scenes to offer his photographic services. He was known to travel the city extensively in his freelance photography work. His sexuality was complicated: a witness testified that he had seen the defendant holding hands with Nathaniel Cater shortly before Cater's death, but Williams vociferously denied being homosexual. And like many serial killers, he had a complex relationship with his parents. Witnesses claimed he had once tried to choke his father, though both parents, who stood by him throughout the ordeal, denied this on the stand. Clearly, Wayne Williams had secrets.

The most compelling evidence, however, was that like so many serial killers, Williams seemed deeply insecure about his own class status. Witnesses testified to his disdain for the poor kids who were being killed, calling them "street grunchins" and "drop shots." A white ambulance driver who knew Williams claimed that he "seemed like he was ashamed of lower-middle-class blacks and lower-class blacks." If so, that shame likely stemmed from his own tenuous middle-class status. His parents, retired schoolteachers, were struggling financially, largely as a result of their investments in Wayne's pipe dreams. They lived on the east side of Dixie Hills, in a leafy neighborhood of modest brick and clapboard bungalows a stone's throw from I-20. A quarter mile west of the Williams home, at the end of Penelope Road, was Verbena Street, and a few blocks west on Verbena sat the wretched Hillcrest Apartments, where two of the victims—Nathaniel Cater and Latonya Wilson—lived. The tiny homes of Dixie Hills, with their neatly kept lawns and single picture windows, were just down the road from real slums. The Williams family lived literally and figuratively on the edge.

The trial lasted two months, during which it dominated the front page of every Atlanta paper. Spectators lined up as early as four a.m. to get one of the eighty-five coveted seats. Reporters from all over the country filed daily updates. Atlantans avidly followed the trial through large sections of the testimony printed in newspapers. On Friday, February 26, the case went to the jury. The jurors deliberated for two hours on Friday and most of Saturday before coming to the judge with a verdict of guilty on both counts. On Sunday, the *Atlanta Constitution* announced that police were planning to disband the task force and close the books on almost all its cases—even the ones not linked to Williams and the ones that still had other active suspects. The only cases left open would be the two girls, whom most people thought had been wrongly added to the list, and—for procedural reasons—Darron Glass. He was, after all, not dead yet. Technically he was only missing.

The Atlanta mainstream immediately began declaring the city exonerated. The trial, they said, was proof that the system was race-blind: it was presided over by a black judge, decided by a predominantly black jury, and overseen by a black mayor and a black public safety commissioner. "This city has always been way out in front of the country as far as race relations is concerned," crowed the former head of the Chamber of Commerce. "Other cities can profit by this example of whites and blacks working and living together."

"Atlanta stands a little taller for handling it in this manner," announced an Atlanta University professor. *Constitution* columnist Lewis Grizzard summed it up in a headline: "Williams Trial Verdict: The City Is Not Guilty."

He was more correct than he realized: it was indeed Atlanta on trial throughout the murders, and the Williams conviction allowed the city to refocus blame not on social failings but on a sick individual. When Wayne Williams's attorney, Alvin Binder, went on ABC's *Nightline* after the trial and pointed out that there had been two unsolved murders that fit the pattern since his client's arrest, there was an immediate angry response. The mayor denounced the attorney and the *Constitution* ran an editorial titled "Trial Is Over, Mr. Binder." Most people were eager to put it all behind them, letting the larger forces at work slip into the dark once more.

The black community's response was more ambivalent. An *Atlanta Daily World* editorial praised the jury, but advocated

taking at least some of the other cases to trial. A poll immediately after the conviction found blacks leery of the justice
system. Even the victims' families expressed skepticism. "The
whole system is unjust," said the mother of Patrick Rogers.
"They wanted to find a scapegoat and they did." Christopher
Richardson's aunt told reporters prosecutors should try Williams for the other cases if they really believed him guilty. "If
they don't have the evidence, they should continue to look for
the killer," she said.

"I think he got a fair trial, but I'm not sure he's guilty,"
declared Nathaniel Cater's father. "I just hope they got the right
man." Many of the victims' relatives expressed the same tenta-
tive hope. But Camille Bell was outraged. "With this conviction," she declared, "Wayne Williams, at 23, became the 30th
victim of the Atlanta slayings."

Under pressure from families and the Southern Christian
Leadership Conference, the Atlanta Metro police department
kept seven of the cases open, disbanding the task force formed
in 1980 but launching a new homicide task force to deal with
murders citywide. The newspapers were busy declaring the
ordeal over. "It is time to put the Wayne Williams case to rest
and move on," declared the *Constitution*'s editors on March 4.
The next day, they practiced what they preached by taking Williams off the front page. He was replaced by the city's plan to
close a spate of schools in poor black neighborhoods.

· · · · ·

"When I was in Atlanta in the fifties," James Baldwin
wrote, "though some Blacks rode buses . . . and some
drove taxis and some drove cars—and many walked—we all
seemed to be in hailing distance of each other, and in sight of
a church or a poolroom or a bar. But now, neither Butler nor
Auburn Street, for example, is what it was and, it seemed to me,
the faces there, now, convey a pained and bewildered sense of
having been abandoned."

In 1982, the year Wayne Williams was tried, three planners published a study of high-crime and low-crime neighborhoods in Atlanta. Their work built on a body of research that, beginning in the seventies, advanced a theory of urban spaces and their effects on human lives. Most famous was architect Oscar Newman's 1972 *Defensible Space,* an influential indictment of public housing architecture and its propensity to increase crime. Others looked at the blight caused by urban roads. The planners' study determined that much of the difference in crime rates in Atlanta could be attributed to physical characteristics. Low-crime neighborhoods were more residential and had fewer arterials or major streets, and their populations were less transient. High-crime neighborhoods had residents who moved a lot, were close to major roads, and included a lot of vacant lots. It seems like a glaringly obvious set of conclusions. But the implications were something that simply could not be said: Atlanta's urban renewal and expressway construction had, at the very least, built the stage on which the tragedy in Atlanta could unfold.

The Atlanta child murders were a strikingly potent symbol for what a quarter century of urban redesign had wrought. The hitchhiking scare of the 1970s was just that—a scare. But what happened in Atlanta showed how the remaking of our built world created an environment conducive to crime, and how it had fostered the victimization of poor children. The national response to the murders reflected this awareness, casting a dark look at community breakdown in the capital of the New South. Once Williams was convicted, however, that awareness was quickly shoved out of sight. It was easier and more pleasant to think the problem could be solved by jailing an obnoxious young man than it was to consider attacking the conditions that made the entire tragedy possible: a racist past, an impoverished—and impoverishing—environment, and a built world that enshrined them both in concrete and brick.

· · · · ·

When I went to Atlanta to trace the geography of the murders, I was surprised to see that, once again, the city is rebuilding itself. The current renaissance is being driven by the return of the middle and upper-middle class to the city. Just as it led the nation in building housing projects, Atlanta is leading the way in eliminating them, becoming the first city in the United States to demolish every single unit of its public housing. I drove from spot to spot on my map, but almost nothing was there. The Hollywood Shopping Plaza, where Clifford Jones was found in a dumpster: razed. Hollywood Courts, where Terry Pue lived: a pile of cement chunks. Hillcrest Apartments, where Latonya Wilson lived and died: boarded up and abandoned. Thomasville Heights, home to at least three victims: scheduled for demolition, a private developer's sign already posted across the street.

Rising up in public housing's place are trendy, tasteful mixed-income private developments, combinations of apartments, townhomes, and single-family dwellings, all lushly landscaped and redolent with features like playgrounds, walking trails, and YMCAs. On the site of the former Perry Homes, there's West Highlands, with apartments, townhomes, and houses grouped around an artificial pond with a fountain. East Lake Meadows—the former "Little Vietnam"—has become The Villages of East Lake, a gated community with a charter school and a golf course. Even the dire McDaniel-Glenn, where Yusef Bell vanished buying a box of snuff, has been replaced by the warehouse-loft-style Mechanicsville Crossing, which boasts security cameras at every entrance.

The new renaissance is driven by the insight that "warehousing the poor" only cements the cycle of poverty. Instead, the city is using housing funds to help low-income families enter the private market: former public housing residents receive rent vouchers and find their own homes. Eighty percent of them will be in new neighborhoods. Advocates say this will lead to more truly mixed-income neighborhoods. Housing activists point out that the vouchers are viewed with suspicion by landlords and that the number of units available to holders is limited. Time will tell whether the approach works or not. Once again, though, transportation is being left out of the picture. Now, in a bizarre inversion of what happened in the sixties and seventies, urban life is attracting the affluent, and the poorest residents are being pushed outward, to the suburban fringe. There, even as the area fills with residents who need public transit, the cash-strapped city is canceling bus service.

Meanwhile, on YouTube, a fascinating community has sprung up to document the vanishing projects. Inspired by the 2005 "blockumentary" *Hood 2 Hood*, former residents have uploaded mash-up videos juxtaposing stills and historic photos of the old projects with interviews and footage of the shuttered, demolition-ready buildings. They're all there: Techwood, East Lake Meadows, Bankhead, Bowen Homes, Thomasville Heights, with locals acting as tour guides. The videos recount the violence and danger of the projects, but they have an odd nostalgic tone. "Bowen Homes R.I.P." someone has spray-painted on one boarded-up low-rise. In the online comments, some Atlantans express skepticism about the new housing program. Once again, they say, the city has simply kicked the poorest people out of real estate it wants to gentrify. "All they did was tear down the old Eastlake Meadows and raised the rent," writes one commenter. "Just like they doin all over the A now. All da folks dat stayed in da old hoods done moved to Lithonia, Clayton Co. and Clarkston."

Dixie Hills, however, looks much the same as it did when Wayne Williams lived there with his parents. Most of the box-like houses are neat and well cared-for, lawns mowed, hedges trimmed. About 10 percent are vacant and boarded up, their unmowed lawns sprouting weeds and foreclosure-sale signs. The former Williams home on Penelope Drive appears to be occupied, its single picture window framed by white shutters, its doors and windows fitted with metal bars. As I stood across

The Williams home in Dixie Hills, a neighborhood of neat, small homes, just blocks from the slums where two victims lived and a stone's throw from I-20. Photo by the author.

the street looking at it, a teenager walked by my car, headed for the bus stop. I could hear the sound of I-20, two blocks away, a steady, dull roar, the sound of people on the move.

. . . . .

The Atlanta child murders and the response to them reveal the legacy of bad faith that followed the interstate highway program's massive restructuring of America's urban spaces, a restructuring that magnified and deepened the race schism in America. Ironically, they also helped launch a new era in the nation, the era of the prime-time serial killer, even as many questions about Atlanta's killer remained open.

A month after the Wayne Williams verdict, a group of concerned black citizens collected more than 1,500 signatures on a petition asking for a retrial. In July, the parents of five victims wrote the U.S. attorney general requesting their cases be reopened. The director of the Southern Christian Leadership Conference, Joseph Lowry, told the *Atlanta Daily World*, "I don't think you will find anyone in the black community who believes Wayne Williams committed all those murders alone." Observers debated whether the "pattern murders" had stopped. Chet Dettlinger lists seven murders that occurred after Williams's arrest that he thinks fit the pattern. In 1985, Abby Mann's made-for-television docudrama *The Atlanta Child Murders* was widely denounced by Atlanta's mainstream for implying that Wayne Williams had been railroaded. In 1986, *Spin* magazine published an account of how the Georgia Bureau of Investigation pursued and then dropped an investigation of a local Klan family, one of whom had bragged to a police informant about killing black kids in Atlanta, and had pointed out Lubie Geter as an intended victim. *Spin* published previously undisclosed transcripts of depositions with the GBI agent in charge about his decision to close the case and destroy all the evidence. The transcripts raise many questions and resolve none.

Camille Bell, fed up with Atlanta, moved to Tallahassee, Florida. She remains convinced that Wayne Williams did not kill her son. Today, few people familiar with the cases believe that Wayne Williams alone committed all the Atlanta child murders—though few consider him totally innocent either. DNA evidence has failed either to exonerate Williams or to prove him incontrovertibly guilty. John Douglas, an FBI profiler who worked with the Williams prosecution, believes that Williams can be considered the killer in eleven of the twenty-nine cases on the list. But he's still convinced that parents and acquaintances were the perpetrators of some of the crimes. "Despite what some people would like to believe," he writes in his book *Mindhunter*, "young black and white children continue to die mysteriously in Atlanta and other cities. We have an idea who did some of the others. It isn't a single offender and the truth isn't pleasant."

As it moved into the 1980s, however, America was not enthusiastic about facing unpleasant truths. In fact, even the phenomenon of the serial killer was about to become a lot less unpleasant. After being the stuff of nightmares, serial killers were about to go mainstream.

*To understand America,
you have to understand
the highways. . . . They
have shrunk the nation,
homogenized the landscape
and strengthened common
lifestyles. The freeways
are not a place but a stage
in our history.*

—ROBERT J. SAMUELSON, 1986

*Serial killers, like society
in general, have become
geographically more mobile.
Unlike their counterparts
in earlier years, some serial
murderers now travel around
the country, leaving a trail of
human carnage.*

—JACK LEVIN AND JAMES
ALAN FOX, 1985

Sprawl followed the interstate: these orchards would soon be gone, replaced by bland edge cities like Walnut Creek along I-680. Development would then sprawl east into the Central Valley and toward I-5. Courtesy National Archives (406G-2-13-65-367).

AMERICAN *ISOLATO*

Lou Ellen Burleigh, age 21, was a secretarial student in September of 1977 when she was invited to interview for a job that sounded too good to be true. A nice monthly wage, good benefits, and she'd be working for cosmetics company Helena Rubinstein. It did seem a bit odd that the interview happened in a parking lot. But the older man with graying hair who met her at the Regency Shopping Plaza explained that his office was under construction nearby. This wasn't surprising: Walnut Creek, California, was a fast-growing "edge city" on the east side of the San Francisco Bay, one of those places where bland office buildings and franchise-packed shopping malls were springing up around a new freeway interchange. The man, who called himself John Brown, interviewed Burleigh in a multicolored van. Everything seemed to go well, and he asked her to return the following day. Though Lou Ellen agreed, the man made her a little nervous, so she asked her boyfriend to come along. He couldn't make it, and Lou Ellen Burleigh went back to the shopping center alone. And then she vanished.

Walnut Creek police were baffled. A nearby construction worker had seen Lou Ellen Burleigh get into a van; he gave them a description of the vehicle and its driver. Other than that, they had no leads. Then, a month later, the Walnut Creek police department got a call from police in Pittsburg, a gritty, industrial town about fifteen miles northwest. A Pittsburg resident named Roger Reece Kibbe had reportedly pulled a knife on a prostitute and threatened to kill her. The woman convinced Kibbe to let her go, and though she declined to press charges, she gave the license plate number of his van to the police. When one of the Pittsburg cops read the newspaper report on Lou Ellen Burleigh, he thought the eyewitness description of the vehicle sounded like Kibbe's van. Walnut Creek police went to Pittsburg and questioned Kibbe, but got nowhere. Then they showed a picture of Kibbe to their eyewitness, but the worker couldn't say if Kibbe was the right man. The guy was just too nondescript.

Lieutenant Ray Biondi, commander of Sacramento County's Homicide Bureau, read the long-forgotten report over a decade later. A lanky man with dark hair, a woolly mustache, and an infectious smile, Biondi had a hunch the Walnut Creek police had in fact questioned the right man. He knew some things the earlier cops didn't. He knew, for instance, that Roger Reece Kibbe had been in trouble with the law for much of his life. Born in 1939, Kibbe had grown up in the southern California city of Chula Vista, a town that went from a sleepy community among citrus groves to a fast-growing wartime boomtown after Rohr Aircraft opened a plant there. The nondescript Kibbe grew up in a nondescript house a few blocks east of the Montgomery Freeway—what would later be known as I-5. It wasn't an idyllic childhood. Like Ed Kemper, Kibbe claimed to have been abused by his mother when his father went off to the Second World War.

As a juvenile, Kibbe had a few run-ins with the Chula Vista police. He was caught stealing women's underwear from neighborhood clotheslines. He staged his own abduction, tying himself up with women's clothing and claiming he had been kidnapped and molested. He had a record by the time he reached adulthood, and he continued to add to it. He was fired from a welding job at National Steel for theft, did time in county jail for burglary, and later did another two years in state prison for stealing parachutes from an airport jump center where he liked to skydive. He was hardly a criminal mastermind, and his demeanor was not aggressive. He just seemed driven by some deep, simmering anger to steal. And not just to steal: to *collect* things. When a Chula Vista officer questioned him about the missing clothing, Kibbe produced a box from his closet. It was full of pilfered women's clothing, cut and slashed with scissors.

But in the mid-seventies, Roger Kibbe seemed to straighten out. In 1975 he married, and his wife Harriet seemed to be just what he needed—someone tough and no-nonsense to take charge of his life. They moved into a tract house in Pittsburg, and Harriet worked in an accounting office. They seemed like a deeply normal couple. They had three cats. Harriet bossed Roger around, but Roger didn't seem to mind. He was physically timid, a soft-spoken man with a mild stutter. He didn't drink. He was good with small kids and revered his younger brother, Steve, a homicide detective in Lake Tahoe, Nevada. Roger Kibbe was not someone you would think likely to commit a murder, let alone do it again and again. But Lieutenant Biondi, in 1985, had some other information that the police in Walnut Creek didn't have in 1977. In the years since Lou Ellen Burleigh disappeared, the American serial killer had come of age. And Ray Biondi had seen more than his share of this newly discovered monster.

• • • • •

A month before Lou Ellen Burleigh went on her fateful interview, New York City police captured a man the media were calling "Son of Sam." David Berkowitz had begun shooting random strangers a year earlier. By the summer of 1977, the city was in a panic. Police had admitted the murders were connected, and newspapers had published rambling missives alleged to be from the killer. But no one called the Son of Sam a "serial killer."

Although there have been multiple murderers throughout history—Jack the Ripper, Countess Bathory of Transylvania, Lizzie Borden—the terms "serial killer" and "serial murder" were not actually used until after World War II. British author Grierson Dickson profiled something he called "series murder," or "multicide," in his book *Murder by Numbers* in 1958. In 1967, John Brophy used the term "serial murder" in his book *The Meaning of Murder*. Brophy separated serial murder—in which the killings are separated by space and time—from mass murder, where multiple killings happened all at once. But even then, the term was not widely used. The *New York Times* first used the construction "serial murder" in May of 1981, in a story about the Atlanta killings. The man most often credited with inventing the term "serial killer" is FBI Special Agent Robert Ressler, who helped shape the bureau's increasing involvement in the topic during the early eighties. Ressler did not invent the term, but it's easy to see why people would think he had. The FBI mounted a campaign in the early eighties that turned serial killers from a rare criminal type noticed mostly by law enforcement into a national obsession—a transformation that served the FBI's purposes. In the process, it cemented America's association of its highways with murder.

But then something truly odd happened. Between the early eighties, when the nation experienced a widespread "panic" about its "epidemic" of serial murder, and the decade's end, serial killers morphed in the public mind from figures of fear to figures of fascination. Murder has always interested the public, but this was a new kind of murder, and new kind of fascination. Serial killers came to be admired, not only as outlaws—we Americans have always loved our outlaws—but as icons of the nation's newly unabashed materialism. This process began with the case of one man: Ted Bundy.

The late seventies had seen a number of high-profile serial murder cases. There was David Berkowitz. In California there was someone known as the Zodiac Killer, as well as the "Hillside Strangler" in Los Angeles—actually two men, cousins

Kenneth Bianchi and Angelo Buono, arrested in 1978. In the Chicago area, the "Killer Clown" John Wayne Gacy, a respected citizen who dressed as a clown at children's parties, was arrested in December of 1978. When nearly thirty bodies were found in the crawl space of his home, he became a media sensation. But the undisputed superstar was Ted Bundy. Handsome, personable, apparently middle class, and with a penchant for victims who made good copy—pretty coeds, ski instructors, sorority sisters—Bundy quickly became the nation's paradigmatic serial murderer.

Bundy first came to the public's notice in 1977. He had been killing women in the Seattle region since the early seventies, but police there didn't have enough evidence to indict him. In 1974, he moved to Salt Lake City to attend law school at the University of Utah, and in late 1974, one of his intended victims got away. She identified Bundy, and he was convicted of kidnapping in 1976. While embarking on Utah's fifteen-year sentence, he was extradited to Colorado to stand trial for murder. While in law school, he had moved his killing activity out of state.

In Colorado, Bundy became a media sensation after he escaped from custody—twice, once from Aspen, the second time from Glenwood Springs. Many people couldn't help but admire his audacity. Aspen locals printed T-shirts saying "Ted Bundy is a one-night stand." An area restaurant offered a "Bundyburger"—an empty bun, which you open to find "the meat has fled." On the lam, Bundy made his way to Chicago, then Michigan, and ultimately, Florida. After a week in Florida, he broke into the Chi Omega sorority house on the Florida State University campus and went on a rampage, brutally bludgeoning and strangling two young women and severely injuring two more. Two weeks later, he abducted, raped, and killed a twelve-year-old girl in Lake City, Florida. He was arrested less than a week later and denied any connection to the Florida killings. But the game was over; he would eventually begin confessing to a shocking, multistate murder career.

Bundy was catnip for the media. Not only was he good-looking and well dressed, he was a former law student, a converted Mormon, and an occasional political worker for Republican candidates and Washington state's Republican Party. News stories depicted him as a bright lawyer-to-be with a promising future in politics. He had worked at a suicide crisis hotline and once saved a small child from drowning. He had run down a purse-snatcher. He wore turtlenecks and nice sports jackets. At his first trial, he conspicuously turned the pages of Solzhenitsyn's *Gulag Archipelago* while the lawyers wrangled. Affable and apparently successful, he looked like the kind of man a woman would proudly bring home to meet Mom and Dad. "All-American Boy on Trial" was the title of the *New York Times Magazine* profile, which called him a "terrific looking man" with a "lean all-American face," a "young man who represented the best of America, not its worst." The *Times* author went so far as to dub him "Kennedyesque."

But Ted Bundy was no Jack Kennedy. On close inspection, his veneer of upper-middle-class sophistication evaporates. Born at a home for unwed mothers in Vermont, possibly the product of incestuous sexual abuse, he was told when very young that his grandparents were his parents. Then his mother took him to Tacoma, Washington, and remarried. He was adopted by his stepfather, a cook in an army hospital. The family, which soon grew to include four more kids, lived in an unimpressive home on Tacoma's west side. Bundy hated being seen in his stepfather's low-class Rambler. "I felt inferior," Bundy later told interviewers, "in part because of the money thing. My family didn't have money problems *per se*, but I was always envious of the kids who lived in all those brick houses where the executives and doctors lived. I felt kind of deprived, at a disadvantage to those people who had the money, the successful parents, all the goodies." It's hard not to hear an echo of Charles Starkweather's resentment for "'uppity' kids from big houses whose old man was a doctor or a president of a bank."

Once at the University of Washington, Bundy worked hard to disguise his humble origins by pursuing a high-end brand-name lifestyle. He bought preppy clothes, drank fancy French wines, forged ski lift tickets. He affected an English-sounding accent. It seems he was most successful in hoodwinking those who were unsophisticated themselves. His first serious girlfriend, the daughter of a wealthy California family, dumped him for his lack of ambition. He later described her as "Saks" to his "Sears and Roebuck." His next girlfriend, Elizabeth Kloepfer, a Mormon secretary from Ogden, Utah, was easier to impress: in her memoir of their relationship, she reports that when she first met Bundy she thought him "a cut above the rest of the crowd," because "his slacks and turtleneck certainly weren't from J. C. Penney." The first time they made dinner together, he impressed her by taking her to a fancy, upscale Safeway to buy steaks. He didn't tell her he had worked there as a night stocker. Kloepfer, who hadn't gone to college, was even impressed by Bundy's academic prowess, though he was a middling undergraduate and, after a round of rejections, did poorly in the one law school that accepted him the first time around, the University of Puget Sound.

Writing after the 1979 trial, Stephen Michaud and Hugh Aynesworth, authors of the most comprehensive account of Bundy's crimes, declare themselves puzzled by the popular image of Bundy. "The press stories about Ted stressed his apparent normalcy, his intellect, his attractiveness, his Republicanism," they write. "They didn't report he was a compulsive nail-biter and nose picker, that he was no genius (I.Q.: 124), that he was at best a fair student in college and failure in law school, that he was poorly read, that he frequently mispronounced words and that he stuttered when nervous and had acquired only a surface sophistication." The authors were swimming upstream. The media persisted in presenting Bundy as brilliant, charming, and promising, and when he announced his intention to defend himself at his Florida trial, 250 reporters from five continents applied for press passes to the courtroom. ABC television paid for a dedicated satellite hookup.

The attention fed on itself. Bundy "fans" sprouted across

the nation. He reportedly received hundreds of letters daily, the majority from adoring women. One of them managed to marry him while he was on death row, where she claimed to have conceived his child. And Bundy himself worked hard to maintain the upper-class image he had adopted. Asked by a prison interviewer to describe his crimes, he replied, "How do you describe the taste of *bouillabaisse*? Some remember clams, others mullet."

After his conviction, Bundy's status as the paradigmatic serial murderer was augmented in print and on film: four books about him were published shortly after the trial. Their titles—*The Stranger Beside Me, The Deliberate Stranger, The Killer Next Door, The Only Living Witness*—highlight both his normalcy and his monstrosity. The most popular of them was by Ann Rule, a hardworking hack writer of parenting and detective-magazine stories who had actually worked with Bundy at the Seattle Crisis Center—a lucky break for a would-be crime writer. Her account *The Stranger Beside Me* launched her career as a best-selling doyenne of true crime. In it, she describes Bundy in terms so glowing she sounds like she's writing his law school recommendation: "a brilliant, handsome senior in psychology at the University of Washington"; "Ted Bundy is a man who learns from experience—his own and others'"; "If Ted is to die, I think he will muster the strength to do it with style." One year later, Elizabeth Kloepfer—writing as "Elizabeth Kendall"—took a similarly admiring tone in her memoir, *The Phantom Prince: My Life with Ted Bundy*.

Bundy fascination spawned a number of false myths about serial killers: that they are predominantly white, middle-class men who prey on beautiful young coeds; that they are intelligent, even brilliant, capable of eluding and tricking the police; and that they are fundamentally divided souls, with a socially acceptable "mask" disguising the dark demon writhing within. Even as academics and criminologists have consistently debunked each of these myths, they persist, not only in movies and novels about serial killers, but in purportedly nonfiction books about them. They serve to make serial killers more likable.

Another myth the Bundy case helped create was the notion that serial killers are mobile predators, roaming the nation in search of victims. Bundy had indeed crossed the continent, inscribing a homicidal arrow across the map from Washington state to Utah to Florida, but before he left Washington the majority of his killings occurred in one very small area—the Seattle neighborhood around the University of Washington. Yet it was his travels that sparked the national imagination. He was said to be "the first coast-to-coast killer, the model of the traveling serial killer who took advantage of what Bundy called 'the anonymity factor.'"

One person who knew better, even in the early eighties, was Lieutenant Ray Biondi. The Sacramento area seemed to have more than its fair share of serial killers, and well before he became aware of Lou Ellen Burleigh's disappearance, or heard the name Roger Reece Kibbe, Detective Biondi had helped capture a number of them. He had tracked down Richard Chase, the "Vampire Killer," a psychotic murderer who drank his victims' blood. He had helped build the case against Gerald Gallego, whose wife Charlene helped him abduct, rape, and murder teenage girls in the Sacramento area in the late seventies. In 1985, Biondi would help solve a series of murders of young boys committed by another young boy—Jon Scott Dunkle. None of these cases fit the stereotype: Chase was psychotic, Gallego worked in a team with his wife, and Dunkle was a diagnosed schizophrenic. And each of them stuck to a very specific "hunting ground." Biondi knew that, although the media presented him as the very model of the modern multiple murderer, Ted Bundy was the exception, not the rule.

· · · · ·

Sometime around 1980, Harriet and Roger Kibbe bought a home in Oakley, a small town about twelve miles east of

Pittsburg. Roger started working as a truck driver, and Harriet began a bookkeeping business. A few years later, using borrowed money, they purchased a furniture warehouse in Modesto, a somewhat grimy agricultural center just outside Stockton, over an hour's drive from their home. Roger was going to make furniture, and Harriet would manage the business's books.

The commute was made possible by the recent completion of I-5. The only interstate connecting Mexico, the United States, and Canada, I-5's California leg was completed in 1979, with the opening of a five-mile stretch around Stockton, thirty miles northwest of Modesto. That October, more than three thousand people joined officials from all three nations in a celebratory ribbon-cutting attended by State Senator Randolph Collier, the "father of the California freeway," and April Vandermoon, a fourteen-year-old girl introduced as "the first baby born on I-5."

The interstate was just one sign of how the region was changing. The Kibbes were part of a wave of development moving eastward from the San Francisco Bay Area. As housing prices soared in the 1980s, suburbs and subdivisions began to spread east from the Coast Ranges, sprawling from the Bay Area into the agricultural Central Valley. Dominating the center of California, the 450-mile-long Central Valley stretches from Redding in the north to Bakersfield in the south. Once home to little more than vast fields of grapes, almond trees, and vegetable farms, the Central Valley began to be devoured by subdivisions in the eighties. Before long, it became California's fastest-growing region, which it remains today.

It was an era of change. As the eighties dawned, the nation was experiencing a profound transition. The seventies—an era of questioning, of self-doubt, of rethinking old beliefs in the face of social breakdown—were about to give way to the eighties, an era of retrenchment, of turning away from what was wrong with society and refocusing on what was right. Some historians even put an exact date on this transition: July 15,

1979, the night President Jimmy Carter gave what came to be known as his "malaise speech." Meant to reinvigorate a nation demoralized by unemployment, economic stagnation, inflation, and a second energy crisis—all following hard on the heels of Watergate and the ignominious conclusion to the war in Vietnam—Carter's speech was a bold call to conscience. At its heart was a startling claim: the nation, he said, was facing a crisis of confidence, in part because it had lost its way. It was time to deal with the fact that America had chosen the wrong path: consumerism. "In a nation that was proud of hard work, strong families, close-knit communities, and our faith in God," President Carter declared, "too many of us now tend to worship self-indulgence and consumption. Human identity is no longer defined by what one does, but by what one owns. But we've discovered that owning things and consuming things does not satisfy our longing for meaning. We've learned that piling up material goods cannot fill the emptiness of lives which have no confidence or purpose." To take "the path of common purpose and the restoration of American values," he proposed a slew of fundamental changes to the American way of life: oil-import quotas, bonds for alternative energy development, legislated reductions in oil use, and reinvestment in public transportation.

At first, the nation was wowed. But then, what he said began to sink in. The president of the United States had declared that the nation shouldn't endlessly consume—that in fact consumption might not equal happiness. Meaning might be found in making and buying less. Conservatives began calling it Carter's "malaise" speech, though he hadn't used that word. Arguments flared up about whether the nation really had lost its confidence, as if the president had been diagnosing a personality disorder and not a structural flaw in society. His self-questioning was dismissed as "navel-gazing."

Carter had done something truly shocking. He had expressed skepticism about what had been American economic dogma since the Second World War: the doctrine of growth. His basic premise—that there might be limits to expanding the economy, to resource use, to consumption—became, as he later wrote in his memoirs, "the subliminal theme" of his entire presidency. It wasn't always subliminal. Dedicating the John F. Kennedy Presidential Library, Carter declared, "We can no longer rely on a rising economic tide to lift the boats of the poorest in our society. . . . We have a keener appreciation of limits now—the limits of government, limits on the use of military power abroad; the limits on manipulating, without harm to ourselves, a delicate and a balanced natural environment."

Carter was not alone in thinking about limits. In 1972, a group of intellectuals calling themselves the Club of Rome commissioned a group of MIT computer programmers to model a range of outcomes to ongoing growth. The geeks assembled a wonky collection of charts and graphs titled *The Limits to Growth*. In model after model, they demonstrated that the endless ramping up of population, industrialization, and resource consumption would lead inevitably to economic collapse and widespread societal meltdown. Although conservative economists immediately denounced the whole project as a doomsday fantasy, the book sold vigorously and was translated into thirty languages. Clearly the idea resounded with a lot of people. Even the money-minded *Business Week*, which rejected the book's conclusions, admitted that "For all the criticism, practically everyone agrees that on a finite planet, growth must end sooner or later."

Growth must end? In fact, there was no such consensus. The nation, as sociologist Amitai Etzioni reported to the 1979 President's Commission on an Agenda for the Eighties, was actually divided against itself, torn between its own commitment to endless growth and its desire to return to the antimaterialist values Carter had described in his speech. It was a state of ambivalence that couldn't last, Etzioni predicted: the nation would have to undergo either "rededication to the industrial, mass-consumption society" or a "clearer commitment to a slow-growth, quality-of-life society."

The choice was made in 1980 with the election of Ronald Reagan. Reagan, articulating boundless faith in the American way, touched a chord in a nation weary of self-doubt and cognitive dissonance. In the campaign's one televised debate, Reagan offered a few simple questions for people to ask themselves in deciding how to vote: "Are you better off than you were four years ago? Is it easier for you to go buy things in stores than it was four years ago?" he began. In stark contrast to Carter's critique of materialism, Reagan's redefinition of the national mission was offered in the simplest terms possible: America is succeeding if its citizens can go buy things. His subsequent landslide victory suggested the message had found an enthusiastic audience: the rededication to mass consumption was on.

The return to a vision of an America without limits was a deep and profound shift in the national sensibility, a turn away from self-doubt and back toward the American dream—defined as unfettered free enterprise, unabashed consumerism, and unflinching military prowess. It was the definition of the American dream that drove the interstate highway program, amped up by eighties upscaling and the affluence of the aging baby boom generation. Suddenly, brand-name awareness like Ted Bundy's was unapologetically everywhere. Shows like *Dallas, Knots Landing,* and *Dynasty* celebrated the arts of getting and spending. *Lifestyles of the Rich and Famous* profiled the conspicuous consumption of real-life counterparts to the Ewings and the Carringtons: host Robin Leach signed off each night by offering his audience "champagne wishes and caviar dreams." It was the era of movies like *Wall Street,* whose antihero Gordon Gekko's speech proclaiming that "greed is good"—however satirically intended by director Oliver Stone—became a rallying cry for would-be corporate raiders.

In the postwar era, Americans had expressed deep reservations about the national commitment to materialism, militarism, and the mobility that underwrote them. Many of those reservations settled on the highway program. In the sixties and seventies, the counterculture led the way to a more thoroughgoing critique of that ideology, including a failed attempt to redefine highways. The eighties would put the critique, and even the reservations, to rest. But not without a struggle. And part of that struggle would center on highway serial killers.

• • • • •

In 1982, Henry Lee Lucas was arrested in Texas for the brutal murder of an elderly neighbor, Kate Rich. If Ted Bundy evoked the serial killer's "mask of sanity," Lucas, a one-eyed former mental patient who had already done time for killing his mother, seemed to embody the monster behind the mask. Born in the backwoods of Virginia, Lucas was a nasty piece of work. His father, according to stories, was a moonshiner who had passed out on a railroad track in a drunken stupor and had both legs severed by a passing train. He hopped around legless for a while before dragging his sorry self into the cold one night to freeze to death. Henry's mother was no better: allegedly she was a prostitute, and it was claimed she forced her family to watch her meetings with "clients," and regularly beat her children with a club. Not surprisingly, young Henry's life of crime began at an early age.

Seemingly remorseless, Lucas admitted upon arrest that he had murdered his elderly neighbor and raped her dead body. But that was only the beginning. Once in custody, he spontaneously began confessing to more murders. First it was around 100 women. Then 150. Then 165. He offered up the name of his frequent accomplice: Otis Toole, who was already in jail in Jacksonville, Florida. Police declared that between them, Lucas and Toole were "good" for at least 28 murders in eight states, including some of what were being called "the I-35 killings"—the late-seventies murders of around 20 hitchhikers and women with car trouble along Interstate 35 in Texas. By October of 1982, Lucas was admitting to 200 murders. Then Otis Toole—perhaps greedy for some of the airtime—confessed to having killed Adam Walsh. The son of a wealthy Florida hotel developer, six-year-old Adam Walsh had been kidnapped in 1981 from a Florida shopping mall. When Adam's severed head turned up sixteen days later, his father John dedicated his life to preventing crimes against children. John Walsh went on to found the National Center for Missing and Exploited Children, and would eventually find his niche as host of the Fox network's longest-running program, *America's Most Wanted*.

The Lucas confessions picked up where Ted Bundy left off. Ted Bundy's travels launched the idea of a new trend: mobile killers roaming the nation's highways. With Henry Lee Lucas, the bond between the killer and the road was drawn even more explicitly. Lucas and Toole, traveling the country, had used the highways and the anonymous exchanges they offered as accessories to murder. Many of their victims were hitchhikers and transients. Their bodies were said to be scattered from Florida to Washington, California to Michigan, many by the side of the road. In the press, Lucas was almost always labeled a "drifter"; articles about him usually featured an impressive list of states whose investigators were on his case.

The exaggerated confessions of Lucas and Toole confirmed what many already believed: the nation was being haunted by increasingly random violence. The Reagan administration had swept into office in part on the promise of "getting tough" on offenders and immediately created a new Task Force on Violent Crime. The FBI also rolled into gear. In April 1983, Senator Arlen Specter wrote FBI director William Webster to request a report on the feasibility of creating a centralized system to "track and analyze serial murders." Webster's report was unveiled at Senate hearings on serial murder in July of that year.

The Senate hearings focused on connecting serial killers to interstate mobility. "Experts" and law enforcement officials were brought in to testify to the dramatic increase in random stranger-murders committed with no regard for jurisdictional boundaries. One expert was Ann Rule. "The thing that I have found about the serial murderers that I have researched," Rule declared, "they travel constantly. They are trollers; while most of us might put 15,000 to 20,000 miles a year on our cars, several of the serial killers I have researched have put 200,000 miles a year on their cars. They move constantly. They may drive all night long. They are always looking for the random victim who may cross their path." Rule's prepared statement referred over and over to serial killers as a "new breed" of criminal. "I cannot really tell you why this new kind of killer has emerged," she declared. "It may be tied in somehow with the fact that we have become an increasingly mobile society." Another witness was John Walsh. His statement was even more emotional. "When we talk about 6,300 unsolved murders in this country last year, random murders, someone is committing these murders and someone is doing these murders, and they are going through this country and police agencies are not linking them up."

Luckily, the FBI was there to offer a solution. Director Webster proposed creating a central repository within the FBI to track and record apparently motiveless violent crimes. Based at Quantico, the division would not only catalog rapes and murders, but would also provide law enforcement with the latest in behavioral analysis of these dangerous, mobile criminals.

In the months that followed, the FBI helped to "educate" the public about this frightening new threat to the nation. On October 26, 1983, Justice Department officials declared that as many as thirty-five serial murderers could be at large in the United States. As reported in the *New York Times*, the statement defined serial murderers as "those who kill for reasons other than greed, a fight, jealousy or family disputes." It distinguished serial from mass murderers, explaining that serial killers "often cross city and state lines, making detection more difficult." It cited the examples of Charles Starkweather and John Wayne Gacy—even though neither fit the model of the mobile, motiveless killer. Starkweather's spree began as a family dispute, and Gacy didn't travel at all, but killed and buried his victims in his own home. Pointing out that 28 percent of the nation's twenty thousand annual homicides went unsolved, the Justice Department hinted darkly that serial killers might be responsible for many of those cold cases—speculating that serial killers were murdering around four thousand people a year. One unnamed city was, according to the research project director, believed at that moment to have five serial murderers roaming its streets.

Skeptics have subsequently pointed out that it was very much in the interest of the FBI, seeking funding for its new national database, to highlight interjurisdictional, mobile killers. As many historians of the Bureau have pointed out, the FBI has always needed to justify its existence by emphasizing the dangers of criminals who can't be dealt with locally because they commit crimes in multiple jurisdictions. It has thus always been part of the Bureau's mission to define an "enemy within," preferably a highly mobile one best fought by a well-equipped federal agency. Gangsters, communists, and "student radicals" all served this purpose at various points. In the eighties, serial killers fit the bill perfectly.

But the story was one the nation found easy to swallow. That's because, underneath all the blood and thunder, the stories about this "new" phenomenon played into the very same anxiety that had been haunting the nation since the postwar years: where was our fast-tracked, on-the-move modernity taking us? The Justice Department dispatched experts to talk about serial murder, and the public eagerly listened. In a January 1984 front-page story titled "Officials Cite a Rise in Killers Who Roam the U.S. for Victims," the *New York Times* reported that there was "growing evidence of a substantial increase in the number of killers who strike again and again, sometimes traveling from city to city, choosing strangers as victims, then moving on to kill again." Serial killers were said to be increasing both in number and in ferocity. "We've got people out there now killing 20 and 30 people and more, and some of them just don't kill. They torture their victims in terrible ways and mutilate them before they kill them," declared the Justice Department's Robert Heck. "Something's going on out there.... It's an epidemic." To explain the epidemic, officials cited all the same reasons trotted out in the juvenile delinquency panic of the 1950s: broken homes, media violence, and increased mobility. Loose sexual morals were thrown in as well.

The story was wildly popular throughout the rest of 1984 and 1985. Articles ran in *Life, Newsweek, Omni,* and a host of other magazines. Every television news magazine, from *60 Minutes* to *America Undercover,* ran at least one serial killer episode. HBO created a full-length documentary called *Murder: No Apparent Motive.* New "infotainment" television shows like *Inside Edition* and *Hard Copy* aired lurid "re-creations" of killers' alleged crimes. All of these stories emphasized the killers' mobility, and most of them repeated the Justice Department estimate of four thousand victims annually, murdered by thirty to thirty-five serial killers roaming the nation. That would mean each killer was dispatching a hundred people annually—an average of two a week. And since they were doing it all across the nation, they could strike anywhere, anytime. No wonder there was a panic.

Mobility was central to the story—but it often didn't fit the crime. Of the eight killers whose photos ran with the "Killers Who Roam the U.S." piece in the *New York Times,* only three could actually be said to have roamed the United States: Bundy, Lucas, and Toole. Randy Kraft, who was known as the "Freeway Killer," did in fact roam the highways, but like Edward Kemper, he stuck to a familiar area in southern California. Wayne Williams—if he was in fact responsible for the majority of the Atlanta child murders—roamed a fairly circumscribed set of streets in Atlanta's ghettos. Angelo Buono and Kenneth Bianchi stuck to the hills above Los Angeles, and John Wayne Gacy chose his victims in the Chicago region and killed them in his own home. But the notion that the highways were behind this frightening rise in violence just made sense to Americans.

Was there an actual epidemic of serial killing in the eighties? Separating an increase in serial murders from an increase in the reporting of them is difficult. A 1992 article in *Criminal*

Justice Research Bulletin concluded there was evidence for a dramatic increase in American serial murder since 1964, but that the number of victims was nowhere near the Justice Department's insinuations. Scholar Philip Jenkins estimated that serial murder accounts for about 2 to 3 percent of American homicides, meaning there are perhaps three to four hundred victims a year. And most serial killers, he declared, do not roam. The public's panic was not only unjustified by the numbers, but it was focused on an image that had little basis in reality.

"In playing up the frenzy," wrote retired FBI profiler Robert Ressler the same year, "we were using an old tactic in Washington, playing up the problem as a way of getting Congress and the higher-ups in the executive branch to pay attention to it." The strategy worked. In June of 1984, President Reagan, addressing the National Sheriff's Association Conference, announced the creation of the National Center for the Analysis of Violent Crime, a federal clearinghouse for information about mobile violent criminals under the auspices of the FBI at Quantico. The NCAVC would be home to the evolving art of criminal profiling, as well as a computer database, known as ViCAP (Violent Criminals Apprehension Program), a centralized, searchable repository of unsolved, apparently random murders and rapes. In developing the questionnaire that local law enforcement agencies would fill out when entering their cases into ViCAP, the FBI consulted with America's favorite expert on serial killers: Ted Bundy.

· · · · ·

Americans and the FBI may have been obsessed with Bundy, but most of the real serial killers out there were significantly less glamorous. Just two months before Reagan announced the creation of the NCAVC, a heroin-addicted prostitute filed a complaint with the Contra Costa County Sheriff's Department accusing Roger Kibbe of rape. Police visited Kibbe at the trucking company where he worked to discuss the case. Kibbe admitted to having given the woman a ride, but denied having had sex with her. Police then tried to contact the woman to follow up with her, but they couldn't find her. Once again, a report on Kibbe was shelved.

Two years later, the bodies began to appear. They were found at varying distances from the I-5 corridor between Sacramento and Stockton, where all of them had vanished. This stretch of freeway zooms through one of the sparser parts of the Central Valley, an area still dominated today by rich agricultural lands. Almonds, corn, and grapes—many of the latter destined for the cellars of Ernest and Julio Gallo—can be seen along the highway. The farms create a complicated patchwork on the flat valley floor, threaded through with a network of channels, distributaries, and sloughs that make up the delta of the Sacramento and San Joaquin Rivers. This part of the Central Valley also features a network of man-made waterways: flood control channels and dams, irrigation canals, and aqueducts, all designed and built during the 1950s to keep water away from places where it wasn't wanted, while bringing it to places where it was.

Stephanie Brown was pulled out of one of those irrigation ditches, near a place called Terminus Island. A vivacious nineteen-year-old bank teller, Brown lived in Foothill Farms, a suburb on the northeast fringe of Sacramento. Late at night in July 1986, she got a phone call from her roommate, whose car had broken down, stranding her and her boyfriend downtown. Stephanie drove over to pick them up, then dropped the roommate and her boyfriend off at his apartment on Sacramento's south side. She didn't know the area well, so they gave her directions back to the northeast suburbs. She never made it. The California Highway Patrol tagged her abandoned car the next morning on the Hood Franklin off-ramp, an isolated highway exit about sixteen miles south of where Stephanie should have gone north on I-5. A crumpled roadmap lay on the ground nearby.

It was easy to imagine what might have happened: lost at night on the increasingly desolate highway, the young woman probably stopped to get her bearings. Perhaps she had been offered aid by a passing motorist. Or perhaps someone posing as a driver in trouble had solicited her help. She didn't live for long after the encounter. Her strangled body was soon found about twenty miles southwest of her car, not far from the intersection of I-5 and Highway 12.

The next month, Charmaine Sabrah disappeared. She had enjoyed a night out in Stockton with her mother, Carmen Anselmi. But as the mother and daughter drove home to Sacramento, Charmaine's car broke down. The two women waited on the shoulder of I-5, hoping the highway patrol would pass by. Eventually, a middle-aged man with a small, two-seater sports car stopped behind them. He asked if they needed help, and when they said they did, he drove the mother, Carmen, to a nearby exit so she could make a phone call. She couldn't reach anyone. The man drove her back to the disabled car, and then offered to drive them home. But one at a time, he said, as he only had room for two in his car. Carmen and her daughter decided Charmaine should go first, since she had an infant waiting for her at home. Charmaine got in the car with the man and waved good-bye to her mother. She was never seen alive again. Her strangled body was found several months later in the old gold mining country of Amador County, on the western slope of the Sierra Nevada.

Detectives talked with Carmen Anselmi at length. She had, after all, ridden in the car with the man suspected of abducting her daughter. She had talked to him as they drove to the telephone, and she had watched her daughter go off with him in his car. She did her best to remember details that might help the police. But the description she gave was vague, and even on further questioning she couldn't fill it in. He was middle-aged, with graying hair. Maybe his nose was a bit big. She desperately wanted to help, but it was dark and she had been drinking. And the man, she told police, was completely nondescript.

Roger Reece Kibbe, the "I-5 Strangler": a killer so bland even a mother who put her daughter into his car couldn't remember any details about him to tell police. Courtesy Sacramento Bee.

Not long after Charmaine Sabrah disappeared, another body was found in the desolate country along I-5. It was Lora Heedick, a Sacramento prostitute. Her case didn't receive the attention paid the pretty all-American girl or the young mother trying to get home to her baby. But Lora Heedick had also been strangled.

• • • • • •

The August that Charmaine Sabrah met her awful fate on the highway, the last five miles of I-80, the first transcontinental interstate, opened to traffic. A celebration was held on the spot, outside Salt Lake City. The occasion reminded some people of industrialist Leland Stanford pounding in the "golden spike" in nearby Promontory, Utah, in 1869. That event, marking the completion of the nation's first transcontinental railroad, had been celebrated with plenty of pomp and national publicity. The completion of I-80, on the other hand, was a small affair that went largely unnoticed. Neither the secretary of transportation nor the director of the Federal Highway Administration attended. The governor of Utah was conspicuously absent. Of the nation's major newspapers, only the *New York Times* covered the story. As Tom Lewis, author of a history of the interstate, points out, what people had come to feel toward the highway system was mostly indifference. "Many accepted the highways as a part of contemporary life and thought little about them," he writes, "except, on occasion, to complain that they were overcrowded, or falling apart."

Throughout the seventies, a number of things had become apparent about the interstate highway program. It had mowed down mountains, plowed through communities, and divided up farms with little regard for the opinions of affected citizens. It had cost at least three times what it was expected to cost. It had accelerated white flight from cities, contributed to urban blight, and abetted the spread of environmentally destructive, aesthetically awful suburbia. It had spawned a monotonous national landscape of homogeneous franchise businesses, ticky-tacky homes, eyesore shopping malls, and hideous commercial strips.

After the first wave of antihighway screeds, an increasingly sophisticated critique had evolved. The focus shifted from what the highways destroyed—landscapes, urban communities—to what they created: sprawl. The highway problem could not be separated from what was called "urbanization," but might better be called "suburbanization." All those land-eating shopping malls and office parks and subdivisions paving their soulless way over countryside and farmland needed to be stopped, before they turned the nation into a nondescript nowhereland. The Task Force on Land Use and Urban Growth issued a report in 1973 declaring that a "new mood" was afoot in the nation. "Increasingly," the report declared, "citizens are asking what urban growth will add to the quality of their lives. They are questioning the way relatively unconstrained, piecemeal urbanization is changing their communities and are rebelling against the traditional processes of government and the marketplace which, they believe, have inadequately guided development in the past." The following year, the Real Estate Research Corporation, an independent research and consulting firm, issued a monumental analysis, *The Costs of Sprawl*, that outlined the fiscal consequences of poorly planned development. It seemed that a new era of "smart growth" was dawning: good urban planning, transit-oriented development, preservation of green spaces and community values. One only had to look at San Francisco, which had canceled its freeways, or Boulder, which had passed slow-growth measures throughout the seventies, or Portland, which drew a growth-management boundary around itself in 1979, to see the future.

The attack on sprawl was part of the seventies zeitgeist, another instance of citizens questioning the doctrine of endless growth and attempting to recenter American life on something other than consumption. But in the eighties, the nation was no more interested in putting limits on suburbia than it was in applying brakes to the economy. In the mood of cultural retrenchment that marked the Reagan years, the antisprawl, antigrowth movement collapsed. "As the boom of the 1980s and 1990s got underway," writes one theorist of sprawl, "it soon became apparent that defeat had been snatched from the jaws of victory and that decentralization and sprawl were far from conquered." What all those tract mansions and office parks and shopping plazas with name-brand stores represented, after all, was greed: developers' greed for land and for profits, individuals' greed for goods and for status. And in the eighties, greed was good.

· · · · ·

In November 1986, Katherine Kelly Quinones, another Sacramento prostitute, disappeared. A month later, the twenty-five-year-old was found strangled by Lake Berryessa in Napa County, forty miles north. Police had no leads.

In May of 1987, the Kibbes moved to the edge of Sacramento. The rising tide of the eighties was not floating all boats: in mid-1986, Roger's furniture-making business had failed. The bank moved to foreclose on their Oakley home. Averting disaster, Harriet Kibbe sold the house. Now she had found a job for herself and Roger. They would manage a ministorage facility called Public Storage, she handling the bookkeeping and customers, Roger maintaining the grounds and doing odd jobs around the place. In addition to receiving modest salaries, they would get to live in a one-bedroom apartment on the premises.

The Kibbes thus moved to the not-yet-incorporated Sacramento suburb of Citrus Heights. Like the nearby Foothill Farms, like so many places in the nation, Citrus Heights was named for what it had displaced. It had begun its growth spurt in the 1970s, when I-80 was completed and a handful of shopping malls and plazas sprouted up not far from the interchange. More retail complexes, office space, and tract housing quickly ate up the rest of the area's rural land, and Citrus Heights said good-bye to the last of its citrus trees. The Public Storage facility the Kibbes moved to was a white strip of building flanking a bland low-end shopping plaza near the Antelope Avenue interchange. It's a classic piece of what developers call "ground cover": a cheap, easily bulldozed business that allows landowners to be cash-flow positive while waiting for the right moment to develop a piece of property. The rental office was at the corner of the building, the manager's apartment adjacent. Rows of garagelike storage units behind reached their fingers toward I-80, its traffic roaring dully by.

That June, a young woman named Karen Finch disappeared. She had spent the day with her daughter at her boyfriend's home in Sonora, an attractive small town up in gold rush territory. At the end of the day, she took her daughter back to her ex-husband's home in Twain Harte, farther up the slope of the Sierra toward Yosemite National Park. She then headed back into the Central Valley to her own apartment in Lodi, a small town between Stockton and Sacramento. She never made it. Her anxious boyfriend found her car on a deserted, mostly agricultural stretch of French Camp Road, between Modesto and Stockton. A week later, her body was found in sparsely populated Amador County, about an hour north of her car. She had been viciously stabbed to death.

Finch's boyfriend and her ex-husband were both brought in for questioning, but Ray Biondi was pretty sure he knew what he was looking at: another victim of the I-5 killer. Like Stephanie Brown, Charmaine Sabrah, and Lora Heedick, Finch had been found mostly nude, with her clothing scattered about the scene. Some of the clothes had been cut up in odd ways: in some cases, the cutting seemed to have been used as a method of removing the clothes, but in others, the slashes and slices were what detectives called "nonfunctional cutting." And Biondi had a gut feeling he knew what those nonfunctional cuts were: a signature.

· · · · ·

By 1987, serial killers were becoming big business. Since the 1980 success of *The Stranger Beside Me*, Ann Rule had been publishing one or two books a year profiling serial killers. Meanwhile slasher films, a horror subgenre centered on a psychopathic murderer and his string of gruesome killings, had become wildly popular. Focusing on a serial killer, they were serials themselves, spawning seemingly endless strings of sequels. *Halloween* began its incredible run in 1978, and was shortly followed by many more: *Prom Night, Friday the 13th, Nightmare on Elm Street*. Slasher films were distinctive in that they often took the point of view of the murderer. The audience, while terrified of the killer, also identified with him: he was what kept the story going. Suddenly, kids wanted to dress up as Jason or Freddy on Halloween.

While audiences flocked to slasher films, they also bought true crime books about serial killers and sensationalist nonfiction books like Jack Levin and James Alan Fox's *Mass Murder: America's Growing Menace*, published at the height of the serial killer panic in 1985. "Despite our emotional distance from the crime," the authors declared at the start, "we must face the fact that the incidence of mass murder is growing. The 1960s mark the onset of the age of mass murder in the United States."

Following hard on the heels of the age of mass murder was the age of mass-murder analysis. A slew of books and television shows about serial killers offered popular takes on law enforcement theories—many of which were being developed at the new National Center for the Analysis of Violent Crime. The profilers there had developed the idea of "signature."

Signature, notes John Douglas, an author and retired FBI profiler, is different from modus operandi. A criminal's MO is how he tends to get the job done—in the case of Ed Kemper, say, picking up hitchhikers, then strangling them. But Kemper's MO changed: when strangling got difficult, he used a knife that he had brought along as a backup. And when he got his hands on a gun, he switched to simply shooting his victims. Eventually, he gave up on hitchhikers altogether. The fact that an MO can and does change flies in the face of the myth that serial killers always use the same method of murder—a myth that has been formed by Hollywood as much as by anyone in law enforcement.

Signature, on the other hand, is more constant. A criminal's signature, according to Douglas, is "what the perpetrator has to do to fulfill himself." It may have little to do with the crime itself—it may even complicate the crime's commission, as in the case Douglas recounts of a bank robber who, during his robberies, made his captives undress and took photographs of them. This was obviously something the robber was doing for his own kicks, rather than as part of the robbery.

To Biondi, the nonfunctional cutting of the victim's clothing was a signature. It convinced him the murders he was investigating were linked. Once he learned about Roger Kibbe's teenage habit of stealing items of women's clothing and cutting them up, he would begin to see how it all fit together. But even before he knew any of that, he felt certain he was on the right track. He became even more certain in August 1987, when an unidentified teenage girl was found dead a hundred miles away in South Lake Tahoe, her body thrown by the side of Highway 50. The young woman—later identified as Darcie Frackenpohl, a seventeen-year-old runaway from Seattle—had been wearing a sleeveless pink dress that had been cut in several places.

Scholars of serial killing—and there are such people out there—have frequently pointed out that signature is often an acquisitive act. Killers keep "trophies" from their victims, whether jewelry or personal effects or—as in Kemper's case—body parts. They become, in essence, collectors. Ted Bundy, typically, is most eloquent on the topic. Discussing his crimes in the third person, he said that he "should have recognized that what really fascinated him was the hunt, the adventure of searching out his victims. And, to a degree, possessing them physically as one would a potted plant, a painting, or a Porsche. Owning, as it were, this individual."

Serial killers reduce people to objects to be added to a list.

Some even keep an actual tally. Randy Kraft, the "Freeway Killer" from southern California, was also called "The Score-Card Killer" by the press: when he was arrested in 1983, he had in his car a list of sixty-five victims he had "collected," written out in a cryptic code. Writers and serial killer "buffs" reinforce the collecting aspect of the crime, arguing over body counts and debating about the most "prolific" serial killers, turning high body count into an achievement, a status-conferring list of possessions. Ed Kemper described killing as a way of making dolls out of living women. A decade later, killers were competing to see who could own the most dolls. As the popular eighties coffee mug slogan went, he who dies with the most toys wins.

· · · · ·

I n September of 1987, Lieutenant Biondi went to Nashville to attend the fifth National Conference on Homicide, Unidentified Bodies and Missing Persons. There, he gave a presentation on the difficulty of tracking serial murders across multiple jurisdictions. As an example, he outlined what he and his fellow detectives were now calling "the I-5 series." He had finally convinced his bosses at Sacramento Homicide to create a task force specifically for these killings. At the conference, he told two hundred of his fellow detectives, hailing from thirty-five states, about the murders along the I-5 corridor. He recounted the nonfunctional clothes cutting that seemed to link the crimes, and the difficulty of getting a bunch of separate agencies to work together on solving them.

Biondi wasn't the only one at the conference looking for ideas about an unsolved series of freeway murders. Public panic about serial killing had abated, but homicide detectives were noticing a disturbing new trend. Bodies were regularly being found along the nation's interstate highways. Biondi attended presentations on freeway murders and the "redhead" killings—unsolved murders of young women who had ended up dumped along interstates in Kentucky, Mississippi, Tennessee, and Arkansas.

Such cases had been increasing in frequency since the late seventies. Donald Henry Gaskins, convicted in 1976, traveled the South's roads in search of victims for what he called his "highway killings" (as opposed to his "serious killings," which were people he knew). Patrick Kearney, who trolled the freeways of Orange County looking for young male hitchhikers, was arrested in 1977. William Bonin, who also killed young men along California highways, was arrested in 1980. Randy Kraft, a Bonin copycat, was arrested in 1983. Kearney, Bonin, and Kraft had each been dubbed the "Freeway Killer." Randy Woodfield, an Oregon bartender who murdered people while robbing homes and businesses along I-5, became known as the "I-5 Killer." He was arrested in 1981 and was quickly made the subject of a book by Ann Rule. And in 1984, Larry Eyler, called the "Interstate Killer" or the "Highway Killer," was arrested in Illinois. Suspected in more than twenty murders, many involving bodies dumped along highways, he was convicted and sentenced to death.

But none of these killers had become a household name, as so many other killers had in the same period. Even Henry Lee Lucas, who had so captivated the nation with his string of confessions, pretty much dropped out of view after the Texas attorney general's office issued a 1986 report debunking the majority of his claims. The report even cast doubt on whether Lucas had murdered "Orange Socks"—the name given an unidentified female corpse found along a Texas interstate wearing nothing but a pair of orange socks. The murder of Orange Socks was what got Lucas sentenced to death, but the attorney general's report pointed out that Lucas was in Florida at the time. Henry Lee Lucas would probably never have made it into print again had he not, in 1998, become the only death row prisoner in Texas to be granted clemency at the request of Governor George W. Bush. His sentence commuted to life, he went back to relative obscurity. He died of heart failure in 2001, largely forgotten.

Something strange was going on. The nation had created a panic over mobile serial killers. But the most-talked-about killers—John Wayne Gacy, Jeffrey Dahmer, Son of Sam, even Ted Bundy—were mostly geographically focused. With the exception of Bundy, they weren't mobile at all. But it didn't matter, because the nation had come to associate freeways and violence. Meanwhile, real freeway killers—mobile predators using the highways to find vulnerable victims—were out there, but they got far less attention. Like the highways themselves, they were bland, unappealing, and lacking in taste. And their victims—gay hustlers, drifters, prostitutes, runaways—were "throwaway" people. The highway killers may have been "collectors," but they were collecting the wrong thing.

· · · · ·

While Ray Biondi was at the Nashville conference, the I-5 case got its first big break. On the night of September 14, Roger Kibbe picked up a prostitute in downtown Sacramento, twenty-nine-year-old Debra Ann Guffie. They drove to an empty golf course parking lot. As they sat in the car haggling over the price of a blow job, Kibbe suddenly grabbed Guffie's arm. He produced a pair of handcuffs and tried to snap them onto her wrist.

Guffie was a hardened heroin addict, but she turned out to be a fighter. When Kibbe grabbed her by the hair, she flailed around and bit him. Then she lunged for the door. As they struggled, a Sacramento police cruiser happened by. Guffie managed to get the car door open, and the officer heard her screaming. He pulled up behind the car. Seeing the cops, Kibbe shoved Guffie out the door and sped off. The police officer gave chase, catching up with him a few blocks later.

Somewhat to the surprise of the police, Debra Guffie was willing to press charges. Kibbe was charged with the assault.

In the interim before the trial, hoping to catch him up to something more serious than manhandling a hooker, police set up twenty-four-hour surveillance of the Public Storage facility where he lived. Kibbe did nothing heinous during this time, so in November of 1987 he was tried for battery, solicitation, and false imprisonment—all misdemeanor charges. Debra Guffie took the stand and testified against him. He was convicted on the first two counts and sentenced to eight months in jail. Detectives decided to put together their murder case against him while he was in jail. They didn't want to give him the chance to kill again.

The first thing they did was hold a press conference warning women in the area that a serial killer was stalking the highways. It made barely a ripple. So early in 1988, Biondi and the Sacramento County sheriff held another press conference to confirm that detectives had linked seven of the murders happening along I-5. They asked the public for help identifying the murderer. "We think he is a frequent lone traveler on major highways in the Central Valley, the Highway 50 corridor and the Tahoe Basin," the sheriff told reporters. "He's probably a resident of one of those areas, more likely the general Valley, as he's familiar, very familiar, with the rural roads and back roads. He has owned or had access to several different makes of vehicles during the recent years and he's probably familiar with and frequents prostitution strolls in the Central Valley cities."

This sounded like exactly the kind of serial killer the FBI and others had been warning the nation about for years: a mobile predator, trolling multiple counties in his search for easy victims. In spite of this, the newly named "I-5 Strangler" got little attention. Some Central Valley newspapers put the story on page 1, but outside the immediate region, it took a backseat position. The *Los Angeles Times*, in its Southland edition, ran it on page 35. In the rest of the nation it didn't play at all.

As Roger Kibbe served his time for battery, Ray Biondi's task force put together their murder case. They gathered behavioral evidence linking the crimes, but it was trace evidence linking victim Darcie Frackenpohl with Kibbe's car that made it possible to get an indictment. Upon his April 1988 release from prison, Kibbe was promptly rearrested for the murder of Frackenpohl.

The first hearing was held in the fall. The judge banned television cameras from the courtroom. He needn't have bothered; the media showed little interest. Not that the public's fascination with serial killers was flagging. In England that autumn, a celebration was being held on the centennial of the Whitechapel murders. Vendors hawked Jack the Ripper T-shirts, mugs, and pins, while newspapers, books, and television specials recounted the murders. A B-movie called *Jack's Back* was released, and a story collection called *Ripper* came out; "Jack the Ripper: He was the first" the cover declared. There was an extra-gory computer game called *Jack the Ripper* and, in pubs, a special, blood-red Ripper cocktail, so people could drink to the forefather of serial killers everywhere.

The following year, Ted Bundy's execution was front-page news across the nation.

• • • • •

After a series of delays, Roger Kibbe's trial for the murder of Darcie Frackenpohl opened on February 14, 1991. That day, MGM Studios released the blockbuster hit *The Silence of the Lambs*. The *Sacramento Bee* hailed it as "the definitive slasher film." Directed by Jonathan Demme and based on the 1988 novel by Thomas Harris, *Silence* was perhaps the most successful pop culture evocation of serial killing ever. The film creates a triangle between FBI cadet Clarice Starling and two serial killers: the "bad" killer Buffalo Bill, and the "good" killer, Hannibal Lecter. Buffalo Bill, who longs to be a woman, kidnaps women, starves them for several days, and skins them to make himself a "woman-suit." Hannibal Lecter, now in prison, was the more civilized murderer: he simply ate his victims.

Played with demonic glee by Anthony Hopkins, Hannibal

the Cannibal immediately became a cultural icon. This serial killer was no monster, but a master of consumer culture; not simply a collector, but a connoisseur. A white-collar killer—he used to be a psychiatrist—Lecter is not only brilliant, but gracious and elegant, rising above his lowly prison circumstances. He makes drawings of the duomo in Florence, quotes Marcus Aurelius, recognizes that Clarice has a "good bag and cheap shoes." He has the soul of an aesthete, and in prison he reaches out to collect the one thing available to him: Clarice Starling's memories. In the film's pivotal scenes, he offers her information that will help her track Buffalo Bill in exchange for her recollections of the miserable, hardscrabble childhood she has repressed to get ahead in the world. He savors her stories just as he once savored a victim's liver, as he famously tells Clarice, with some fava beans and a nice Chianti. In comparison, poor, social-climbing Ted Bundy—the Safeway stockist—looks pitiably obvious in his attempts to ape highbrow tastes. Hannibal the Cannibal is no poser but the real deal: sophisticated, high-class, and educated. Audiences loved him for it. At the film's end, he has escaped, and the final scene shows him following an obnoxious prison warden who has tormented him: viewers know another grisly meal is about to take place, and they can't help but relish it too.

Was it inevitable that the serial killer would metamorphose in the eighties from figure of repulsion to figure of adulation, from bogeyman to icon? Serial killing is, after all, a kind of greed: Jeffrey Dahmer fixating on his victim's body parts, Ed Kemper hoarding his trinkets, Henry Lee Lucas piling up the confessions. Hannibal Lecter, too, is nothing if not greedy; "*Thank you*, Clarice," he breathes when she finally yields up her most painful memory, the one for which the film is named, the one he was waiting for all along. His materialism verges on camp. "Love your suit!" he tells a desperate senator whose daughter is missing, in a line that always gets a laugh. Was embracing the serial killer just one more way to insist that greed was good?

The year *Silence* hit theaters, Bret Easton Ellis published his widely reviled novel *American Psycho*. Its protagonist and narrator, yuppie Wall Street executive Patrick Bateman, spends much of the novel recounting his flashy, brand-name-obsessed lifestyle in exhaustive detail. He uses the same flat tone to describe the increasingly brutal murders he commits as the novel progresses—in fact the two merge. In one scene, for instance, he tortures a victim by making her watch a video of himself killing another woman: "I'm wearing a Joseph Abboud suit, a tie by Paul Stuart, shoes by J. Crew, a vest by someone Italian and I'm kneeling on the floor beside a corpse, eating the girl's brain, gobbling it down, spreading Grey Poupon over hunks of the pink, fleshy meat."

Unpleasant as it is to read, *American Psycho*—like Oliver Stone's *Wall Street*—was clearly intended as a satirical critique of eighties materialism. The controversy that exploded upon its publication—and reignited over the subsequent film adaptation—suggests that it may have been a little bit too close to the bone. Critics declared it "repulsive," "revolting," "garbage," and "designer porn." The author received death threats. The nation was more ready to accept a serial killer as hero than to contemplate the consequences of doing so.

The Silence of the Lambs was not only a box-office smash hit; it won five Academy Awards. Host Billy Crystal was brought onto stage at the awards ceremony dressed up as Hannibal Lecter, demonstrating conclusively that it was no longer a bad thing to be identified with a serial murderer, as long as it was the classy kind. If the nation was fascinated by serial killers before, it was absolutely crazy about them now. "Somehow it has happened," declared Joyce Carol Oates in a 1994 *New York Review of Books* essay, "that the 'serial killer' has become our debased, condemned, yet eerily glorified Noble Savage, the vestiges of the frontier spirit, the American *isolato* cruising interstate highways in van or pickup truck that will yield, should police have the opportunity to investigate, a shotgun, a semiautomatic rifle, quantities of ammunition and six-packs and junk food, possibly a decomposing female corpse in the rear."

I had to look up *isolato* when I read the piece. It means a person who is not just isolated, but out of step with the times or the culture. This seemed like the opposite of what Oates was saying. The serial killer in the nineties had become an antihero, "condemned yet eerily glorified," but completely in-step with the times, not least for his unapologetic materialism.

Bland, blue-collar Roger Reece Kibbe was the one who was out of step: an economic loser in an age that loved winners, he was getting no such glorified status. Even as the media couldn't get enough about Hannibal and those they took to be his real-life counterparts, they were barely interested in the case of the I-5 Strangler. The *Sacramento Bee* ran intermittent stories about the trial in its Metro pages; outside Sacramento, it was barely covered at all. The hundreds of reporters who had jostled for seats at Ted Bundy's trial were no-shows. An Associated Press reporter doggedly filed stories from court, but few newspapers picked them up.

As Operation Desert Storm gripped the nation and California coped with a devastating drought, the trial of Roger Kibbe went stolidly on. The first soup kitchen in Citrus Heights opened as he sat in the courtroom, leading some to note that suburbanization often pushed the vulnerable into the ranks of the underclass. The trial took just over a month. In his closing statement, the prosecutor told the jury that Kibbe's actions were "a road map of the most repugnant behavior possible in a human being." Jurors deliberated for a little less than four hours before delivering a verdict. *The Silence of the Lambs* was still raking in admissions fees when Kibbe was declared guilty.

A few regional papers took note of the conviction in their "Around the Nation" sections. In May, Kibbe was sentenced to a mandatory twenty-five years to life. The event was given a single column in the *Los Angeles Times*. *USA Today* gave it thirty-four words. No other major newspaper even mentioned it.

The media were not the only ones who felt the case was hardly noteworthy. As the sheriff's deputy escorted him from the building, Kibbe made small talk with the man.

"I've killed a few women," he said. "What's the big deal?"

• • • • •

The *New York Times* used the phrase "serial killer" or "serial murderer" 108 times in the 1980s. In the 1990s, one or the other appeared 781 times. In the aughts, 1,199. The vast majority of mentions, however, were not in news stories but in arts and entertainment contexts: movie, book, and television reviews. The nation is still crazy about serial killers—but they have to fit the bill. *The Silence of the Lambs* is widely touted as one of the best thrillers of all time. *American Psycho* is available on DVD in an "uncut Killer Collector's edition." And today the nation is entranced with its latest serial killer hero, the handsome and winning Dexter of the popular television series.

Highway killers, however, rarely enjoy top billing in the serial killer ranks. Outside the world of serial killer "buffs"—admittedly a growing subculture—the names Larry Eyler, Randall Woodfield, Randy Kraft, and Roger Reece Kibbe are little known. Kibbe, up for parole in 2009, got a small flurry of coverage in the local media when DNA evidence led prosecutors to indict him for six more murders. He was linked not only to Stephanie Brown and Charmaine Sabrah, but also to prostitutes Lora Heedick and Katherine Quinones. Prosecutors added Barbara Ann Scott, who had disappeared in early 1986 and was not originally linked to the I-5 series. And they charged him with the murder of Lou Ellen Burleigh, the hopeful secretary "John Brown" had interviewed in his van thirty-two years earlier. In order to avoid the death penalty, Kibbe pled guilty to all six murders and received a sentence of life for each.

Like the highways and their soulless sprawlscape of big-box stores, parking lots, strip malls, and ground cover, highway killers have become a part of life in America—one that is ugly, unpleasant, and no fun to think about. It's much more fun to ignore them in favor of their glamorous fictional counterparts. The nation adores Hannibal Lecter, not Roger Kibbe. It wants to live in Knots Landing, not Citrus Heights.

When I drove from San Francisco to see the stretch of I-5 between Stockton and Sacramento where so many women had vanished, boxy housing developments were still spreading along I-580 from the East Bay into the Central Valley. I-5 looks much the same as it must have in the eighties—lined with agricultural fields and a complicated system of dikes and canals. The Hood Franklin off-ramp is still desolate and French Camp Road still a low-traffic byway through farmland. One thing, however, had changed. Along I-5, about every five miles, were bright blue emergency telephones.

Meanwhile, as Roger Kibbe serves out the remainder of his natural life in Pleasant Valley State Prison, the FBI has turned its attention to a new and insidious kind of serial killer. These murderers, more invisible even than Kibbe and his ilk, are said to be roaming the nation's interstates. Hundreds, perhaps thousands, of victims can be mapped onto the highway network. There's even a whole new division at the NCAVC to analyze them. The FBI claims are meeting with skepticism from many in local law enforcement who feel the FBI has cried wolf too many times. The irony is that this time, the Bureau may be dead right.

> *Fed by the prosperity of the last decade, the 46,567-mile network of limited-access roads that make up the Interstate System is a linear economy-on-wheels, a distinct and self-sustaining 51st state, in a sense, that generates life and commerce.*
>
> —PETER T. KILBORN, 2001

> *Crime is a process, depending on the convergence of offenders and targets in the absence of guardians. The transportation system generates these convergences.*
>
> —MARCUS FELSON AND RACHEL BOBA, 2010

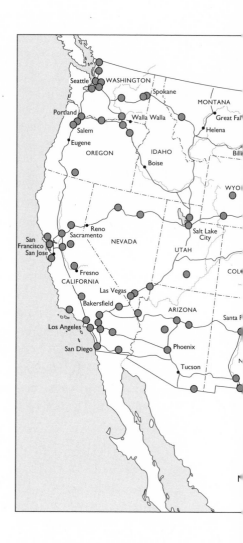

A map the FBI released when it announced its Highway Serial Killings Initiative. The dots represent bodies spread across the nation like a pathogen carried by car. Courtesy FBI.

≡ DRIVE-BY TRUCKERS ≡

Sometime on June 25, 2007, twenty-five-year-old Sara Hulbert went to Nashville's seedy Cowan Street with a pair of guys named Lee and Hollywood. According to Lee, the three scored some crack and smoked it together. After a while, an argument broke out about divvying up what was left. Sara got annoyed and left. Lee figured she was headed for the nearby T.A.—a truck stop with a lively prostitution trade— to make some cash. He watched her disappear between a pair of empty truck trailers. He never saw her again. Somewhere in that row of warehouses, truck washes, and vacant lots, as traffic on I-24 roared by overhead, Sara Hulbert climbed into the wrong truck. Around 12:50 in the morning the T.A. security guard called the cops. He had found Hulbert face-up in the back lot, near the sagging fence hookers squeezed through to do business, a half-inch hole in her head.

Looking at the crime scene, Nashville Metro Detective Pat Postiglione thought he might be dealing with a serial killer. Postiglione, a small, wiry man, with black hair, nearly black eyes, and the trace of a Queens accent, had encountered serial killers before. During his nearly thirty years at the Nashville Metro Police Department, he had helped track down Paul Reid, who had killed seven people while robbing fast-food joints.

He worked the case of Michael Scott Magliolo, a "lumper," or person who does odd jobs for truckers, who claimed to have killed twelve people across several states. In the Hulbert crime scene, Postiglione saw several things that said "serial killer" to him. Hulbert was naked, not just dumped there but carefully posed, the soles of her feet pressed together so her legs made a diamond. There was no sign of a struggle. And there appeared to be little or no physical evidence. In fact, Nashville police really had only two things to go on: a sneakerlike footprint and a grainy T.A. surveillance tape. It showed trucks streaming in and out of the lot all night, but there was one that seemed suspicious: it had stayed only sixteen minutes. All that could be made out was a yellow cab pulling a white trailer with some kind of writing on the side. As a lead, it wasn't much.

Postiglione knew that another prostitute had been killed just a few weeks earlier in Lebanon, Tennessee, about thirty miles east of Nashville on I-40. That woman had been shoved butt-down in a truck stop trash can, garbage carefully piled on top of her stomach. The detective contacted the FBI's Violent Criminals Apprehension Program (ViCAP) and asked agents there to query their national database for similar crimes along highways connecting to the Nashville region. An FBI analyst confirmed that there were cases that looked similar, including a prostitute killed at a truck stop in Alabama. Postiglione and his partner, Lee Freeman, decided to ask for every credit card receipt from the T.A. on the night of the murder. They figured they had a trucker to find.

At least twenty-five former truckers are currently serving time in American prisons for serial murder. There's Robert Ben Rhoades, who converted his truck cab into a torture chamber, now serving a life sentence in Illinois. There's Scott William Cox, a trucker who pled no-contest to two murders in Oregon. There are Dellmus Colvin, who pled guilty in five murders to avoid the death penalty in Ohio, Keith Hunter Jesperson, serving life sentences from four different states, and Wayne Adam Ford, who finally got sick of killing and walked into a California sheriff's office carrying a woman's breast in a plastic bag. When trucker Sean Patrick Goble was arrested in North Carolina and confessed to several murders, ten states lined up to question him about their own cold-case highway homicides. It seems our interstate highway system has become our Whitechapel, with truckers its roving Rippers.

• • • • •

A soft-spoken woman from Oklahoma first saw the pattern. Terri Turner is a supervisory intelligence analyst with the Oklahoma Bureau of Investigation. In September of 2003, a homicide case landed on her desk. A body had been found along I-40 in eastern Oklahoma, and because of jurisdictional issues, the OBI was asked to work the case. Turner, a homicide and sex crime specialist, immediately put out a teletype seeking other female bodies that had been found, like hers, nude, near interstates, and with signs of having been bound. Within seventy-two hours, two responses came back: agencies in Arkansas and Mississippi had similar cases. At that point, Turner knew she might be looking at linked crimes. She had her communications specialists monitor the teletypes for further cases that might be related. In seven months, they had seven homicides. She calls them "my seven girls."

The bodies were all unidentified at first, but eventually investigators identified two of the women. Both had worked as truck stop prostitutes. This was the breakthrough moment for Turner.

"We hold the trucking industry as a whole in very high regard," she told me. "The vast majority of truck drivers are good, hardworking people, and without them our nation would come screeching to a halt. But there are a very few who have found that that particular job is very suited to this particular type of crime."

Turner began reaching out to people in the trucking industry, as well as bringing the different investigators together, making sure they knew about one another's cases. In the spring of 2004, she decided to have a meeting in Oklahoma City for all the investigators working on her seven cases—and any others that might be related.

"I anticipated maybe twenty, twenty-five individuals," she told me, "but by the time word got around about the kind of cases we were going to be talking about, I ended up having sixty investigators from seven different states show up for that meeting. That was really the beginning of the initiative."

FBI analysts at ViCAP had even more surprising news. When they queried their database, they found more than 250 homicides connected to I-40 in the existing files, spread out across Oklahoma, Arkansas, Mississippi, and Texas. A trucker arrested for rape and assault in Lincoln, Nebraska, in late 2004 was eyed as a possible suspect. But in the end, it was John Walsh's show *America's Most Wanted* that broke the case. The show aired the story of an Oklahoma City prostitute killed and thrown from an overpass in Texas. A woman called in and reported that her nephew, already in jail, had bragged about doing something similar. She gave police his name: John Robert Williams, a twenty-eight-year-old long-haul trucker.

"We had never considered the interstate highway system as a common linkage system," ViCAP head Mike Harrigan told me. "We know now it's been going on for years, but we had never picked out the pattern."

$\cdot$ $\cdot$ $\cdot$ $\cdot$ $\cdot$

"Are there more serial killers out there today than there ever have been?" Jim McNamara asked. "No. It's just that there are units that specialize in helping catch and identify them, and through the increase in communications and technology, linkage is better." Jim is a supervisory special agent in the FBI's Behavioral Analysis Unit—the profiling unit made famous in *The Silence of the Lambs*. We were sitting in a windowless conference room in a nondescript office building near

Quantico, Virginia. There are no signs outside the building, just a sea of very clean cars; no name on the front door, just a buzzer commanding "Press here." This is the National Center for the Analysis of Violent Crime, created after the serial killer panic of the mid-eighties. Countless commuters drive by the brick office plaza daily without ever knowing that inside it, FBI agents wearing business attire and sidearms are attempting to connect the dots between some of the nation's most inexplicable crimes.

FBI agents are quick to deny that there is an "epidemic" of serial killing along America's highways, but they seem to be working at cross purposes. On the one hand, they are exceedingly careful not to overstate the danger to the public. That's partly because, after using the wave of public hysteria in the early 1980s to build enthusiasm for funding the NCAVC, the FBI faced a backlash. The numbers they had fed the press—the four thousand annual unsolved murders committed by thirty-five roving serial killers—were declared inflated. Scholars took the FBI to task for fanning the flames of hysteria. The FBI, wary of becoming the federal agency that cried wolf, now backs away from such sweeping claims.

On the other hand, the Bureau has a clearly defined problem, and a program designed to address it. In early 2009, it announced the Highway Serial Killings Initiative (HSKI), focused on killers who choose their victims and dump their bodies along highways. As in the past, the media jumped eagerly on the story. After decades of popular culture linking mobility and murder, who isn't convinced there are killers on the road? Who doesn't fear rest areas or half-expect to see bodies dumped in the right-of-way's scrub? Road trip violence has become such a cliché that films have taken to playing with its gender dynamics: the 2007 film *Interstate* gave us a pair of female hitchhiking murderers, and the same year's remake of *The Hitcher* swapped the male character's heroism for that of his girlfriend. When the psychotic serial killer John Ryder ties one of them to a truck to be torn limb from limb, it's young Jim who gets quartered, not Grace. She must then pursue and kill the hitcher herself.

The Highway Serial Killings Initiative includes Hollywood's favorite victims—hitchhikers and stranded motorists—in its mission definition. But most of the database's victims are truck stop prostitutes. And while the FBI may be fearful it will be accused of inflating the stats again, in fact recent studies suggest that the numbers of serial murder victims have continually been *underestimated*—even during the eighties panic. The undercounting stems from the fact that the vast majority of victims have always been prostitutes—as many as 75 percent according to one scholar. Research into prostitute mortality suggests that the homicide rate for prostitutes is 229 out of every 100,000, making it the leading cause of death in the profession. The U.S. national average for all homicides in 2009: 5 per 100,000.

Press releases introducing the Highway Serial Killings Initiative included a frightening-looking map pinpointing more than five hundred bodies found on or near highways and already entered into the ViCAP database. Represented by red dots, the bodies cluster around major transfer points in the interstate network: Los Angeles, Oklahoma City, Nashville, Indianapolis, Chicago, Atlanta, Pittsburgh, Philadelphia. But no state is immune: the red dots spread along the interstates like a pathogen carried by car. It looks like a connect-the-dots puzzle where the picture is the interstate highway system. The map is the perfect culmination of the evolving link between highways and violence. At the top of its online release, the FBI inserted a stock photograph of a road, white line bisecting the pavement like a scar.

Reporting the story, the media noted that the majority of victims were drifters and prostitutes, but they played up the menace to average Americans. *USA Today* immediately filed a Freedom of Information Act request with the FBI, asking for details of where the bodies were found. "Many families drive from state to state and need accurate information to determine where they should and should not stop," the newspaper sanctimoniously declared. The FBI denied the request. *USA Today* ran a story reporting on its refusal, with a sidebar offering tips on how to "avoid being a victim." The most obvious precaution—don't turn tricks at truck stops—seemed to go without saying.

In 2007, its first full year of operation, the HSKI assisted in the clearing of twenty-five murders committed by three truckers. Excitement grew among law enforcement agencies about addressing a backlog of unsolved murders. Massachusetts has never cracked the case of nine prostitutes discovered dead along highways near New Bedford. Miami has thirty-one murdered prostitutes with unknown perpetrators on the books. San Diego has more than forty, all of whom vanished from truck stops. A series of bodies found along highways in four Southern states is known as the "redhead murders," because several of the victims had red hair. There may not be an "epidemic" of serial killing menacing average Americans this time either, but if you restrict the population to truck stop prostitutes and truckers, it does look like there's an epidemic going on. The list of around two hundred suspects, the FBI press release bluntly said, was mostly long-haul truckers. But even there, the FBI— once bitten, twice shy—is hesitant to make any broad claims.

"No one here is saying, 'Well, they're obviously truck drivers,'" FBI Supervisory Special Agent John Molnar told me. "No, the only obvious assumption you can make is that it's somebody using that road."

· · · · ·

A few weeks after Sara Hulbert's murder in Nashville, Pat Postiglione and his partner Lee Freeman arranged to meet at the T.A. and go through the receipts. As Postiglione was driving over, he noticed a yellow truck with a white trailer cruising slowly down the Cowan Street "stroll." It looked like his suspect vehicle—but no doubt thousands of trucks did. Still, a truck had no reason to be on this road, other than a truck wash, prostitution, or drugs. The truck didn't get a wash, and it didn't stop for anything else. With Postiglione following, the truck passed the spot where Hulbert was last seen alive and then entered the T.A. As soon as it parked, the driver shut all the curtains in the cab.

Detective Postiglione radioed Freeman to let him know where he was, then approached the truck and knocked on the door. After a few moments, the trucker opened it. A heavy man with stringy brown hair and glasses, he was yawning and stretching as if he'd just been awakened. Postiglione explained that he was working on a murder investigation and asked to see the guy's license. The trucker handed it over. Bruce Mendenhall was the name on it. It didn't mean anything to the detective. But he noticed what looked like spots of blood on the inside of the cab door. And there was blood on Mendenhall's thumb.

It's a detective's job not to jump to conclusions. Postiglione didn't mention the blood. He told Mendenhall that police were asking all drivers of yellow cabs with white trailers to volunteer DNA samples. Would Mendenhall agree to the test? The trucker said he would. Lee Freeman had arrived by this point, and he went to his car to get a consent form. Mendenhall came out of the truck to sign it. As he did, a voice in Pat Postiglione's head told him to look inside that cab. He asked Mendenhall for permission to search his truck.

"Are you going to tear it up?" Mendenhall asked. Postiglione said no, he just wanted to look around. Mendenhall agreed, and Postiglione climbed into the cab. He was surprised at how spacious it was. He edged between the seats and into the living area behind. The top bunk was folded up; he sat down on the bottom bunk. Nearby, he could see a pair of black shoes. He picked them up. The tread looked a lot like the cast made of the shoe tread at the crime scene. There was a garbage bag near the bed, and Postiglione pulled it to him. It was filled with paper towels, women's clothing, and shoes, all of it soaked with blood.

Mendenhall had jumped onto the running board and was

watching Postiglione with an inscrutable expression. Postiglione asked him about the bloody paper towels. He had cut his leg, Mendenhall said. He pulled up his pant leg and displayed a smooth calf. Postiglione pointed out that it didn't seem to be injured. Mendenhall switched his story. He'd had a girl from Indianapolis in the cab, he said, and she had cut herself. Postiglione asked if he had any women's clothing in the truck. Yes, the trucker answered, his wife and daughter had some clothes there. Postiglione looked in the bag again. There was a lot of blood. Later DNA testing would link it to at least four women, all of whom were missing or dead.

"Bruce, am I sitting in the right truck?" he asked. Mendenhall shrugged. Postiglione asked again. "Is this the truck we're looking for?"

"If you say it is," Mendenhall replied.

"Are you the guy we're looking for?" Postiglione asked.

"If you say so."

· · · · ·

To someone like Detective Pat Postiglione, it makes a kind of intuitive sense that long-haul truckers might be behind many of the highway killings. There were roughly 3.5 million truckers on the road as of 2006, and the workforce has changed along with the job.

"I've dealt with truckers a lot and truckers are a different breed," Pat Postiglione told me. "A lot of them are regular good family people but a lot of them are not."

Interstate highway construction led to a boom in the trucking industry. In the years since the interstate era began, the proportion of freight going over the road has steadily increased. Then came the Motor Carrier Act of 1980 deregulating trucking, and the number of trucks on the road shot up even more. In the last twenty years alone, according to OSHA, there has been an increase of 44 percent in registered large trucks and a leap of 86 percent in how many miles those trucks travel. Today, roughly 70 percent of all domestic freight goes over the road, and more than 80 percent of the nation's communities are served exclusively by trucks.

To survive cutthroat competition, trucking has become leaner and more efficient. Unionized trucking companies have dwindled, while smaller, low-wage ones have multiplied. Today, trucks have become what economist Michael Belzer calls "sweatshops on wheels," with truckers driving harder, longer, and faster, for lower relative pay. Most are paid by the mile—on average around thirty-nine cents.

Drive any interstate and you'll read a variety of "We're hiring!" ads on the backs of the big rigs you pass. As the need for drivers has expanded, the bar to entry has been lowered. Today, neither a high school diploma nor a clean criminal record is required to drive a truck. In fact, beginning with welfare reform in 1996, employers could get a federal Work Opportunity Tax Credit for hiring convicted felons, and many in the trucking industry did. Most trucking companies don't care if drivers have a permanent address. It's possible even to drive a truck with drunk driving convictions on your regular license. Quickie trucking schools of varying quality are everywhere, offering a commercial driver's license in as little as two weeks. Often the training is paid for by a trucking company in return for a period of indenture. Annual employee turnover at these companies is around 100 percent.

As trucking has changed, it has attracted a new demographic: less educated, less stable, less tied to unions, less rooted in family life. Has it also begun attracting a criminal element? Or as Supervisory Special Agent Mark Hilts, head of one of the FBI profiling units, puts it: "Are some of these guys migrating to truck driving as a lifestyle that allows them to do what they do? We don't know enough yet to make conclusions."

The FBI may not want to draw conclusions, but the public already has. The mythology of the trucker has changed along with the industry. In the sixties and seventies, the independent trucker was celebrated in country music and in movies like *Smokey and the Bandit* or *Convoy.* The trucker was a working-class hero, the last American cowboy, a skilled handler of twenty thousand pounds of pure power who outfoxed county mounties, bears in the air, and prissy hours-of-service rules in his patriotic dedication to American commerce. It took a special breed, as Merle Haggard sang, to be a truck driver. But as frustration with the interstate system grew and the association between highways and violence was cemented in the public mind, truckers, too, started to look like a menace to public safety. Today, the public image of the trucker is closer to the deranged driver who gets his comeuppance in *Thelma & Louise.* No longer heroic asphalt cowboys, truckers are frequently seen as ill-educated rednecks, amped up on meth, shoving themselves up your tailpipe or spewing misogyny over their CB radios. And sometimes, as in the case of 1997's *Breakdown,* they are depicted as cold-blooded killers.

· · · · ·

"At the end of this testimony," declared deputy district attorney Tom Thurman, "there will be no doubt that there is a cold-blooded killer in the courtroom." It was May 2010, nearly three years after the murder of Sara Hulbert, and day one of Bruce Mendenhall's trial. From the windows of Courtroom 6A you could see, across the Cumberland River, the muddy, shuttered T.A. where Hulbert was found, a collection of hazmat trucks scattered with debris around its lot. One week earlier, the Cumberland had risen and raged through Nashville. The historic floods had closed the courthouse and had nearly swept the T.A. off the map: the fuel tanks filled with raw sewage, and one trucker had to be rescued by boat. To Sara Hulbert's relatives, a row of women with feathered hair and dressy pants sitting behind the prosecution's table, it must have seemed like poetic justice.

Bruce Mendenhall sat impassively between two of his lawyers. Mendenhall is no Dexter. In fact, even as real serial killers

In prison, they called him "Truck." Bruce Mendenhall, a trucker convicted of one murder so far, enters the Nashville courtroom. Associated Press photo / Christopher Berkey.

go, he gets low marks for mediagenics—which might explain why, besides me, there were only a couple bored-looking local reporters in the room. He isn't dashing like Ted Bundy, passionately deranged like Charles Manson, or eerily normal like John Wayne Gacy. He's not even impressively nondescript like "I-5 Strangler" Roger Reece Kibbe. Mendenhall looks like someone you'd see eating alone at a truck stop. He is fifty-nine, and not a youthful fifty-nine. He has a cartoon trucker's body— beer belly, sloping shoulders, trudging gait. He is diabetic. His cheeks sag in deep hollows, and his limp hair could use a trim.

The prosecution and the defense agreed on the basics. Sara Hulbert was killed in Bruce Mendenhall's truck with Bruce Mendenhall's gun. But they took differing positions on who had done the killing. There were no eyewitnesses, and Mendenhall claimed from the time of his arrest that someone else had killed her—in his truck, with his gun. Two guys followed him around, he said, killing women in his truck and leaving him to clean up the mess. That was the story he had told Detective Postiglione immediately after his arrest.

· · · · ·

Pat Postiglione had little doubt, when he sat down to interview Bruce Mendenhall, that he was dealing with a serial killer. "We seem to have more than our share of them in Nashville," he told me. "I think it has to do with the interstates."

We were sitting outside the courtroom. Postiglione was waiting to testify, and the judge had barred witnesses from the trial when they weren't on the stand. The benches outside the courtroom faced a floor-to-ceiling plate glass window that looked out on the city's tangle of freeways.

Three interstates converge in Nashville: I-40, the main east-west route across the southern United States, I-65, a straight line between the Gulf of Mexico and Chicago, and I-24, a diagonal route across southern Illinois and Tennessee that serves as the main corridor between St. Louis and Atlanta. At Nashville the confluence of the three routes creates a ten-mile, eight-lane ring road that encircles downtown, splitting five times. The splits cause massive backups as everyone on the right suddenly needs to go left just as everyone on the left needs to go right. The whole road is always packed with trucks.

If you're driving south, from Indianapolis say, the Nashville T.A. comes right after the I-65/I-24 split. It's not well marked. But truckers knew it well enough; before the floods, it was always busy. Truckers tend to frequent one truck stop chain—the chains encourage it by giving loyalty points or making deals with trucking companies to give their credit card to drivers. But truckers also know which truck stops cater to "four wheelers," as they call motorists in cars, and which ones are "truckers' truck stops." Often the latter are the ones that offer them the extra services they require.

Truck stops are populated not only by truckers, but by many other people who labor unofficially in the trucking industry:

"polishers" who work on the trucks, "lumpers" who help truckers load and unload, and, of course, "lot lizards," the truck stop prostitutes. Many of these workers-for-hire are transients; some are homeless. Some double as drug dealers. The back row at truck stops is known as the "party row," because it's typically where the truckers who want sex or drugs park. Private security guards at truck stops attempt to stop the sex trade with varying levels of enthusiasm, but prostitutes arrive in cars or slip onto the property from the back; they ply their trade by moving unseen between the trucks, rapping on doors. Truckers who aren't interested post a sign in their windows—a drawing of a lizard behind a circle with a bar through it—so they can sleep without being awakened by the unceasing knocks.

"You go to the truck stop and you stand there and 100 percent of the girls who come around there have a pimp within twenty feet," Postiglione told me. "The girl's so strung out you can spot it a hundred yards away. And she's ready to get into the truck with Ted Bundy, Bruce Mendenhall."

It clearly bothers Postiglione that young women become so vulnerable. It bothers him that he arrested Bruce Mendenhall on July twelfth. Had he arrested the trucker one day sooner, another young woman might still be alive.

"What made this case unique," he said, "is we were chasing him as he was killing. Because he killed a girl June twenty-fifth and a girl July first . . . so it wasn't like he'd killed and he stopped. When he came back to the truck stop that night he'd killed a girl the night before. We were kind of chasing a phantom."

· · · · ·

Clark Fine has chased the same phantom. Fine is a classic cop's cop, a detective in the sheriff's office in Hendricks County, just west of Indianapolis. Even over the phone, you can hear the ghosts of thousands of cigarettes in his raspy, unfiltered voice. "What can I do for you, darlin'?" he drawled when I reached him at his desk.

In 2004, Fine had a cold case involving a murdered prostitute named Buffie Brawley. Brawley was found dumped in an abandoned truck stop on Indianapolis's south side. She had been beaten up, strangled, and run over with a truck. Fine attended Terri Turner's Oklahoma City confab on the I-40 killings. Indianapolis is on I-70, but truckers frequently travel up from the Southwest to the Midwest via I-44 out of Okalahoma City, intersecting with I-70 at St. Louis. Anything going on in Oklahoma City could easily find its way to Indy. At Turner's meeting, Clark Fine became friends with a police sergeant from Grapevine, Texas. Like Fine, the Grapevine sergeant had a case similar to Terri Turner's—a truck stop prostitute who had been killed and thrown from an overpass.

"It's kind of mind-boggling how many girls get killed every year doing that," Fine told me. Eventually, John Robert Williams—the suspect in Terri Turner's series—confessed to the Grapevine crime from prison in Mississippi. The sergeant called Clark Fine and told him he ought to talk to the guy too.

"Myself and a partner drove down to Mississippi and we had specific things about our case—she had certain tattoos on her— to see if this might be the guy," Fine recalled. At the Mississippi State Penitentiary at Parchman, John Williams told the detectives he remembered their Buffie Brawley, though he hadn't known her name. Fine asked a few questions about the crime scene, and Williams got some right and some wrong. Fine asked him if he remembered a tattoo on the woman's buttock.

"You have to remember, I don't have sex with them, I just kill them," Williams said. Fine was losing interest in Williams fast. He figured he had a serial confessor on his hands, someone like Henry Lee Lucas, who got a thrill bragging to cops about all the murders he'd supposedly gotten away with. But then Williams volunteered that he did remember a tattoo on Brawley's leg. It said Ebony, he recalled. He told the detectives he thought that was funny, since Brawley was white and "Ebony is usually a black girl's name."

"But the thing is," Fine told me, "that girl had a daughter

named Ebony, and so she had that tattoo. And then I knew this asshole was the guy that did it."

For Fine, it closed what had been a long, sad case. At the start of it, he had gone down to the local truck stop to talk to other prostitutes who might know something. One woman he spoke to was Carma Purpura, a young blonde with a broad, infectious smile. "I interviewed her down at the truck stop and I said, 'This is a dangerous life.' And she said, 'I know, but I gotta make a living.'"

On July 11, 2007, Carma Purpura got into Bruce Mendenhall's truck at a Flying J in Indianapolis. Her cell phone and clothing were in the bag of bloodied items discovered by Pat Postiglione the very next day. Some of the blood in the truck matched DNA provided by her parents. Her body has yet to be found.

"People think all cops are jaded and go home and get drunk every night, but we do care," Fine said. "We do care about these people and we want them to have someone working on their behalf. Because they're throwaway people. Sometimes the only people that give a shit are the cops. Even the family sometimes gives up on them."

· · · · ·

Sara Hulbert's family did not give up on her. Throughout Mendenhall's trial, they sat behind the prosecution's table, looking alternately angry, bored, and stricken. Their Sara had gone down the wrong road, and now the elaborate machinery of the state had clanked into gear to bring her justice. If an effort anywhere near this size had been mounted to help her kick drugs, she would probably be alive today, raising her kids, shopping with her sister, dating men her grandmother didn't like. But she had fallen in with the wrong sort, gotten addicted to drugs, sold her body at truck stops, and fallen through society's cracks. After her various run-ins with the law—two charges of criminal trespassing, one of driving with a revoked license— she had now returned to its bosom. Hulbert's relatives jumped to their feet like boot camp recruits every time the jurors entered or left the room. Those twelve citizens held justice for Sara in their hands. As for the defendant, Hulbert's family avoided looking at him.

Mendenhall didn't look at them either. For most of the trial he sat impassively and watched. His lawyers sometimes spoke to him and he would murmur back. But he showed no emotion as forensics experts recounted Hulbert's injuries, as investigators held up the weapons found in his truck, as his former boss told the jury how he had teased Mendenhall about fending off lot lizards and how Mendenhall had replied, "I just shoot them." The exception was when the prosecution played the video in which Mendenhall told Pat Postiglione the story about the "real" killers. As Postiglione, on-screen, deftly maneuvered him into waiving his right to have an attorney present, Mendenhall shook his head slightly, then hunched down in his seat, one hand pressed to his sagging cheek. It was the only show of emotion from a man who otherwise sat very still and stared straight ahead, concentrating on where this very large machine was taking him. It seemed appropriate that his prison nickname was "Truck."

The tape had an electrifying effect on the jury: it's rare that juries get to hear defendants' stories from their own mouths, and Mendenhall's was a strange combination of evasive and guileless. On the tape, Postiglione moves very quickly to the events on the night of Hulbert's death. Mendenhall declares that he had been driving all night, coming down from Indy. He stopped to fill up and get a sandwich at another truck stop, the Nashville Pilot. But as he was in the fuel lane, two men he knew walked up.

"Where you going now?" they asked.

"None of your *bus*iness," Mendenhall told them.

"Well, we'll *make* it our business," they said. One of them got in his truck, determined to ride with him. Mendenhall relates all of this to the detectives with the kind of overemphasis four-year-olds use when they're making up a story. It would be disarming if the man weren't talking about a murder.

Mendenhall says he was so upset by seeing the two men, he forgot to get his sandwich at the Pilot. So he stopped at the T.A. and, hoping they would leave, went inside for some food. But when he came back out, the men were in his truck with a dead girl. She was sprawled out in his bed, naked, with a bloody plastic bag over her head.

"I said, 'You guys, what the *hell* . . . ?'" he continues. "And they go, 'It's your problem, not ours.' And they got out and left." He figured they had killed her with his gun, he says, because "they've did it before." Mendenhall says he cleaned up the mess in his truck and put the body on the grass for the T.A. grounds crew to find. As Postiglione is pressing him for further details about the killing, Mendenhall interrupts him.

"They do it all the time," he declares. "I don't know. . . ."

"Okay," Postiglione says. He was born in Queens and raised on Long Island, but he has picked up the Southerner's way of saying "okay," gently, the last syllable rhyming with *lie*. "You don't know these guys."

"Yes," Mendenhall says, "I know one."

"How did they know you were at the Truck Stops in Nashville?" Postiglione asks, and Mendenhall says, "That's what I don't know. They . . . they meet me everywhere."

Postiglione is a deft interviewer. It's clear throughout the tape that he's nudging Mendenhall to give up details about the murder without ever confronting him directly. The more Mendenhall knows, the worse it will be for him. So the detective plays along with Mendenhall's story like a parent indulging a child's imaginary friend. When Mendenhall tells him that the other two men had sex with Hulbert, Postiglione carefully puts the next question in the third person: "Did Bruce have sex with her?" Bruce insists that Bruce did not. Finally Postiglione asks Mendenhall for the men's names. Mendenhall then makes his big mistake: he names two men he really knows, men with alibis two states away, men against whom he holds grudges. In the part of the videotape that the jury was not allowed to see, Mendenhall goes on to describe a number of other incidents involving these fantasy killers. They caught up with him at a Flying J on I-465 in Indianapolis the night before, he says, and just as in Nashville, they killed a girl in his truck. He ran into them in Birmingham, Alabama, and he suspects they killed someone there because his gun was gone for a while, and "wherever them two are, them, they're like killin'." And, when Postiglione prods him to think about whether he's ever been on I-40 east of Nashville, he recalls running into the killers again at the Pilot in Lebanon, Tennessee—where the girl in the garbage can was found. He went into the arcade to play video games and returned to find his cab full of blood.

It's the lamest story imaginable, and Postiglione plays along gently, nonthreateningly, without ever really suggesting he does or doesn't believe it. He uses the same neutral tone when he finally tries to get Mendenhall to back off from the lie.

"We're not going to treat you any different now," he says, "if you tell us you were the one who actually did it. And these guys, even though they were mean and nasty to your family, they really had nothing to do with the homicides. If you're the guy that did these killings...."

He leaves it hanging, and in the pause, Mendenhall seems to realize the jig is up.

"Get me a lawyer," he says.

After his arrest, Mendenhall attempted to have Pat Postiglione killed. The person he hired for the hit, a fellow prisoner about to be paroled, turned state's witness. Wearing a wire, the informant had several conversations with Mendenhall in which they plotted the hit, and how Mendenhall would pay for it by driving a truck for the other man after his acquittal. Mendenhall refers to Postiglione throughout the recordings as "the wop" and "the queer." When I talked to him, Postiglione mentioned the fact often enough to suggest it bugged him.

• • • • •

B ruce Mendenhall is not clever. He is not charming. He does not fit popular culture's preferred image of a serial killer, an evil genius who makes fools of the cops until a brilliant detective brings him down. It's not clear if he even fits the profile the FBI has built over the last three decades using case studies and interviews with convicted killers. That profile depicts serial murderers as predominantly psychopaths, with deep pathologies that can often be detected in childhood. For instance, criminologists frequently refer to the "MacDonald Triad," a trio of behaviors that are highly correlated with later homicidal behavior. The three symptoms—fire-starting, bedwetting past the normal age, and cruelty to small animals— don't obviously predict a life of crime, but the combination has been noted in a large number of criminals. Criminologists agree that if your nine-year-old displays all three, it's a good idea to seek counseling.

The trucker killers, however, may have a different pathology, one that isn't necessarily there from an early age. Eric Hickey, dean of the California School of Forensic Studies at Alliant International University and a frequent law enforcement consultant, thinks the truckers may be a different type of serial murderer than we've come to expect. He's planning on adding a section on truckers who kill to the new edition of his classic book, *Serial Killers and Their Victims.*

"If we developed a profile of truck driver serial killers, we'll find some things that are different from other serial killers," he told me. "But overall they're predators, and they like to control people, and they probably have some very bizarre paraphiliac sexual interests." Predation, the urge to control, paraphilia, aka perversion—those things are in keeping with other serial killers. But Hickey thinks there's one possible distinction: he believes the truckers are more likely to be sociopaths than psychopaths. "It's such an opportunistic murder," he said.

Sociopaths tend to have below average intelligence. They are capable of feeling emotion, but bad at controlling it. They tend to commit crimes of opportunity. Charles Starkweather was probably a sociopath. Psychopaths, on the other hand, tend to be smart—average or above average intelligence—but they lack normal emotional responses such as remorse, empathy, and sorrow. They are capable of deliberation and self-control, and thus more likely to plan a crime carefully. The planning—the "hunt"—is part of the appeal. Ed Kemper, Ted Bundy, and Roger Reece Kibbe seem more like psychopaths. Hickey doesn't think the truckers fit that profile.

"Part of it is the type of work it is," he told me. "It doesn't appeal to a lot of psychopaths in general. And you're limited in your victims. Most people who are truckers are going to be killing prostitutes and hitchhikers. What about those people like Ted Bundy who would never want to kill a prostitute?"

Given that the murders are opportunistic, Hickey says, a big part of the problem could be the truck stops themselves. "I was just looking at one truck stop in Alabama, and they had over five hundred people who were given citations in one year," he told me. "Men having sex with men, prostitution, thieves, people buying and selling drugs. Often it's quite common to see deaths occur at truck stops. Truck stops are absolutely fascinating places for criminal activity. If you've ever been to a truck stop late at night you'll know what I'm talking about. If you walk out among the trucks you'll see a lot of things going on that you don't want to see."

· · · · ·

Truck stops followed in the footsteps of interstate construction. The highway system put more trucks on the road and made it possible for them to cover enormous distances. Naturally, the system required places to refuel both machine and driver. There are roughly ten thousand truck stops in the nation today, ranging from seedy dives like Nashville's T.A. to places like the Iowa 80: a huge, well-kept T.A. complex containing restaurants, stores, theater, showers, laundry, even a barber and a dentist. Typically, truck stops service four wheelers as well, which is why in the late nineties T.A. changed its name from Truck Stops of America to Travel Centers of America. Even so, like all truck stops, T.A. facilities keep four wheelers and truckers separate. Motorists and truck drivers enter at separate entrances, gas up at separate pumps, park in separate lots, and often pay at separate counters. Special lounges and shower facilities are designated for truckers exclusively. Frequently the restaurants will be set up to quietly divide the populations by offering counter seating for individual diners and a separate room of booths for groups.

Truck stops emerged to meet truckers' bodily needs, but they do a bad job. Truckers need to eat: truck stops offer an array of salty snacks, giant bags of candy, factory-made sandwiches and hot dogs. Often there's a whole aisle dedicated to meat snacks—beef jerky in various forms. In-house restaurants are either greasy spoon diners or fast-food franchises like McDonald's and Taco Bell. Truckers need to stay awake: truck stops sell extra-caffeinated coffee, cans of Red Bull bigger than any you've ever seen, energy drinks with names like Amp and Monster. Given sustenance like that, it's not surprising that truck stops usually feature another whole row of extra-strength headache powders and antacids.

Driving, particularly driving an eighteen wheeler on the freeway, is not kind to the human body. It's not hard to imagine how truck stops might counter the rigors of driving: they might have salad bars and dog runs and fitness centers. Instead they offer arcades and dingy drivers' lounges—a row of easy chairs all facing a giant TV, as if what a driver should do when he stops driving is go and sit some more. Truck stops ought to offer a place to unwind and get a good night's rest; instead they offer CDs and DVDs and a parking lot full of idling or exiting trucks. They ought to offer human interaction, friendly chat at the very least, but instead they provide, unofficially, lot lizards who knock on the door of each cab and offer—for about thirty bucks—fifteen minutes of relief from the lonely life of the road. Truckers sometimes pay them just to talk.

Add to this the fact that many of the nation's truck stops have become magnets for all kinds of crime: robbery, drug deals, assaults. Truckers have to deal with the constant threat of becoming crime victims themselves, from an all-out hijacking of their freight to pilferage of their spare tires while they sleep. To criminals, a truck is a rolling opportunity. Even a fifty-three-foot truckload of toilet paper, boosted and sold on the street for a dollar a pack, is a relative gold mine.

"We are targets for crime because criminals see us as money," Desiree Wood, a trucker who blogs as "Trucker Desiree," told me. She doesn't carry a gun; many trucking companies ban them in their trucks, though some truckers carry them anyway. Other truckers simply avoid truck stops, preferring to sleep at rest areas or in Walmart parking lots.

In fact, individual truck stops can become so notorious for criminal activity that larger trucking companies declare them off-limits to their drivers. Interstate Distributors keeps a list of banned truck stops. Desiree Wood drives for Covenant, and when the GPS on her truck shows that she has entered an area near one of Covenant's off-limits truck stops, her communications device gives her a message warning her to stay away. Truck stops in West Memphis, Arkansas, for instance, are no-go, and Covenant drivers are not allowed within twenty-five miles of Atlanta's outer loop, I-285. The warnings, Wood noted wryly, always refer to the problem truck stops as "high pilferage" areas, rather than mentioning any danger to the truckers.

Wood told me that T.A. was concerned enough about the problem of truck stop crime that it was instituting a host of new security features. But when I contacted company representatives several times asking for details, they declined to comment.

. . . . .

"All the research in this field shows that problems are highly concentrated," Ron Clarke told me. "So you will find that the vast majority of truck stops are no problem and that there's just a few that account for quite a large percentage of the problem. It's called the 80/20 rule." Eighty percent of the problem, in other words, will be caused by 20 percent of the truck stops. Criminologists call them "risky facilities." Clarke is a leading authority on situational crime prevention, a discipline founded on the startlingly simple assertion that every crime requires the intersection of three elements: a criminal, a victim, and a place. You can reduce crime—not just relocate it, but reduce it—by focusing on any or all of those elements. You can try to dissuade the criminal. You can try to remove the victim. But the easiest thing to do is to redesign the place.

Situational crime prevention grows out of the work of Jane Jacobs on urban design in the sixties and of architect Oscar Newman in the seventies. Both Jacobs and Newman discussed "natural surveillance," a community's propensity to reduce crime by being alert to problems before they get out of hand. Jacobs called it "eyes on the street," Newman, "defensible space." But criminologists and planners soon showed that there were many additional ways to "design out crime." A famous case is New York's Port Authority Bus Terminal, an infamous haven for prostitution, gun sales, drug-dealing, larceny, and panhandling in the eighties. A task force was convened to study the problem, and in 1992, the Port Authority began instituting hundreds of changes to the terminal's design. Some were obvious: securing ceiling panels and locking doors to stairwells, hiring bathroom attendants, improving lighting, creating programs to move transients into shelters. Others were less obvious: reducing the size of support columns, straightening sight lines, moving ticketing to a central location, enlarging entrances, repainting walls in light colors. Special attention was paid to shining up the floors. Fourteen key changes were made in the restrooms, including reducing the sink size, shortening the doors, straightening the walls, and increasing the

A setting that creates crime? The Bloomsbury, New Jersey, truck stop that makes its small town the most crime-ridden in Hunterdon County. A blog requesting truck drivers to name "truck stops so dangerous even truckers don't stop there" yielded the reply "all of them in New Jersey." Photo by the author.

tile size. The redesign was an unqualified success: robberies, assaults, and public disorder rates plummeted. People no longer think of the Port Authority as a crime gauntlet.

"Somewhere like the Port Authority Bus Terminal *created* crime," Clarke said over a bowl of chili. "It produced all the conditions for crime to happen." We were sitting in the diner of the T.A. truck stop in Bloomsbury, New Jersey. Bloomsbury, an adorable town in a rolling, rural part of the state near the Pennsylvania border, has a population of 857, mostly living in charming Victorian homes. But the tiny burg had the highest crime rate in Hunterdon County in 2009—because of the town's two truck stops. Two-thirds of the town's crimes happened at this T.A. After lunch, we took a walk around the facility.

"At the moment it doesn't look particularly dangerous," Clarke said with some surprise as we stood in the back lot watching a never-ending stream of big rigs clanking and snarling their way into the T.A. parking area. "It's probably perfectly safe right now."

Ron Clarke doesn't usually spend much time at truck stops; he seemed a little taken aback when I invited him to lunch at one. A university professor at the Rutgers School of Criminal Justice, he has a PhD in clinical psychology and an incredibly long list of publications on crime prevention. He has a genteel British accent, and he looks a little like Anthony Hopkins; he even slides down the hill of his "yes"—*Yeeeyas*—in a way that sounds like Hopkins at his most diabolic, which is vaguely disconcerting. Some people find his ideas disconcerting as well: his work proceeds from the assumption that we are who we are in part because of where we are.

"Criminal disposition isn't something totally independent of environment; it's interacting with it," he explained. "If you produce a whole lot of crime opportunities, you will create a criminal disposition. People will be tempted to do things they wouldn't otherwise do."

The interstate highway system and the environments it creates—rest areas, service plazas, truck stops, motel and gas station clusters, not to mention the blighted urban areas alongside or underneath the highway itself—might very well be creating such opportunities. Our transportation system could be an enabler.

Much of situational crime prevention looks like plain old common sense: harden targets. Reduce the vulnerability of victims. Take away the anticipated rewards for crime and increase the perceived risks. It seems very straightforward, and yet, it has by no means become standard practice. People are resistant to an approach that feels so deterministic.

"People like to demonize criminals, don't they?" Clarke said by way of explanation. "They like to think that criminal people are different from other people. It makes them feel more secure in their own morality and their own lives. They don't like to think that in a slightly different environment they might behave very badly."

As we strolled around the truck stop parking lot, threading our way between trucks in the fuel lanes and cruising the aisles of the convenience store, Clarke pointed out all the possible places where a situational crime prevention approach might intervene. Increasing security at those places would involve a variety of obvious efforts—more security cameras, better lighting, some sort of "check-in" function or license plate scanner—as well as some less obvious ones. Perhaps, Clarke said, the truck stops that enable murder are the ones that tend to be closer to or farther from the on-ramp. Perhaps they tend to be in rural areas—or maybe in urban ones. They might be the ones with more landscaping, or different video games. The layout of the place could make a difference. The correct approach to the problem would begin with collecting data: identify the risky facilities through crime rates, then survey how they differ from the nonrisky ones.

Anonymity, Clarke speculated, is probably a big part of it. Looking at the row of trucks with their extensive private cabs, his first thought was what a dangerous place it would be for a sex worker to go looking for customers. It would be easy for no one to know she was there besides the truckers. Paradoxically, he said, one of the best things for the truck stops to do would be to ease up on the prostitution trade a bit.

"Say that this place had a place where you could sit comfortably and drink coffee and so on," he mused. "Prostitutes could use that and come to be known. You know how hotels often have prostitutes in the bars, and they're friendly with the bartender. And everyone knows what's going on and it's not legal but it's not interfered with because it's not causing a problem."

Anything that makes the prostitutes less anonymous could make them seem less disposable. And anything that makes the truckers feel less anonymous themselves will also conduce to better behavior. Pointing to a table of burly truckers eating sandwiches nearby, Clarke noted that one of them could easily be a psychopath. "But you'd never know. Most of the time, he's behaving in a perfectly law-abiding, sociable way, because of the environment he's in that's guiding his behavior." But what about when he's alone in the truck?

"When you think about the trucking environment, it isn't just the truck stop; it's the truck as well," Clarke said. "The whole thing is creating prostitution actually: lonely guys who have a bedroom with them, girls appearing out of the blue without any effort. When you think about it all, you're tailor-making a prostitution problem, and some of that will turn bad. And the turning bad is probably made easier by the circumstances of the truck stop and the truck."

· · · · ·

On the Mendenhall trial's third day, the state brought out a long line of experts from the Tennessee Bureau of Investigation to introduce the evidence found in Bruce Mendenhall's truck. This included fingerprints, blood and semen evidence, a nightstick, a collection of knives, and the murder weapon, a .22 rifle. It also included the sex toys.

The defense objected before the prosecution could even

mention the sex toys. Once the investigator who was going to bring them up took the stand, the jury was sent out of the room and the haggling began. The witness was questioned for the judge, and the lawyers argued over each item. First up was the penis pump. The assistant prosecutor, a striking woman in dramatically high heels, insisted the penis pump was relevant because of the kind of genital damage the victim suffered. The judge examined the photos over his bifocals. "What does one do with a penis pump?" he demanded. "Does anyone know?"

The trial then entered a zone so darkly comic that no one dared look at anyone else. The court officers stared straight ahead with faces of stone. The reporters looked intently at their notebooks. The lawyers hovered helplessly over their files. The one person in the room who could surely explain how a penis pump was used, Bruce Mendenhall, kept his eyes on the table in front of him. The prosecutor explained that this was why the jury needed to see the packaging: so they could read the instructions.

"Which box is it?" demanded the judge.

"The one with the baseball player."

The judge read the box aloud: "Rookie of the year pleasure pump for the novice enlarger." No one laughed, but the invisible vapor of self-control that always filled the courtroom could briefly be discerned. A trial is a fascinating and horrific experience. The most awful acts and injuries are described, but rarely does anyone scream or cry or call down curses on the killer. Sara Hulbert's grandmother left the room every time she even started to weep. By the same token, no one ever laughs. The point of a trial is to drain every emotion away until the truth appears, square-cornered and solid as a building amid the waters of a receding flood.

The sex toys were ultimately allowed, but in truth they proved nothing. There was no DNA evidence on them. Like much of the prosecution's evidence—such as the knives, which were also ultimately allowed—they served a different purpose: to help the jury construct a story. The prosecution introduced the items to make Mendenhall seem like a person who would kill, though none of these items is unusual for a trucker to have. Truck stops almost invariably sell the exact type of nightstick he had in his truck, and they frequently have large glass display cases showing off an astounding array of hunting knives. Being ready to defend yourself is part of the ethos of the independent trucker. It is not unreasonable. The combination of on-the-job violence and vehicular accidents makes truckers six times more likely than average to die on the job. Driving a truck is among the top ten most dangerous jobs you can hold, according to the Department of Labor. It does not, of course, provide data for prostitution.

As for the sex toys, they are generally not sold at truck stops, but there's no shortage of adult video stores along the interstate that cater to truckers, as anyone who drives the freeway knows. These items might be seen as proof that truckers are a tribe of sex-crazed perverts, but they can also be seen as simply testimony to the fact that, after a long day of grueling driving, some kind of unwinding is desired. The defense could have pointed this out. But to do so would have asked the jury to consider the lives of long-haul truckers and how difficult and damaging they must be. And that is something almost no one seems willing to think about.

· · · · ·

C onsigned to the stressful world of interstates and truck stops, known to their dispatchers as a number, to the law as a license plate, and to their clients as a set of GPS coordinates, truckers are the gears that keep the machinery of global commerce running. But what's going on in their heads? I asked Pat Postiglione if he thought there might be something about trucking that could push some people predisposed to violence over the edge.

"Sure," he said. "You're on the road for hour after hour after hour and all you're doing is thinking. You're not communicating with anybody. If you're that type of person, it could evolve out of you. But it might also be that you're a trucker because you are a serial killer type person."

There has been almost no work done examining the mental health of the nation's truckers. The only paper on the topic I could find was deeply disturbing. In a qualitative survey done at a seedy Southern truck stop, truckers reported very high levels of stress related to time pressures, loneliness, bad health, and separation from their families. They related anxiety about what they saw as their bad public image, and they reported that the loneliness of the road led them to risky encounters with sex workers and to drug use. A surprising number of truckers reported using crack to keep alert while driving and pot to go to sleep when stopped.

"Basically trucking is an unhealthy occupation," Mona Shattell, one of the paper's authors, told me when I called her up to discuss it. Shattell and some of her coauthors also published a paper on truckers' physical health. Surveying all the literature they could find on the topic, they reported that the job imposed a host of health-damaging conditions on drivers, including long work hours; fatigue; sleep deprivation; postural fatigue; exposure to noise, vibration, and diesel fumes; a sedentary lifestyle; and a miserable diet. As a result, truckers were disproportionately likely to suffer musculoskeletal disorders, cancer, cardiovascular problems, respiratory problems, disrupted biological cycles, risky behaviors such as drug use and unprotected sex with prostitutes, and psychological and psychiatric disorders. "It's a public health issue," Shattell said. She said she had another paper on trucker mental health under review—this one with a much larger data set—supporting the conclusions of the first.

Shattell finds the psychological issues particularly intractable. "There is a lot of depression, a lot of loneliness, a lot of sleep problems, a lot of anxiety, a lot of chronic fatigue—and not much treatment," she said. "Access to care is a big issue. Even for people who do have primary care providers it's not a fun thing, especially for men, to get treatment for mental heath problems, so many of them are not treated." Shattell reported that truckers, in addition to being horribly lonely, often feel hemmed in and stressed out by conflicting demands on them.

"They have a lack of control—about their time, about their schedule," she said. "There's this pressure to deliver on time—everything is working against them and it's not in their control. There are the federal guidelines that say they have to rest a certain number of hours. They may not be tired at that time. Then they have their employers who need this load here at a certain time. And then they can get delayed by so many things. They're really stuck a lot of the time and without a lot of support."

Shattell's truckers also reported feeling vulnerable to physical violence. But the loneliness of the job was what came through most clearly. Everything truckers experience is made worse by being so isolated.

"I'm sacrificing pretty much my sanity," one trucker in the study told researchers. "My ability to talk to people. It is total isolation." Another reported that the job dehumanized him, because "sometimes you feel like a machine, like part of that truck . . . you're self-contained in your own world."

The people who share that world—both at truck stops and sometimes in the trucks—include lumpers and prostitutes. It's a standard fact of serial killing that the killers rarely choose their victims from a radically different social class. Most often, a killer's victims are all either one small step above him on the social scale or one small step below. In the latter case, the murder can often be seen as a way of saying "This is not me. I am better than my victim, and to prove it I will take her life."

To truckers, the lives of truck stop hookers must feel uncomfortably familiar. They are freelance workers, paid not by the hour but by the job. They are prone to drug use. They are poorly remunerated, and their working life, spent in truck stops, destroys their health and sabotages their attempts at family life. They are little more than a call sign to the people who hire them, and their task is simply to take on someone else's burden for a time. One criminologist refers to this kind of victim as the "less dead." Their lives are accorded so little value, their deaths mean less as well.

Those devalued lives, like the truckers', are unimaginable outside the landscapes highway federalism built: the anonymous world of exit ramps, right-of-ways, and travel plazas where places are numbers, people are anonymous, and human interaction is entirely mediated by commerce. Lot lizards are the by-products of a global economy built on the easy flow of cheap goods and cheap labor, people numbered for the bottom in a world that has grown comfortable assigning dollar values to human beings. When they are discovered in truck stop dumpsters, or discarded like litter in the interstate right-of-way, their relative value is being totted up.

When Bruce Mendenhall put a gun to Sara Hulbert's head, was he trying to reassure himself that he was something more than just a cog in the machinery of commerce, as undervalued and inconsequential as a truck stop whore?

• • • • •

For the closing arguments of Bruce Mendenhall's trial, Carma Purpura's family came to Nashville. Purpura's sister was small, with short, straightened brown hair and an easy smile. In the hallway outside the courtroom, Carma Purpura's relatives embraced Sara Hulbert's like long-lost family, bonded by an unspeakable sorrow. Then they all hugged Pat Postiglione, who had also come for closing arguments. He and Lee Freeman were both sharply dressed, in sport coats and pressed pants. They bristled with controlled anticipation. In the courtroom, the Purpura relatives sat in the front row with Sara Hulbert's family. The detectives sat a couple rows behind, on the same side. They had all been waiting for this day for three years.

The prosecution's closing argument was accompanied by a PowerPoint presentation. It was the most complete circumstantial case imaginable. It added up to a complete story. But—

and this is one of the many places where real trials differ from the ones in movies and on television—it didn't tie up every loose end. There were gaps and inconsistencies in the testimony. There were witnesses who hadn't appeared. There was a tire track and a second footprint at the crime scene that had never been matched. And there was the semen evidence, none of which matched Mendenhall. The state just let these things hang in the air.

The defense, in its summation, highlighted every one of them, declaring that the state had simply not made its case. There were enough loose ends to leave a reasonable doubt. Even if they believed Bruce Mendenhall to be guilty, it was the jury's obligation to acquit. The attorney methodically went through the state's case, masterfully phrasing every gap in the story as a question the jury could not answer: "Is that answer good enough?" "Should we just take him at his word?" "Is this coincidental?" "Whose semen was it?" As he spoke, you could see the family growing noticeably upset. Before he began talking, acquittal was like a ship sailing by on a distant horizon. As he talked, it turned and headed for shore. You could make out its contours.

"I'm asking you to do something difficult," he told the jury in closing. "I'm asking you to follow the law."

The prosecutor, on rebuttal, asked them to do the exact opposite. He offered them a story that made sense. He referred to the truck as a "killing chamber." He told the jury Sara Hulbert was "doing the only thing she knew to do to support her habit." He painted a picture of the actual murder, "probably under the interstate, so you couldn't hear the noise." In the final moments, he put up a slide of Sara Hulbert, a young woman happy and hopeful, her brown hair restrained by a headband.

"She had a right to live," he declared. "She had a right to change her life and raise her children." Sara's relatives, pictures of control until that moment, silently wept. At least one of the jurors wept as well.

Once the jury retired to their deliberations, family members were whisked off to the room set aside for them. The detectives headed out to get things done. The lawyers vanished into other parts of the courthouse. Only the reporters hung around outside the courtroom, unwilling to risk missing the verdict. The reporter from the *Tennessean* worked on another story. Two members of the local TV news crew fiddled with their camera. I sat on the bench before the plate glass windows, watching the never-ending stream of cars and trucks flow around Nashville on its way toward St. Louis, Indianapolis, Chicago, Lincoln, Sacramento, Atlanta.

This is the world we have made. It's worth asking what effect it might have on people who spend a long time in it. In the late nineties, an outbreak of interest in "road rage" and aggressive driving led scientists to research what happens to people at the wheel. Driving, they reported, has psychological—even physiological—effects on drivers. This is your brain on the road: being at the wheel—especially if you are alone—noticeably changes human responses to stimuli. It renders us anonymous and deprives us of verbal interaction, body language, eye contact. Sociologists call this "asymmetry of communication": we are rendered mute, our identity reduced to a make and model. Frustrated in our innate desire to be perceived as humans, we become paranoid. We attribute hostile motives to oblivious others. How many times have you found yourself screaming something in your car that you couldn't imagine saying to a live human being? Deprived of the human reciprocity we are hardwired to crave, we may begin to see other people as objects. Behind the wheel, we are all psychopaths.

One day after Pat Postiglione knocked on the door of Mendenhall's truck, Darlene Ewalt, a Pennsylvania homemaker, was found murdered on her back patio. She had been talking on the phone late at night when someone crept up in the darkness and slit her throat. Her husband, sleeping upstairs, was considered the prime suspect. Two weeks later, Monica Massaro, a thirty-eight-year-old woman who ran a home-cleaning business, was slashed to death in her bed in Bloomsbury, New Jersey. The next night, parents of fifteen-year-old Shea McDonaugh heard whimpering coming from their daughter's bedroom in their home in Chelmsford, Massachusetts. Rushing in, they found a man dressed in black crouched on top of their daughter with a knife to her throat. Incredibly, the two suburban parents wrestled the intruder to the floor, disarmed him, and held him down while Shea dialed 911. The man turned out to be Adam Leroy Lane, a trucker from North Carolina.

In Lane's truck, police had found a variety of knives and ninja-style weapons, a B-movie about a serial killer called *Hunting Humans*, and a receipt for a radar detector bought at the T.A. in Bloomsbury, New Jersey. One of the Massachusetts investigators e-mailed the details of the case to ViCAP. It didn't take long for analysts to link the three states' knife assaults: all of the women lived near interstate exits. Their homes were walking distance from large truck stops. In each case, Lane had simply left his rig parked in the lot while he wandered into the nearby residential area, checking for unlocked doors.

Investigators from the Hunterdon County, New Jersey, prosecutor's office went to Massachusetts to talk to Lane. The trucker confessed to having killed Monica Massaro "by accident" in a botched robbery attempt. "I was looking for money," he told the detectives. "I was losing everything I had."

I wrote to Adam Leroy Lane and asked him about that statement. What did he mean by saying he was losing everything? Was it because of his work as a trucker, or in spite of it? "I don't know where you get your information," he wrote back, "but I was never on the verge of losing anything. I never had anything to lose." The line was eerily reminiscent of Charles Starkweather's response when asked if he regretted throwing his life away. "I threw away nothin' cause I didn't have nothin'."

Adam Leroy Lane is now serving a twenty-five-year sentence from Massachusetts, a fifty-year sentence from New Jersey, and a life sentence—reached on plea—from Pennsylvania. He is an anomaly: trucker violence has been largely confined to truck stops and other places created by the interstate highway system. Lane took his homicidal rage on the road—or rather, *off* the road, and onto Main Street instead.

Predictably, the media response to Lane, like the response to the FBI's announcement of the Highway Serial Killings Initiative, focused on the interstates. No television story on the topic failed to run some B-roll of cars and trucks rolling down a divided highway. "They are marvels of engineering," intones a grave voice over a montage of interstate highways opening a *Dateline* episode about Lane. "Vast webs of highways and roadways, spun from human ingenuity and grit. Connecting distant points, and strangers in the night. Only no one was thinking much about exit and entrance ramps when they found her . . . A beautiful woman attacked in the night—viciously." As it moves from one murder to the next, the show offers a map showing I-80 intersecting with I-78: "All he needed was another exit ramp, and another unlocked door." By the time the program reaches Massachusetts, where Lane was caught attacking Shea McDonaugh, the *Dateline* writers connect the dots: "It had to do with where they lived—or what they lived near." Another shot of the highway hammers the point home.

Dateline's focus on highways was typical. During the Bruce Mendenhall case, Nashville's News 5 created a special logo for reports on the trucker that included his picture, a menacing truck grill, and the interstate shields for I-40 and I-65. Exit: Metropolis Utopia has morphed into Exit: Murder.

· · · · ·

On the last day of the Mendenhall trial, around three p.m., a runner burst from the Davidson County courthouse conference room. Suddenly, everyone reappeared, as if by magic: the families, the detectives, the attorneys, thronging down the hallway toward the courtroom. I had never spoken to Hulbert's relatives—it was lame reporting, but I couldn't bear the thought of intruding on grief so profound. But Sara Hulbert's grandmother walked right up to me outside the courtroom and grabbed my arm with the bony, fragile grip of an older woman. "I hope it goes okay," she said, fixing her eyes on me with watery intensity.

"Me, too" is all I could say.

The crowd filled the courtroom and listened to the forewoman read the verdict. She paused slightly before the word "guilty." The judge stated that Mendenhall would receive a mandatory life sentence. The trucker gave no response as he stood to leave. For Bruce Mendenhall, this was only trial number one. He had been indicted by Tennessee for another murder, as well as by Indiana and Alabama. Sara Hulbert's family looked relieved. For them, at least, this ordeal had reached its end.

[The Interstate System] will never be finished because America will never be finished.

—FRANCIS C. "FRANK" TURNER, FORMER FEDERAL HIGHWAY ADMINISTRATOR, 1996

The overall increase in crime and possible ineffectiveness of government services to manage the problem had made boundaries become blurred. This helps create a sense of anonymity, which makes a ripe playing field for serial murder. Thus a change in the ecosystem leads to a new phenomenon appearing or mutating.

—GERARD LABUSCHAGNE, 2001

The marker near the spot where Charles Starkweather murdered his last victim memorializes not Merle Collison, but earlier victims of road violence: pioneers killed by Indians. Photo by the author.

A PRAYER FOR
≡ THE BODY BURIED ≡
BY THE INTERSTATE

In 1998, retired FBI profiler Robert Ressler was invited to Mexico by the state government of Chihuahua. The border city of Juárez, officials told him, was being haunted by murder. Young women, many of them teenagers with long brown hair and pretty faces, were disappearing, often on their way to work in the city's many maquiladoras, the plants where consumer goods are assembled for export. Some young women simply vanished. Others were later found dead in vacant lots, irrigation ditches, or the scrubby desert outside of town, raped and often brutally tortured. They had usually been strangled. Authorities thought they might have a serial killer on the loose, and they invited the famed American expert in serial murder to help them look for the pattern. Who better than the Americans, after all, to help them puzzle out a problem the United States had been grappling with for years?

Mexico, like much of the developing world, had been modernizing rapidly in the last decades of the century. That modernization was changing life in the nation, and the changes were most dramatic in places where transportation was driving the transition. Juárez was one of those places.

Part of one of the largest binational urban areas in the world, Juárez is linked by four bridges to its American sister city, El

Paso, Texas. It had long been a typical border town, its restaurants, bars, and nightclubs offering Americans a south-of-the-border night out since Prohibition. But it was more than just a tourist trap. Its location made it a hotspot for U.S.-Mexican trade. Juárez is one of the rare international cities serviced by the U.S. interstate highway system—I-110 branches off from I-10 and takes traffic directly to the Cordova Bridge—and is well connected to the rest of Mexico, mainly via the Ciudad Juárez–Mexico highway. And in the nineties, Mexico, like so much of the world, was increasingly taking to the road.

President Carlos Salinas de Gortari was investing in upgrades to the Ciudad Juárez–Mexico highway. He had also spurred nationwide road travel by licensing eighty companies to build and operate $12 billion worth of private toll highways. The new roads, along with proximity to American freeways, had made Juárez into not only a major manufacturing center but a transportation hub. American companies had been setting up maquiladoras since 1965 in the border area's free trade zone, where they could take advantage of cheap, nonunion Mexican labor. This intensified after the 1992 signing of the North American Free Trade Agreement, or NAFTA. Negotiated by Mexico's President Salinas, Canadian Prime Minister Brian Mulroney, and U.S. President George H. W. Bush, the three-nation treaty sought to eliminate the remaining trade barriers between Canada, Mexico, and the United States. And indeed, in its first decade, it helped to create 1.2 million Mexican jobs. NAFTA was meant to reduce pressure on the border area, letting plants open elsewhere in the nation, but in fact, most of the jobs it created were in the established free trade zone—around a quarter of them in Juárez. There, assembly plants, warehouses, and trucking terminals were already in place, with connections to the American highway network.

The killings began in the early nineties. There had been murders of women earlier, but they suddenly surged in 1993, as Juárez experienced an influx of residents. When NAFTA bolstered industry, thousands of workers streamed north from

Mexico's less industrialized south to take jobs assembling brake pads, vacuum cleaners, car seats, Blackberry components, plasma TVs. Parts were shipped tax-free to Mexico, and assembled products were shipped back across the border, en route to American households. Juárez swelled to an official population of around 1.3 million—but many estimated the real number was more like 2 million. The 80 percent of the maquiladoras that were American-owned were exempt from paying local taxes, so the city had a hard time providing services to this massive influx of workers. New residents lived in the rapidly expanding *colonias,* or shantytowns, on the city's edges. Houses were makeshift structures cobbled together from pallets or cardboard, streets were dirt lanes, water came by truck, and electricity usually came from illegally tapping into one of the city's rare streetlights.

The maquiladoras offered long hours and low wages—around a tenth of what similar jobs paid on the other side of the border. Workers found it difficult to finance life in the border town: the cost of living in Juárez was roughly 90 percent that in El Paso. But the plants were clean and modern, with amenities like free meals and indoor showers, and working in them beat the grinding poverty of the countryside. They offered women in particular something that had previously been hard to come by: a route out of stifling domestic drudgery and into a more modern life. More than half the workers hired in the assembly plants were female. As long as they could prove they weren't pregnant, women were actually preferred by the maquiladoras: they could be paid less, and they had the patience to stick to tedious, repetitive tasks for long hours.

"We are again transforming the world by bringing progress to all people, but especially to women," declared a maquiladora manager. Mexican women seemed to agree. In the nineties, forty thousand to sixty thousand women a year flooded into Juárez in search of a better life.

And then they began to die. In January 1993, Alma Chavira Farel was found beaten, raped, and strangled. That same month, Angelina Luna Villalobos, a pregnant sixteen-year-old, was found strangled. Graciela Garcia turned up dead four days later. Soon it began to seem like a steady drumbeat of death. In February, one woman's body found. In March, two. In April, one. In May, four. Often, the women had disappeared in broad daylight, while walking to work or waiting for the city bus. Two more were found in June. Two in August, one in September, two in October, one each in November and December. That was year one, and those women were the ones whose bodies were found and whose deaths were reported and counted. Activists declared there were many more: women whose bodies could not be identified, women who weren't reported missing, women who had simply vanished. "They were murdering women," women's rights activist Esther Chavez said, "and throwing them out like garbage."

The murdered women were the city's poorest residents, factory workers and store clerks and schoolgirls. Some were underage, using forged birth certificates to work in the maquiladoras. Some had no families and were not reported missing. Others had families who searched for them in vain. It went on with no sign of slowing through 1994 and 1995. María Rocío Cordero, age 11, raped and strangled on her way to primary school. Silvia Elena Rivera Morales, 16, a high school student who worked in a shoe store, found strangled with her breasts mutilated. Olga Alicia Pérez, 20, found eight days later, stabbed, strangled, her right breast removed, her left nipple bitten off. Both Rivera Morales and Pérez, like many of the victims, were found in the Lote Bravo, an area on the southern edge of the city where the dirt streets of squatter settlements give way to desert scrubland. The Lote Bravo sits between Mexican Federal Highway 2, leading to the coast, and Federal Highway 45, the link to the nation's interior, a crossroads where many of the town's most vulnerable residents had washed up. First they lived there in the struggling shantytowns; then they turned up dead in the brush beyond.

In December 1995, police announced a breakthrough. They

had solved the series of crimes, they said, with the arrest of an Egyptian immigrant, Abdel Latif Sharif Sharif. He was charged with the murder of Elizabeth Castro. Castro was a seventeen-year-old factory worker last seen boarding a shuttle bus from her maquiladora—in response to the murders, some maquiladoras had begun running shuttles to take their workers from the plants to public bus stops. It had not been enough to protect Castro: she was found strangled with her own shoelaces and covered with bite marks in the Lote Bravo, four days after she vanished.

Abdel Latif Sharif Sharif had come to law enforcement's attention three months earlier, when he was accused of rape. His accuser subsequently disappeared and the charges were dropped, but police looked into his record and discovered he had a long history of rape and assault charges in the United States. He had served time in a Florida prison for rape and attempted murder, after which he moved to Midland, Texas, to work as an engineer for the oil company Benchmark. Threatened with deportation in 1993, he had moved to Juárez, where Benchmark had a maquiladora. There, authorities said, he had indulged his taste for violence. Witnesses had seen him with Castro, and also with Silvia Rivera Morales, the high school student found dead in the Lote Bravo. A local stripper told police that Sharif admitted to her he had murdered nine women she had introduced him to.

Abdel Latif Sharif Sharif was branded "the Juárez Ripper" and "El Monstruo." He was eventually convicted for Castro's murder, though questions were raised about the quality of the evidence. Police ignored all doubts, insisting they had put the city's serial killer in jail. But then, with Sharif incarcerated, the murders continued.

In April 1996, Rosario García Leal, an eighteen-year-old worker at the Philips maquiladora, turned up dead outside of town. She was wearing her factory identification card when she was found. Facing public pressure, police conducted raids on the city's red light district, where they said several of the women had been spotted before their deaths. They arrested nine members of an alleged gang called Los Rebeldes, the Rebels. They announced that the gang members had been carrying out murders-for-hire paid for by Abdel Latif Sharif Sharif, as part of a plan to make himself look innocent. Families of the alleged gang members pointed out that the charges were absurd: the boys had no serious criminal records, and their "confessions" were tortured out of them. Nevertheless, "Los Rebeldes" remained in jail.

And still the murders continued. By late 1997, more than 170 women were dead. The state attorney general formed a Special Task Force for the Investigation of Crimes Against Women. As in Atlanta, bizarre conspiracy theories circulated. Satanists were said to be responsible. A ring of organ-harvesters was purported to be at work. The notoriously corrupt police and the similarly suspect army were each blamed. In return, Juárez authorities, like some in Atlanta, blamed the women, claiming that they were prostitutes, or loose women, or at the very least provocatively dressed. What did they expect, going out to bars with men? In cases where the women had never gone to a bar, police insisted that their husbands or boyfriends were the likely culprits. And if the girls were very young, police blamed their families for being inattentive: "Do you know where your daughter is tonight?" demanded the mayor in one statement. Many families reported having difficulty filing missing persons reports, even when their missing daughter was a young teenager. Police refused to fill out the forms, insisting the girls had probably gone off with their boyfriends.

Women's rights activists pointed out that the sudden explosion of women working outside the home was a huge upheaval for a very traditional culture. Many pointed to Mexico's ancient gender "cults" of *machismo* and *marianismo*, which prescribe public, dominant roles for men and passive, domestic roles for women. Economically unsuccessful men were frustrated in their failure to achieve *machismo* and might be displacing that frustration onto the bodies of women who "took men's jobs."

Like so many of the highway killer cases, the Juárez murders could be interpreted as an expression of economic rage by those "numbered for the bottom," an angry acting out of the "disposable" nature of others by people who may fear that they themselves are disposable.

Into this heated environment came former FBI profiler Robert Ressler, invited as a private consultant to advise the Chihuahua state government. Ressler took three trips to Juárez, during which he pored over the 160 cases the police had on file. Then he and the state attorney general held a press conference to announce the expert's findings. Out of the 160 cases, Ressler told Mexicans, 76 were likely to be linked, because they all fit a similar pattern: a young, attractive girl abducted on her way to or from work in a maquiladora, and then raped and strangled. Ressler declared that the cases might be the work of one or more perpetrators, and he suggested that the serial killer or killers could be coming from across the border. "My leading theory," he declared, "is that there's a person living in El Paso who is going over to Mexico to take advantage of these less-sophisticated women."

Mexicans were puzzled. Oscar Maynez, chief of the state's forensics department, pointed out that there had never been a study of Mexican serial killers, but that didn't prove there weren't any. Besides, the person who had murdered the young women was clearly familiar with the deserts outside Juárez. Why would the American crime expert be so quick to assume the pathology must have been spawned in his own nation?

In fact, there was an odd propensity among Americans who paid attention to the Juárez tragedy—and their numbers were admittedly few—to feel that the United States must somehow be at fault. True crime author Simon Whitechapel, in his 2002 book *Crossing to Kill*, played up the theory that serial killers were coming from the United States to murder Mexicans, calling Juárez "the serial-killer playground," as if those exaggerated hordes of mobile serial killers from the eighties panic had suddenly turned their vehicles south, toward Mexico. It's a made-for-TV notion, but serious scholars were also revealing a quiet conviction that the United States must bear some responsibility for the Juárez tragedy. They were increasingly insisting the real culprit, rather than mobile serial killers, was NAFTA.

"NAFTA has not only increased jobs but also increased opportunities for criminal victimization and exploitation in the maquiladoras," one scholar declared. Many feminist scholars linked the murders to the devaluation of women by the maquiladoras—and by globalism in general. The academics weren't the only ones making the connection. A Carnegie Council report in 2003 found that "the impact of free trade policies and the ensuing population growth have weakened the city's social fabric." The ABC News program *20/20* did an episode on the murders in 1999. "These workers make things that you buy," Sam Donaldson said, announcing the segment. "But you may be surprised to see how they live." And in a long story about the killings, the *Washington Post* noted that "Ciudad Juárez epitomized the promise of the 1994 North American Free Trade Agreement," but pointed out how that promise had quickly developed a dark side: "The killer or killers were preying on victims furnished in part by the global economic forces so vital to Juárez's boom."

Beneath all of these assertions lies a startling suspicion: that the violence in Mexico is the inevitable result of a culture that adopts American-style growth capitalism. In other words, the murders are not only the high cost of low prices, but an exaggerated reflection of something that happened in the United States too. Violence is what happens when a poor nation, a more vulnerable nation, is swept up in the same growth fever that transformed our own nation in less insidious but still significant ways. Mexicans, just as Americans had done fifty years earlier, were betting that a rising tide would lift all boats. To encourage that rise, they were building their lives on wheels. And as they became a nation of anonymous, mobile strangers, they, too, were experiencing an increase in violence, just as Americans had in the sixties.

The murders continued as the nineties wore on into the new millennium, with drug cartel violence becoming an increasing part of the mix. One of Mexico's major drug cartels was based in Juárez, and the increased trade across the border had made drug trafficking even easier. The thousands of tons of legal goods crossing the border daily were a perfect cover for illegal goods, hidden in secret compartments, beneath false floors, or inside packages of apparently legal items. Once they got across the border, narcotics could travel via I-10 or I-25 throughout the United States, the world's largest market for illegal drugs.

In July of 1997, in a bizarre turn that almost seemed scripted by Hollywood, the leader of the Juárez cartel, Amado Carrillo Fuentes, died on the operating table while undergoing surgery to transform his appearance. Two of his three doctors quickly turned up encased in cement-filled drums left by the side of a road; authorities said they had been tortured to death. But the pain quickly spread as a war of succession began. The level of violence in Juárez increased dramatically. Thirty-eight women were counted as murdered there in 1998. But now there were many men dying as well.

In early 1999, state officials invited a new crop of FBI profilers, this time current agents, to review the cases and weigh in on the murders again. News agencies were reporting that between five and ten women had been murdered in the first two months of 1999 when the four profilers from the Behavioral Analysis Unit arrived in Juárez that March. They spent five days reviewing the case files. Their conclusions were starkly different from Robert Ressler's. Most of the murders, they said, were isolated events. There was probably no serial killer at loose in Juárez, though Sharif might very well have been guilty of a number of the earlier killings. They were not, however, convinced by the evidence that Sharif had orchestrated subsequent murders from prison, a conclusion largely ignored by the Mexican authorities.

After the FBI agents left town, a fourteen-year-old maquiladora worker was raped, strangled, and left for dead in the desert. Amazingly, she survived and identified her assailant: the bus driver of her maquiladora shuttle. He was arrested and allegedly confessed, naming three other men who were involved. Those men were also arrested, and police reported that they, too, confessed. The Chihuahua special prosecutor then told newspapers an incredible story: a ring of bus drivers had been committing the murders, and they had also been hired by Sharif. This story was received with more skepticism than previous ones. Once again, the suspects claimed their confessions had come about as a result of torture. Once again, the police were claiming that Sharif had orchestrated murders from prison with an efficiency that seemed highly improbable. The previous alleged coconspirators, the young men of the "gang" called Los Rebeldes, had by now been in jail for three years, awaiting trial. It seemed there wasn't enough incontrovertible evidence to convict them, so police simply kept them locked up. They would wait five more years before being convicted in a trial considered by many observers to be a sham.

But the American mainstream media had lost their taste for the intricacies of official corruption and inscrutable violence in Mexico. The U.S. press took to blaming the drug war for everything. After newly elected Mexican President Felipe Calderón announced a drug cartel crackdown in 2006, the violence reached astonishing levels. In 2010 Juárez racked up around 2,800 murders, a number double that of the murders of New York, Los Angeles, Chicago, and Houston combined. Wealthy people have been leaving the city, and many businesses have pulled out. Bars and restaurants that once catered to tourists are shuttered. Juárez is now considered the most dangerous city on earth that is not an active war zone.

But whether blaming NAFTA, American serial killers, or drug traffic—which is, in the end, just another kind of traffic headed for the United States—all accounts of the unfolding violence along the Mexican border reveal a detectable tone of misgiving. Mexico is modernizing, just as we did, committing itself to a world of national mobility and global flows.

The dark underside of that new mobility is a loosening of the bonds that tie people to one another and to place. This must at least partly explain our feeling of deep discomfort as we watch the developing world striving to emulate the mobile lifestyle Americans built after the Second World War. Even as Americans themselves have come to recognize all the problems that automobility brings—pollution, traffic, sprawl, community breakdown—the developing world is buying cars and building highways as fast as it can, seeing them, as we once did, as a route to the good life.

"Highways and country roads are synonymous with progress," declared Mexican President Felipe Calderón in a speech on transportation in August 2010, "because every new road creates more opportunities for everyone. That is why, in my government, we have invested in highway infrastructure as never before. Roads are followed by electricity, water and drainage; schools, universities and hospitals are built; trade and investment increase and above all, jobs are created."

In 2007, the *Financial Times* group declared Juárez the number one "Large City of the Future" in North America, citing it in particular for its cost-effectiveness. Journalist Charles Bowden had beat *FT* to it by ten years. In 1996, he declared Juárez the city of the future. "This future," he wrote in *Harper's*, "is based on the rich getting richer, the poor getting poorer, and industrial growth producing poverty faster than it distributes wealth. We have these models in our heads about growth, development, infrastructure. Juárez doesn't look like any of these images."

What does Juárez look like? It looks like an extreme example of what's going on in many parts of the developing world. Where economic development and modernization go, serial killing frequently follows. China, for instance, appears to be experiencing an uptick in serial murder, much of it explicitly tied to the nation's fast-growing mobility. Having declared roads essential to the nation's economic growth, the Chinese government began building modern expressways in the 1990s, quickly building some thirty thousand miles of new roads. Officials proudly report that they expect to surpass the United States in highway mileage by 2020.

Not long after the highway construction program began, reports of Chinese serial murder began to emerge for the first time. There was Li Wenxian, a farmer who moved to Guangzhou, the rapidly growing industrial and transportation hub of south China. After being cheated by a prostitute, he began to kill them. Li allegedly confessed to thirteen murders after his 1996 arrest and was executed later that year. A few years later came Hua Ruizho, a cement truck driver in Beijing, who picked up prostitutes along his truck routes in Beijing and murdered them. He was arrested and executed in 2002.

In late 2003, China arrested four serial killers within the space of a few weeks. A couple in the southern Chinese industrial city Shenzhen reportedly lured twelve women to their deaths with offers of work. A drifter named Yang Zhiya, who worked as a cook at construction sites, was arrested for breaking into homes in four provinces and bludgeoning sixty-five people to death. And a migrant farmworker from central China, Huang Yong, was accused of murdering seventeen boys over the course of two years. "I always wanted to be an assassin since I was a kid," he told reporters, "but I never had the chance." It's another strange echo of Charlie Starkweather: *I always wanted to be a criminal, but not this big a one.* The official Chinese news agency declared that Huang was driven to violence by movies and television, just as many in the 1950s had insisted that delinquents like Starkweather were the product of crime comics and violent films.

The next year, Wang Qiang was sentenced to death in Liaoning province for killing forty-five people, starting in the late nineties, and a gang of men was arrested in Shandong province for murdering at least thirteen women after luring them to a rented home to have sex for cash. "Reports of serial killings began appearing with unusual frequency in the media late last year," mused the *South China Morning Post*. Serial murder may not be as new to China as the government insists, but pubic discussion of it is.

India has also recently begun a giant highway program based on America's interstates. The National Highways Development Project, begun in 1998, is part of a national commitment to economic growth. Less than ten years after it started, in 2007, the rapidly growing city of Delhi experienced an outbreak of serial murder similar to that of Juárez in the early nineties. A local businessman named Moninder Singh Pandher—manager of an earth-moving equipment dealership—was arrested along with his servant Surendra Koli. Both were charged with murder after the remains of seventeen children were discovered in drains outside Pandher's upscale suburban home. Newspapers reported a surprising fact: children had been disappearing for over a year from a nearby slum called Nithari, but little attention had been paid. "One of the villages which had been gradually engulfed by the burgeoning suburb over three decades," wrote *India Today*, "Nithari is now a slum spilling over with thousands of dirt-poor migrants from West Bengal and Bihar." These "dirt-poor" migrant laborers from the countryside were ignored by police when they attempted to file reports about their missing children. "They always told me she had run away with someone," reported the mother of a missing thirteen-year-old. Other parents claimed they were beaten or asked for money when they sought police help. By the time the gruesome cache of body parts was discovered, thirty-eight young people, half under age 14, had disappeared. Upon hearing news that human remains had been found, frantic parents showed up at the site to dig through the drains for clothing and bones. After the arrests, enraged crowds threw rocks at both the suspects and police. Six policemen were ultimately suspended for dereliction of duty.

As in Juárez, economic change was fingered. "The globalised world is throwing up new variations in criminal behavior, especially in a society which is alienated and where the administrative system is on the verge of collapse," a psychiatrist told *India Today*. Less than two weeks later, the bodies of nine sodomized and murdered laborers were discovered in the fast-growing technology hub Hyderabad. Police arrested three men they said had collaborated in the killings. Then the bodies of four children were found in an abandoned rice mill in the northern state of Punjab. They too were reported to be the children of migrant laborers.

Indian newspapers ran articles analyzing the "new" phenomenon of serial killing. Earlier cases were mentioned: Raghav Raman, a schizophrenic arrested for killing forty-one "pavement dwellers," or vagabonds, in the sixties, allegedly in an attempt to avert war with Pakistan; Auto Shankar—so nicknamed because he drove an auto rickshaw—arrested for killing nine teenagers in the 1980s and executed in 1995. News stories even brought up the Thuggies, an allegedly ancient group of murderous highwaymen, often said to be worshippers of the goddess Kali and believed to have killed millions of travelers along India's roads between the seventeenth and nineteenth centuries. Yet still Indians felt like they were seeing something new: India "had never before witnessed such an act of barbarism" as the Delhi murders, declared the *Statesman*. A commentator in the *Hindustan Times* called it "the silence of our lambs." "Was I the only person to think as I read *The Silence of the Lambs*: could it ever happen here?" he asked. The answer to that question seemed clear after the Delhi murders came to light. The Indian press began using the term "serial killer" much more frequently.

In India, as in Mexico and China, the new order of violence was linked to the nation's increased mobility, the migrations of hundreds of thousands of people, and the new, more anonymous communities of a rapidly changing culture. As in the United States at an earlier point, the anxiety about the violence seems to reflect fears for where the nation is heading: toward a culture, as Bowden put it, where the rich get richer and the poor sink further into miserable destitution. The *Hindustan Times* put it succinctly: "We imagine we live in a perfect shining India where there are no serial killers and where new malls

open every week. . . . But for millions of Indians, there is no justice, there is no security, and when their children go missing,
there is nobody who will even listen to them."

The mark of an intelligent person, F. Scott Fitzgerald
famously said, is the ability to hold two opposing ideas in mind
at the same time. Trade and economic growth, and the mobility that underwrites them, are good. They improve people's
lives, as their advocates claim, and help spread the blessings
of democracy. But they can also be dangerous. If they bring
increasing inequality, they eventually lead to increased violence. Sociologists have dedicated reams of paper to parsing
the statistical connections between development and homicide rates across cultures. The widely accepted consensus is
that development decreases homicide—up to a point. That
point is the point of extreme income inequality. When income
disparity creates an underclass, homicide rates begin to rise
again, and a culture grows more violent. Inequality is the fly
in the ointment of growth, just as John Kenneth Galbraith
pointed out in 1954, right at the beginning of it all.

Galbraith was talking about America, but in a globalized
world, we must look at inequality globally, too. Trade and economic growth and mobility may seem to be reaching some sort
of natural limits in the United States, but a whole new world
of commerce and mobility awaits us, a world where goods,
money, people, drugs, and violence increasingly cross borders,
and where the underclass one economy creates often lives
in another nation. Once again, our misgivings about this are
reflected in a frightening figure, a new killer on the road whose
features we have yet to fully discern. Like his predecessors, he
is surely part of the world that made him, the underside of a
dream that is increasingly not just America's, but the world's.

· · · · ·

Just west of Douglas, Wyoming, near the spot on the road
where Charles Starkweather came upon the sleeping Merle

Collison, there's a small turnoff with a tombstonelike marker at its edge. When I was driving Starkweather's route, I had passed it before I had a chance to stop: old U.S. 20 has been turned into I-25 here, so I was moving fast. I was curious enough to turn around. Had someone installed a monument to the poor shoe salesman, thuggishly shot through his car window as he awoke from his roadside nap?

I drove to the next interchange, changed direction, drove back to the previous exit, and retraced my steps to the marker. A truck was parked at the turnoff's edge, the trucker nowhere in sight. There was nothing but interstate and brownish-yellow grass as far as the eye could see in any direction, so it didn't seem likely he'd taken a walk. He was probably in the back of his cab, napping.

I got out and walked to the marker. A picture and a block of text were carved on its face. The line drawing showed a covered wagon with some oxen resting nearby. By the wagon wheel was a bush, a man's legs poking out from behind it.

Three men named Sharp, Franklin, and Taylor, and one unknown man were killed by Indians July 12, 1864 where the Oregon Trail crosses Little Box Elder Creek 2 1/2 miles S.W. of here. They are buried 4 miles S.W. by the grave of Mary Kelly who also was killed July 13, 1864.

The marker stood before a barbed-wire fence. It was August, and dry. The wind was bending the yellow grass backward in a graceful dancer's dip. Cars thudded by behind me. The road, I thought, has always been a dangerous place.

Below the text was the date the Landmarks Commission erected this marker: 1954. That was the year President Eisenhower and his advisors were scheming about how to get Congress to approve federal outlays for a national highway network. General Lucius Clay was being brought on board to help. In Lincoln, Nebraska, Charlie Starkweather and Bob Von Busch bought their first car together. In southern California, the six-year-old Ed Kemper listened to his parents arguing, and fifteen-year-old Roger Kibbe was sneaking out to snatch women's clothing off clotheslines. And one year earlier, in nearby Los Angeles, a city already hard at work building freeways, a California Highways Department bulldozer operator named Mack Rae Edwards murdered an eight-year-old girl named Stella. He buried her beneath his worksite: the Santa Ana freeway. Stella's death was the start of an unusually long killing career. For seventeen years, Edwards lured elementary-school-aged boys and girls to his car or his home while remaining a respectable and apparently normal citizen. The children were simply never seen again, and no one suspected the reliable highway employee.

It was a more trusting age, and because he could so reliably dispose of the bodies, Edwards succeeded for years. But in 1970, he kidnapped three little girls and botched the murder. Once the girls, who knew him, got away, Edwards knew he was finished. He walked into a Los Angeles police station and handed the officer at the front desk a loaded gun. "I have a guilt complex," he said, and proceeded to confess to the murders of six children, beginning in the mid-fifties. Later, on death row, he told confidants it was more like eighteen. The bodies were going to be hard to find, however, since they were beneath the LA freeways he had helped to build. Any help he could give authorities was scotched when he hanged himself with the electrical cord of a prison television.

While I was working on this book, new information surfaced about the locations of some of the missing victims of Mack Rae Edwards. A crime author researching the case found a man who had worked with Edwards and had detailed records of where the murderer had been working every day. Based on the records, the LAPD decided to go looking for the body of Roger Madison, a sixteen-year-old boy who had disappeared in 1968. Police, FBI agents, and cadaver dogs descended on an off-ramp on the Moorpark freeway near Simi Valley and began digging for remains. They worked for several days but found nothing.

The dogs continued to indicate there was something there. The workers concluded that the child's bones must be under the freeway itself. But they couldn't dig beneath the freeway; to do that, they would have to close it.

A memorial service was held next to the off-ramp. Roger Madison's sister Sharon placed a bouquet of roses between the highway and the empty pit. The construction crew, helmets in hands, stood solemnly by her side. The dogs sat alert on their leashes, their eyes bright in the wind. Nearby, over the concrete road that would serve as Roger Madison's tombstone, the afternoon traffic roared by, Americans, as ever, on the move.

SOURCES AND ACKNOWLEDGMENTS

Introduction: Killer on the Road

Throughout this book, I have used primary sources wherever possible to trace the story of the creation of the interstate highway system. I am grateful to the Eisenhower Foundation for a travel grant to visit the Eisenhower Presidential Library (cited here as EPL) in Abilene, Kansas, as well as for the loan of a bike (!) while there. Archivists Catherine Cain, Chalsea Millner, and Herb Pankratz were especially knowledgeable and helpful. The library itself is a stunning example of Eisenhower-era design, and well worth even a casual visit.

Among the various boosterish interstate histories and antihigh-way screeds, Tom Lewis's multifaceted *Divided Highways* (Penguin, 1997) stands out for its fair-mindedness. I have also relied on Mark Rose, *Interstate: Express Highway Politics* (University of Tennessee Press, rev. ed. 1990); Owen Gutfreund, *Twentieth Century Sprawl: Highways and the Reshaping of the American Landscape* (Oxford University Press, 2004); and Stephen Goddard, *Getting There: The Epic Struggle between Road and Rail in the American Century* (University of Chicago Press, 1994). Jane Holtz Kay's *Asphalt Nation: How the Automobile Took Over America and How We Can Take It Back* (University of California Press, 1997) is as delightfully furious as it sounds. Phil Patton's *Open Road: A Celebration of the American Highway* (Simon and Schuster, 1986) is more thoughtfully critical than its title suggests. And of the boosters, the best is surely the Federal Highway Administration itself: *America's Highways 1776–1976* (U.S.

Department of Transportation, 1976) is a gigantic, detailed delight for the highway buff. Many thanks to Joe Conway, highway buff and researcher at the Turner-Fairbank Highway Research Center, for giving me a copy.

To understand Lucius Clay I used Jean Edward Smith, *Lucius D. Clay: An American Life* (Henry Holt, 1990), a compelling, thorough biography of an unsung American of integrity and enormous influence.

vii *"Every time we merge with traffic"*: David Brodsly, *L. A. Freeway: An Appreciative Essay* (University of California Press, 1981): 5.

vii *"We mass-produce everything"*: Henry Taylor Fowkes Rhodes, *The Criminals We Deserve: A Survey of Some Aspects of Crime in the Modern World* (Oxford University Press, 1937): 1.

1 *the nation's murder rate shot up in the sixties and seventies*: According to the FBI Uniform Crime Reports (available through a fabulous table-making tool at http://www.ucrdatatool.gov/Search/Crime/Crime.cfm), the murder rate per 100,000 Americans rose every single year between 1963 and 1974, from 4.6 to 9.8. It then hovered around 9 until the mid-nineties, going as low as 7.9 (1984) and as high as 10.2 (1980). Since 1995 it has generally fallen; in 2009 it was 5.0, lower than any year since 1964.

3 *"maimed whatever it touched"*: Kay, *Asphalt Nation*: 244.

4 *"what the program could contribute to economic growth"*: Reminiscences of Gabriel Hauge (March 1967), Columbia University Oral History Collection, EPL Oral History 190: 77. The Federal Highway Administration website includes a page debunking various interstate myths, including the whole idea that the interstates were predominantly for civil defense, http://www.fhwa.dot.gov/interstate/interstatemyths.htm.

4 *"The defense angle was a very persuasive part"*: Reminiscences of Prescott Bush (1967), Columbia University Oral History Collection, EPL Oral History 31: 166. Quoted by permission of the Oral History Research Office, Columbia University.

5 *called defense . . . "an afterthought"*: Charles M. Noble, memo to John Stewart Bragdon, April 6, 1960, John Stewart Bragdon Papers, EPL.

5 *overpasses were being built too low for its purposes*: In 1960 the Bureau of Public Roads briefly suspended interstate highway projects, including bridges, after the Department of Defense stated its need for seventeen feet of clearance. Congressman

SOURCES AND ACKNOWLEDGMENTS

Henry S. Reuss, letter to John Stewart Bragdon, January 12,
1960, John Stewart Bragdon papers, EPL.

6   *"what was good for the country is good for General Motors
    and vice versa"*: typically Wilson is misquoted as having said,
    "What's good for General Motors is good for the nation," a subtle
    but significant change. Jean Smith cites the actual quote in
    Lucius D. Clay: 611.

7   *"leveling off in automobile use would certainly be disruptive to
    our economy"*: Lucius Clay, speech to Washington Conference of
    Mayors, December 3, 1954, Lucius Clay Papers, EPL.

8   *"make another pie and everybody has a bigger piece"*: Remarks of
    George M. Humphrey to the National Governor's Conference,
    April 1954.

8   *"[T]he automobile," declared the Labor Department*: U.S. Bureau
    of Labor Statistics, *How American Buying Habits Change* (U.S.
    Department of Labor, 1959): 196.

9   *"leaves a self-perpetuating margin of poverty"*: John Kenneth
    Galbraith, *The Affluent Society* (1958; Houghton Mifflin 40th
    anniversary edition, 1998): 79.

10 *large-scale economic effect of highway building was to drive
    up inflation*: part of a good analysis of the economic effects of
    highways in Phil Patton, *Open Road*: 87.

Chapter 1: What a Mean World This Is

For the facts of the Starkweather murders, I have relied predominantly
on typescripts of the trial transcripts available at the Nebraska Historical Society and on newspaper reports from the *Lincoln Journal* and
the *Lincoln Star* (since merged), many of which are collected in Earl
Dyer's *Headline Starkweather* (Journal-Star Printing Co., 1993). Newspapers, however, printed many inaccurate details, so I have used them
with caution. Governor Victor Anderson's papers in the Nebraska
State Archives were helpful in re-creating the political context; they
include a fascinating trove of letters people wrote to him advocating or
denouncing mercy toward Starkweather. Many thanks to librarians at
the state archives and at the Nebraska Historical Society, the University of Nebraska, Lincoln, and the Lincoln Public Library.

Quotes from Charles Starkweather come from Dr. James Reinhardt's *The Murderous Trail of Charles Starkweather* (Thomas, 1960),

229

based on his extensive prison interviews with Starkweather. He
revisits some of this material in *The Psychology of Strange Killers*
(Thomas, 1962). Two "true crime" accounts of Starkweather's spree
have been written: William Allen's *Starkweather: Inside the Mind of a
Teenage Killer* (Emmis Books, 2004 ed.) relies heavily and effectively
on Reinhardt's transcripts. Michael Newton's *Waste Land* (Pocket
Books, 1998) is more of a novelization. Additional facts about Caril
Ann Fugate come from *Caril* by Ninette Beaver, B. K. Ripley, and Patrick Trese (Lippincott, 1974), a work of advocacy but a good source of
detail about Caril and her family. Marilyn Coffey's "Badlands Revisited" in the *Atlantic Monthly* (December 1974) describes the panic in
Nebraska following the Ward murders.

Nebraska highway history comes from local newspapers and
from George Koster's *A Story of Highway Development in Nebraska*,
published in 1997 by the Nebraska Department of Roads, as well as
James C. Creigh, "Constructing the Interstate Highways System in
Nebraska," *Nebraska History* 72 (Spring 1991). I also used the book
Nebraska Historic Highway Survey, prepared by the Nebraska State
Historical Society and the Nebraska Department of Roads. For the
histories of Lincoln and Capital Bridge I also used Neale Copple,
Tower on the Plains (Lincoln Centennial Commission, 1959).

My view of the fifties was shaped by David Halberstam, *The Fifties*
(Random House, 1993); Lizabeth Cohen, *A Consumer's Republic: The
Politics of Mass Consumption in Postwar America* (Vintage, 2004);
and Karal Ann Marling, *As Seen on TV: The Visual Culture of Everyday Life in the Fifties* (Harvard UP, 1994). Fifties car culture is illumi-
nated by Christopher Finch, *Highways to Heaven: The Autobiography
of America* (HarperCollins, 1992).

I am grateful to the Hartmann Center at Duke University for a
travel grant that allowed me to spend time in its wonderful advertising
archive looking at the history of car ads. Special thanks to my Lincoln,
Nebraska, research assistant, temporary Husker Miranda Strand. And
a shout-out to Nebraska Bowhunters Association members for letting
me camp with them at their annual retreat while I was retracing
Starkweather's flight, and for not shooting my tent full of arrows.

12   *"This new highway program will affect"*: Robert Moses, "The New
      Super-Highways: Blessing or Blight?," *Harper's*, December 1956.
12   *"There will always be differences"*: James Reinhardt, *The*

Murderous Trail of Charles Starkweather, Police Science Series (Charles C Thomas, 1960): vii.

15 *written up in . . . U.S. News & World Report*: February 7, 1958.

19 *nation's production of goods and services doubled in the decade between 1946 and 1956, and median and mean family income doubled between 1949 and 1973*: Cohen, *A Consumer's Republic*: 121.

19 *Detroit would ship 8 million of them*: Marling, *As Seen on TV*: 134.

20 *"We were all a little like that then"*: Bob Von Busch, quoted in Allen, *Starkweather*: 31.

20 *"The relationship is, of course, reciprocal"*: President's Advisory Committee, "A 10-Year National Highway Program: A Report to the President," January 1955, John Stewart Bragdon Papers, EPL.

21 *"I hope so," du Pont replied*: quoted in Helen Leavitt, *Superhighway—Superhoax* (Doubleday, 1970): 45.

23 *The Boom Is Just Beginning!*: *Business Week*, September 29, 1956.

34 *doubt there was any measurable increase in juvenile crime*: see, for instance, James Gilbert, *A Cycle of Outrage: America's Reaction to the Juvenile Delinquent in the 1950s* (Oxford University Press, 1988).

35 *"juvenile delinquency in America is largely a reflection"*: Irving Sarnoff, *New Republic*, January 18, 1960.

Chapter 2: Forklift

Edmund Kemper's story has attracted quite a few tellers, but the only complete book dedicated to him is Margaret Cheney, *The Coed Killer* (Walker & Co., 1976), which is the source of my Kemper quotes. He is analyzed at length in Elliot Leyton, *Hunting Humans: The Rise of the Modern Multiple Murderer* (Carroll & Graf, 2001); Peter Vronsky, *Serial Killers: The Method and Madness of Monsters* (Berkley Books, 2004); and the more scholarly *Murder and Madness* by Donald Lunde (Portable Stanford, 1975). Lunde, a psychiatrist who served as an expert witness in all three Santa Cruz trials, also discusses Herbert Mullin and John Linley Frazier. Ward Damio, a Santa Cruz journalist, also wrote about all three murderers and the way they affected Santa Cruz in *Urge to Kill* (Pinnacle, 1974).

My interpretation of the "hitchhiker panic" was influenced by Jeremy Packer's excellent study, *Mobility without Mayhem: Safety,*

Cars and Citizenship (Duke University Press, 2008). The story of the growth of the antihighway movement is best told by the era's screeds, particularly Helen Leavitt, *Superhighway—Superhoax* (Doubleday, 1970); Ben Kelley, *The Pavers and the Paved* (Donald W. Brown, 1971); Ronald Buel, *Dead End* (Prentice-Hall, 1972); and, for the California specifics, John Robinson, *Highways and Our Environment* (McGraw-Hill, 1971) and William Bronson, *How to Kill a Golden State* (Doubleday, 1968).

The classic book on the counterculture and its values is Theodore Roszak, *The Making of a Counterculture*, first published in 1968 (University of California Press, rev. ed. 1995).

53 *"American are living in the midst"*: Robert Paul Jordan, "Our Growing Interstate," *National Geographic*, February 1968: 195.

53 *"As the Woodstock generation"*: "Rules of Thumb," *Newsweek*, February 19, 1973: 38.

56 *"a virtual Möbius strip of money"*: Tom Lewis, *Divided Highways*: 127.

57 *a plan to drop twenty-two nuclear bombs to vaporize the Bristol Mountains*: "Creation of Mountain Pass by Atom Blast Studied," *New York Times*, December 24, 1963: 36.

57 *"As 1970 draws near"*: Richard Lillard, *Eden in Jeopardy* (Knopf, 1966): 204.

57 *"a monument to materialism"*: Bronson, *How to Kill a Golden State*: 104.

61 *"a beautiful, groovy way to travel"*: "A New Rule of Thumb," *Newsweek*, June 16, 1969: 63.

61 *"Mostly you just feel"*: "Youth on the Move: A Look at the Hitchhiking Scene," *Santa Cruz Sentinel*, July 11, 1971.

66 *"Where Are Those Superhighways?"*: Richard Thruelsen, *Saturday Evening Post*, December 14, 1957.

68 *A 1966 Sports Illustrated feature*: "Rule of Thumb," *Sports Illustrated*, June 6, 1966.

74 *"they are asking for a lot more than a ride"*: "Women Mobilize for War on Rapists," *Cabrillo Times & Green Sheet*, February 15, 1973.

75 *they "liked to hitchhike"*: "Thumbs Down on Hitchhiking!," *Reader's Digest*, January 1970.

82 *the cops stopped handing out the cards—except to women seen hitchhiking*: reported in *Jet*, March 22, 1979.

Chapter 3: The Cruelest Blow

Several books have been written about the Atlanta child murders: Cliff Dettlinger and Jeff Prugh, *The List* (Philmay Enterprises, 1983), take a skeptical approach toward the Williams verdict, as does James Baldwin in *The Evidence of Things Not Seen* (Henry Holt, 1985). Jack Mallard, *The Atlanta Child Murders* (self-published), does not— which is not surprising, since the author was the prosecutor. Bernard Headley connects the murders to the city's politics in *The Atlanta Youth Murders and the Politics of Race* (Southern Illinois University Press, 1999). He borrows from Steve Oney's insightful feature "A City Robbed of Light," *Atlanta Journal-Constitution Weekly Magazine*, April 19, 1981. John Douglas makes an argument for the FBI's importance to the case in *Mindhunter: Inside the FBI's Elite Serial Crime Unit* (Pocket Star, 1995). More useful to me were the declassified FBI files on the case, available at the FBI's online Freedom of Information Act Reading Room: http://vault.fbi.gov. Kim Reid's affecting memoir *No Place Safe* (Dafina, 2007) paints a picture of what it was like to be a black child in Atlanta when black children were regularly turning up dead.

Freeway racism and freeway revolts are discussed in many of the early antihighway screeds, including Helen Leavitt, Ben Kelley, and Ronald Buel (all cited above), A. Q. Mowbray, *Road to Ruin* (Lippincott, 1969), and Richard Hébert, *Highways to Nowhere: The Politics of City Transportation* (Bobbs-Merrill, 1972). More recent histories include Paul Mason Fotsch, *Watching the Traffic Go By: Transportation and Isolation in Urban America* (University of Texas Press, 2007); Brian Ladd, *Autophobia: Love and Hate in the Automotive Age* (University of Chicago Press, 2008); and Henry Moon, *The Interstate Highway System* (Association of American Geographers, 1994).

The Atlanta History Center is not only a refrigerated haven on hot summer days, but a gold mine of documents painting a dramatic picture of Atlanta's housing, highway, and economic development programs. Charles Rutheiser's brilliant *Imagineering Atlanta: The Politics of Place in the City of Dreams* (Verso, 1996) helped me sort through the city's planning history. Also useful were Ronald Bayor, *Race and the Shaping of Twentieth-Century Atlanta* (University of North Carolina Press, 1996); Larry Keating, *Atlanta: Race, Class and Urban Expansion* (Temple University Press, 2001); Tamar Jacoby, *Someone Else's House: America's Unfinished Struggle for Integration*

(Basic Books, 2000); Clarence N. Stone, *Economic Growth and Neighborhood Discontent: System Bias in the Urban Renewal Program of Atlanta* (University of North Carolina Press, 1976); Barbara L. Jackson, "Desegregation: Atlanta Style," *Theory into Practice* 17, no. 1. In thinking about Atlanta's redevelopment of its business district, I was influenced by the always eye-opening work of Mike Davis, especially "Urban Renaissance and the Spirit of Postmodernism," *New Left Review* 151 (May–June 1985), as well as by simply spending time walking around there.

85 *"Every major city from Boston"*: the editors, "Highways vs. People," *New York Times*, November 20, 1966: E12.

85 *"The War on Black Children"*: Pamela Douglas, "The War on Black Children," *Black Enterprise*, May 1981: 22.

88 *"you have to hack your way through with a meat ax"*: quoted in Robert Caro, *The Power Broker: Robert Moses and the Fall of New York* (Vintage, 1975): 849.

88 *displaced around a million Americans*: Raymond Mohl, "Race and Space in the Modern City," in Mohl and Arnold Hirsch, eds., *Urban Policy in Twentieth Century America* (Rutgers UP, 1993): 101.

89 *"they hadn't the faintest notion of what they were doing"*: Lewis Mumford, "The Highway and the City," *Architectural Record*, reprinted in *The Highway and the City* (Harcourt Brace Jovanovich, 1953): 234.

89 *"Autos are strangling cities coast to coast"*: "Senate Unit Told of Transit Crisis," *New York Times*, March 21, 1961.

90 *everything progressive planners advocate today*: EPL, John Stewart Bragdon Papers.

92 *one-third of the city's existing housing stock was demolished*: Rutheiser, *Imagineering Atlanta*: 153; Keating, *Atlanta*: 93.

93 *Atlanta would lead the nation in public housing*: Atlanta Housing Authority, http://atlantahousingauthority.blogspot.com/2008/07/public-housing-projects-in-atlanta-are.html.

93 *Twelve percent of its population*: Dettlinger and Prugh, *The List*: 102.

93 *planners had once infamously attempted to build a wall*: see Ronald Bayor, "Roads to Racial Segregation: Atlanta in the Twentieth Century," *Journal of Urban History* 15:1 (November 1988).

93 *configured to eliminate portions of poor black neighborhoods*: Keating, *Atlanta*: 205.

93 *the city insisted on moving I-75/I-85*: Stone, *Economic Growth and Neighborhood Discontent*: 53.

95 *might easily be called "a slum"*: *Sweet Auburn: A Comprehensive Urban Design Plan for Auburn Avenue* (Georgia Institute of Technology College of Architecture, December 1975): 3.

96 *"Rats and roaches infest every building"*: "Cities: Recipe for Riot," *Time*, June 30, 1967.

97 *decried the "racial double standard"*: Richard Whalen, "The American Highway," *Saturday Evening Post*, December 14, 1968.

97 *"blacks found themselves receiving at best"* and *"they most certainly are dealing them the cruelest blow"*: Hébert, *Highways to Nowhere*: 105, 189.

98 *population of many counties surrounding Atlanta*: U.S. Dept. of Commerce, Bureau of the Census figures; cited in *Decade of Decision* (Research Atlanta, 1981): 4.

98 *warned of the "extreme separation"*: *Back to the City: Housing Options for Central Atlanta*, technical report commissioned by Central Atlanta Progress, June 1974: 3.

98 *"stock the Chattahoochee with piranha"*: Rutheiser, *Imagineering Atlanta*: 99.

99 *"heroic mirror towers surging up one after another"*: Philip Diamond, "Capturing the Great Town," *Real Estate Atlanta* 5:1 (1975): 8.

100 *"everything is within reach of the pedestrian"*: *John Portman: Art and Architecture*, walking tour guide by the High Museum of Art, 2010.

100 *"the suburban couple can ice skate"*: Mike Keza, "Atlanta Straining to Be Top Convention City," *New York Times*, March 17, 1976.

101 *Yusef was buried beneath concrete*: Dettlinger and Prugh, *The List*: 57.

103 *"geography had become a parameter in and of itself"*: Dettlinger and Prugh, *The List*: 125.

110 *"Somehow Atlanta is on trial in this thing"*: "Still No Solution: Atlanta on Trial," *Washington Post*, March 12, 1981.

110 *"inward-looking, cold, impersonal and inhuman"*: "Experts Find Environment a Factor in Vulnerability of Slain Atlanta Children," *New York Times*, March 18, 1981: A24.

110 *"the placement of the bodies"* and *"the proximity of highways"*:

"Investigators Feel Many Killers, Separately, Slew Atlanta Children," *New York Times*, March 15, 1981: A1.

113 *The district attorney said he still believed*: "An Arrest in Atlanta, But Has There Been Too Much Pre-trial Publicity?," *Christian Science Monitor*, June 23, 1981.

120 *Housing activists point out*: "Atlanta Is Making Way for New Public Housing," *New York Times*, June 21, 2009.

121 *city is canceling bus service*: "Going to Extremes, as the Downturn Wears On," *New York Times*, August 7, 2010.

123 *previously undisclosed transcripts*: Bob Keating and Barry Cooper, "A Question of Justice," *Spin*, September 1986, and Bob Keating, "Atlanta: Who Killed Your Children?," *Spin*, October 1986.

Chapter 4: American Isolate

The investigation of Roger Reece Kibbe is the subject of one book, Bruce Henderson's *Trace Evidence* (Lisa Drew/Scribner, 1998). For Ted Bundy's story, I mainly used Stephen Michaud and Hugh Aynesworth, *The Only Living Witness* (Linden Press, 1983), as well as their collection of interviews, *Ted Bundy: Conversations with a Killer* (Signet, 1989). I also used Elizabeth Kendall's *The Phantom Prince: My Life with Ted Bundy* (Madrona, 1981); Steve Winn and David Merrill, *Ted Bundy: The Killer Next Door* (Bantam, 1979); and, to a lesser extent, Ann Rule, *The Stranger Beside Me* (Norton, 1980). Bundy is also discussed in Elliot Leyton, *Hunting Humans*. Henry Lee Lucas is discussed in Peter Vronsky, *Serial Killers: The Method and Madness of Monsters* (Berkley, 2004), though for facts I primarily used contemporary newspaper accounts.

My understanding of the eighties was shaped by two fascinating books by historian Robert M. Collins: *Transforming America: Politics and Culture in the Reagan Years* (Columbia University Press, 2007) and *More: The Politics of Economic Growth in Postwar America* (Oxford University Press, 2000). On suburbanization and sprawl, my thoughts were mainly shaped by a few sources both pro and con. The pro-sprawl thinkers are Robert Bruegmann, *Sprawl* (University of Chicago Press, 2005) and Joel Garreau, *Edge City: Life on the New Frontier* (Doubleday, 1991). The antis include Jane Jacobs, *The Death and Life of Great American Cities* (1961; Modern Library, 1993);

Kenneth T. Jackson, *Crabgrass Frontier: The Suburbanization of the United States* (Oxford University Press, 1985); James Kunstler, *The Geography of Nowhere* (Touchstone, 1993); and Andres Duany, Elizabeth Plater-Zyberk, and Jeff Speck, *Suburban Nation: The Rise of Sprawl and the Decline of the American Dream* (North Point, 2000). FBI history is engagingly recounted in Rhodri Jeffreys-Jones, *The FBI: A History* (Yale University Press, 2008). My understanding of how the Bureau used the serial killer panic to its advantage was shaped by David Schmid's fun and smart book, *Natural Born Celebrities: Serial Killers in American Culture* (University of Chicago Press, 2005), as well as Philip Jenkins, *Using Murder: The Social Construction of Serial Homicide* (Aldine de Gruyter, 1994).

126 *"To understand America, you have to understand"*: Robert J. Samuelson, "Highways to Everywhere," *Newsweek*, June 30, 1986: 50.

126 *"Serial killers, like society in general"*: Jack Levin and James Alan Fox, *Mass Murder: America's Growing Menace* (Da Capo Press, 1985): 18.

132 *"Ted Bundy is a one-night stand"*: see Jane Caputi, "The New Founding Fathers: The Lore and Lure of the Serial Killer in Contemporary Culture," *Journal of American Culture* 13:3 (1990): 5.

133 *a "terrific looking man" with a "lean all-American face"*: Jon Nordheimer, "All-American Boy on Trial," *New York Times Magazine*, December 10, 1978: 24.

133 *"I felt inferior"*: Michaud and Aynesworth, *Ted Bundy: Conversations with a Killer*: 25.

134 *"The press stories about Ted stressed his apparent normalcy"*: Michaud and Aynesworth, *The Only Living Witness*: 14.

134 *250 reporters from five continents*: Michaud and Aynesworth, *The Only Living Witness*: 10.

135 *"How do you describe the taste of bouillabaisse?"*: quoted in Elliot Leyton, *Hunting Humans*: 128.

136 *"the first coast-to-coast killer"*: Roy Hazelwood, foreword to Michaud and Aynesworth, *The Only Living Witness*: 5.

137 *"the first baby born on I-5"*: "Mexico, U.S. and Canada Linked by 4.6-Mile Road Completing I-5," *New York Times*, October 13, 1979.

139 *"the subliminal theme"*: Jimmy Carter, *Keeping Faith: Memoirs of a President* (University of Arkansas Press, 1995): 23.

139 *"We can no longer rely on a rising economic tide"*: quoted in Collins, *Transforming America*: 25.

139 *"rededication to the industrial, mass-consumption society"*: quoted in Collins, *More*: 164–165.

142 *"The thing that I have found about the serial murderers"*: all quotes from the hearings are from Serial No. J-98-52, Hearing before the Subcommittee on Juvenile Justice of the Committee on the Judiciary, United States Senate (Government Printing Office, 1984).

143 *"those who kill for reasons other than greed"*: "35 Murderers of Many People Could Be at Large, U.S. Says," *New York Times*, October 28, 1983.

144 *"growing evidence of a substantial increase"*: Robert Lindsey, "Officials Cite a Rise in Killers Who Roam U.S. for Victims," *New York Times*, January 21, 1984. Robert Heck's quote below is from the same story.

145 *A 1992 article*: Philip Jenkins, "Myth and Murder: The Serial Killer Panic of 1983–85," *Criminal Justice Research Bulletin* 3:11 (1988). Robert Stote and Lionel Standing, in "Serial and Multiple Homicide: Is There an Epidemic?," *Social Behavior and Personality* 23:4 (1995), concluded that serial homicide did in fact increase in the eighties, but only as much as all homicide did.

146 *"In playing up the frenzy"*: Robert Ressler, *Whoever Fights Monsters: My Twenty Years Tracking Serial Killers for the FBI* (St. Martins, 1992): 229–230.

150 *"Many accepted the highways"*: Lewis, *Divided Highways*: 259.

152 *"As the boom of the 1980s and 1990s got underway"*: Bruegmann, *Sprawl*: 203.

155 *"what the perpetrator has to do to fulfill himself"*: John Douglas, *Mindhunter: Inside the FBI's Elite Serial Crime Unit* (Pocket Books, 1995): 252.

155 *signature is often an acquisitive act*: see, for instance, Mark Selzer, *Serial Killers: Death and Life in America's Wound Culture* (Routledge, 1998): 64. See also Sara Knox, "The Serial Killer as Collector," in Leah Dilworth, ed., *Acts of Possession: Collecting in America* (Rutgers UP: 2003).

155 *"should have recognized that what really fascinated him was the hunt"*: Bundy quoted in Winn and Merrill, *Ted Bundy: The Killer Next Door*: 123.

159 *"He's probably a resident of one of those areas"*: "I-5 Strangler Blamed for 7 Deaths in North," *Los Angeles Times* (Southland edition), January 9, 1988: 35.

162 *"I'm wearing a Joseph Abboud suit"*: Bret Easton Ellis, *American Psycho* (Vintage, 1991): 328.

162 *"Somehow it has happened"*: Joyce Carol Oates, "'I Had No Other Thrill or Happiness': The Literature of Serial Killers," *New York Review of Books*, March 24, 1994.

163 *"a road map of the most repugnant behavior"*: *Sacramento Bee*, March 15, 1991.

Chapter 5: Drive-by Truckers

My heartfelt thanks to Pat Postiglione, who never seemed to enjoy talking about himself but dutifully did so whenever I asked him to. Lee Freeman, Terri Turner, and Clark Fine were also open and kind. Eric Hickey very generously discussed his work with me, as did researcher Mona Shattell. Extra thanks to Marcus Feltsin and Ron Clarke, who let themselves be convinced to speculate about truck stops, and especially Ron for actually visiting one with me. And I am extremely grateful to the FBI agents who met with me, some of them multiple times, to make sure I understood how both ViCAP and the Behavioral Analysis Units work. Supervisory Special Agents Mark Hilts and James McNamara of Behavioral Analysis Unit 2; Supervisory Special Agents Mark Nichols, Mike Harrigan, John Molnar, and John Raleigh of ViCAP; Crime Analyst Nathan Graham of ViCAP; and of course Special Agent Ann Todd, my loyal companion from Public Affairs, were all very generous with their valuable time. Unless otherwise cited, all quotes in this chapter are from interviews by me.

My understanding of trucking was shaped by Shane Hamilton's fascinating book *Trucking Country: The Road to America's Wal-Mart Economy* (Princeton University Press, 2008). Another useful book, though old, was Charles Perry, *Deregulation and the Decline of Unionized Trucking* (Wharton School Labor Relations and Public Policy Series no. 28, 1986).

166 *"Fed by the prosperity of the last decade"*: Peter T. Kilborn, "In Rural Areas, Interstates Build Their Own Economy," *New York Times*, July 14, 2001.

166 *"Crime is a process"*: Marcus Felson and Rachel Boba, *Crime and Everyday Life*, 4th ed. (Sage, 2010): 206.

169 *At least twenty-five former truckers are currently serving time*: list compiled from newspaper archives. Janet McClellan lists twenty-two American trucker serial killers arrested before 2008 in "Delivery Drivers and Long-Haul Truckers: Traveling Serial Murderers," *Journal of Applied Security Research* 3:2 (2008).

173 *serial murder victims have continually been underestimated*: Kenna Quinet, "The Missing Missing: Toward a Quantification of Serial Murder Victimization in the United States," *Homicide Studies* 11:4 (November 2007): 319–339.

173 *the homicide rate for prostitutes is 229 out of every 100,000*: J. J. Potterat et al., "Mortality in an Open Cohort of Prostitute Women," *American Journal of Epidemiology* 159 (2004); cited by Quinet: 323. The U.S. homicide rate comes from the FBI Uniform Crime Reports, available at http://www.ucrdatatool.gov.

173 *"Many families drive from state to state and need accurate information"*: Blake Morrison, "Along Highways, Signs of Serial Killings," *USA Today*, October 5, 2010.

177 *roughly 70 percent of all domestic freight goes over the road, and more than 80 percent of the nation's communities are served exclusively by trucks*: U.S. Department of Agriculture, *Study of Rural Transportation Issues*, April 2010, http://www.ams.usda.gov/AMSv1.0/RuralTransportationStudy.

177 *"sweatshops on wheels"*: Michael Belzer's fascinating study of how trucking has changed since deregulation is *Sweatshops on Wheels: Winners and Losers in Trucking Deregulation* (Oxford University Press, 2000).

187 *MacDonald Triad*: the original article describing the triad is John M. MacDonald, "The Threat to Kill," *American Journal of Psychiatry* 120 (1963).

191 *A famous case is New York's Port Authority Bus Terminal*: this case was outlined in great detail in Marcus Felson et al., "Redesigning Hell: Preventing Crime and Disorder at the Port Authority Bus Terminal," in Ronald Clarke, ed., *Crime Prevention Studies* 6 (1996), http://www.popcenter.org/library/crimeprevention/volume_06/01_Felson.pdf.

197 *makes truckers six times more likely than average to die on the job*: In 2008, 856 truckers died on the job, a fatality rate of 24

per 100,000. U.S. Bureau of Labor Statistics, U.S. Department of
Labor, http://www.bls.gov/iif/oshwc/cfoi/cfch0007.pdf.

198 *survey done at a seedy Southern truck stop*: Mona Shattell,
Yorghos Apostolopoulos, Sevil Sönmez, and Mary Griffin,
"Occupational Stressors and the Mental Health of Truckers,"
Issues in Mental Health Nursing 31 (2010): 561–568.

198 *a paper on truckers' physical health*: Yorghos Apostolopoulos,
Sevil Sönmez, Mona Shattell, and Michael Belzer, "Worksite-
Induced Morbidities among Truck Drivers in the United
States," *AAOHN Journal* 58:7 (2010).

200 *"less dead"*: the phrase is from Stephen Egger, *The Killers among
Us* (Prentice-Hall, 2002).

202 *research what happens to people at the wheel*: see, for instance,
John Urry, "Inhabiting the Car," UNESCO International
Conference, Universidade Candido Mendes, Rio de Janeiro,
May 2000, http://www.lancs.ac.uk/fass/sociology/papers/
urry-inhabiting-the-car.pdf. Tom Vanderbilt summarizes much
of this research in the first chapter of his eye-opening book
*Traffic: Why We Drive the Way We Do (and What It Says about
Us)* (Knopf, 2008).

204 *"They are marvels of engineering"*: "A Stranger in the House,"
Dateline, aired August 3, 2009 (NBC).

Chapter 6: A Prayer for the Body Buried by the Interstate

For information on the murders in Juárez, I have relied on newspaper
stories, as well as Charles Bowden's hypnotic and horrifying book
Murder City (Nation Books, 2010); and Teresa Rodriguez, Diane
Montané, with Lisa Pulitzer, *The Daughters of Juárez* (Atria, 2007).
Also important were Jessica Livingston, "Murder in Juárez: Gender,
Sexual Violence and the Global Assembly Line," *Frontiers*, 2004; and
Katherine Pantaleo, "Gendered Violence: An Analysis of the Maquila-
dora Murders," *International Criminal Justice Review* 20:4 (2010).

206 *"[The Interstate System] will never be finished"*: Francis C. Turner,
quoted in the *Richmond Times-Dispatch*, August 19, 1996.

206 *"The overall increase in crime"*: Gerard Nicholas Labuschagne,
"Serial Murder Revisited: A Psychological Exploration of Two

South African Cases," PhD diss., (University of Pretoria, 2001), quoted in Brin Hodgskiss, "Lessons from Serial Murder in South Africa," *Journal of Investigative Psychology and Offender Profiling* 1:1 (January 2004): 72.

210 *"We are again transforming the world"*: quoted in Livingston, "Murder in Juárez": 62.

211 *"They were murdering women"*: quoted in Molly Moore, "An Anguished Quest for Justice," *Washington Post*, June 26, 2000.

213 *"Do you know where your daughter is tonight?"*: quoted in Livingston: 63.

214 *"My leading theory"*: quoted in Patricia Price, *Dry Place: Landscapes of Belonging and Exclusion* (University of Minnesota Press, 2004): 139.

215 *"NAFTA has not only increased jobs"*: Pantaleo, "Gendered Violence": 351.

215 *A Carnegie Council report*: Lydia Alpízar, "Impunity and Women's Rights in Ciudad Juárez," *Human Rights Dialogue* 2.10 (Fall 2003), http://www.carnegiecouncil.org/resources/publications/dialogue/2_10/articles/1056.html.

215 *"Ciudad Juárez epitomized the promise"*: Molly Moore, "Young Women Follow Journeys of Hope to Factories—and Then, to Violence," *Washington Post*, June 25, 2000: A1.

218 *"Highways and country roads are synonymous with progress"*: IV Report of Government, Presidency of the Republic, Mexico, DF, August 29, 2010, http://mexidata.info/id2792.html.

218 *"This future is based on the rich getting richer"*: Charles Bowden, "While You Were Sleeping," *Harper's*, December 1996.

219 *quickly building some thirty thousand miles of new roads*: Business Monitor International, *China Infrastructure Report* (Second Quarter 2011): 40.

219 *"I always wanted to be an assassin"*: quoted in the Reuters story on his execution, "Execution for China Serial Killer," CNN.com, http://edition.cnn.com/2003/WORLD/asiapcf/east/12/09/china.killer.reut.

219 *"Reports of serial killings began appearing"*: He Huifeng, "Four Held over Serial Murders of 12 Women," *South China Morning Post*, December 13, 2005: 8.

220 *"One of the villages which had been gradually engulfed"*: Sandeep Unnithan and Shyamlal Yadav, "Butchers of Suburbia," *India Today*, January 15, 2007.

221 *India "had never before witnessed"*: Shreya Basu, "Butchers of
Mankind," *Statesman* (India), February 15, 2007.

221 *"Was I the only person"*: "The Silence of Our Lambs," *Hindustan
Times*, January 27, 2007.

222 *The widely accepted consensus is that development decreases
homicide—up to a point*: a good summary is Steven Messner,
Lawrence Raffalovich, and Peter Shrock, "Reassessing the
Cross-National Relationship between Income Inequality and
Homicide Rates," *Journal of Quantitative Criminology* 18:4
(December 2002).

224 *Mack Rae Edwards murdered an eight-year-old girl named
Stella*: a good summary of the Edwards crimes is Kenneth Todd
Ruiz, "Police Back Theory on Missing Boy," *Pasadena Star
News*, March 19, 2007: 1.

My heartfelt gratitude goes to Mark Crispin Miller, for believing in
this odd book from the start. Copious honor is due Hal Clifford, my
first reader and an invaluable wellspring of writing wisdom. Thanks
are also owed to my editor Theresa May at the University of Texas
Press, my wonderful agent Nat Sobel at Sobel Weber Associates, and
all the stellar folks at both those institutions. And as always, love and
gratitude to my family and friends for putting up with the long process of creating this book, and for listening patiently to accounts of
murder, mayhem, and infrastructure. I know it hasn't been easy.

≡ INDEX ≡

Program (ViCAP), 146, 169,
171, 173, 203
Von Busch, Bob, 20, 21, 25, 26,
31, 223

Walker, Curtis, 109
Walsh, Adam, 141–142
Walsh, John, 142, 143, 171
Ward, Charles K., 23–24
Ward, Clara, 39–41; home of,
39
Ward, Lauer, 23–24, 37, 40, 49;
home of, *39*
Ward, Michael, 26, 37, 38
Webber, Harry, 111
Webster, William, 142, 143
Wenxian, Li, 219
White, Lawrence, 71
Whitechapel, Simon, 214

white flight, 11, 95–96, 105, 121,
150
Williams, John Robert, 171, 182
Williams, Wayne Bertram, 112–
118, 145; home of, 112, 116, 121,
122; photograph of, *114*
Wilson, Charles, 6
Wilson, Latonya, 101, 106, 116, 120
Wood, Desiree, 190
Woodfield, Randy, 157, 164

Yellow Book, 90–92; image from,
91
Yong, Huang, 219
Young, Andrew, 110

Zhiya, Yang, 219
Zodiac killer, 131
Zuniga, Linda, 70